Touring Literary Mississippi

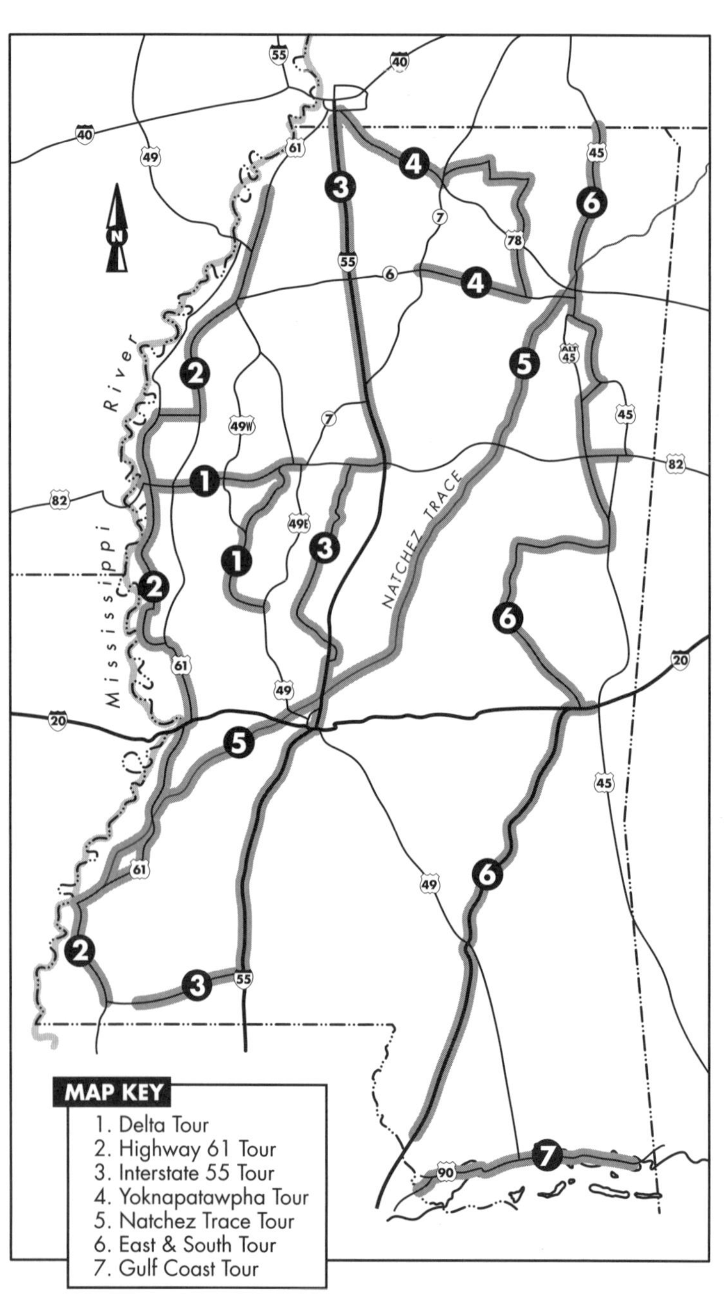
MAP KEY
1. Delta Tour
2. Highway 61 Tour
3. Interstate 55 Tour
4. Yoknapatawpha Tour
5. Natchez Trace Tour
6. East & South Tour
7. Gulf Coast Tour
Mississippi River
NATCHEZ TRACE
N

Touring Literary Mississippi

Patti Carr Black
and
Marion Barnwell

University Press of Mississippi / *Jackson*

Publication of this book was made possible in part by Mary Jayne G. Whittington.

www.upress.state.ms.us

Manufactured in the United States of America

Designed by Todd Lape

10 09 08 07 06 05 04 03 02 4 3 2 1

Library of Congress Cataloging-in-Publication Data

Black, Patti Carr.
Touring literary Mississippi / Patti Carr Black and Marion Barnwell.
p. cm.
ISBN 1-57806-367-1 (alk. paper) — ISBN 1-57806-368-X (pbk. : alk. paper)
1. Literary landmarks—Mississippi—Guidebooks. 2. American literature—Mississippi—History and criticism. 3. Authors, American—Homes and haunts—Mississippi. 4. Authors, American—Mississippi—Biography. 5. Mississippi—Intellectual life. 6. Mississippi—In literature. 7. Mississippi—Guidebooks. I. Barnwell, Marion. II. Title.
PS144.M7 B58 2002
810.9'9762—dc21 2002000632

British Library Cataloging-in-Publication Data available

For Beth Griffin Jones

For Claiborne Barnwell

Contents

Preface

Recently, writing guru Natalie Goldberg drove to Mississippi from her home in Taos, New Mexico. As she explains in her book *Thunder and Lightning*, Mississippi's abundance of extraordinary writers had beckoned. She visited Beth Henley's family home in Hazlehurst, then drove on to Jackson and Oxford. While she was looking over Faulkner memorabilia at Rowan Oak, the curator took what seemed to be an important telephone call. She hung up, then shared the news that Richard Ford had just won the Pulitzer Prize. "Not another one," thought Goldberg, leaning against a wall. There were times in our research when we felt the same way.

This book is intended to be a helpful guide for travelers who, like Goldberg, want to see homes and other sites associated with Mississippi writers. With well over a hundred pictures, it is also designed for the armchair tourist.

Shelby Foote once remarked that Mississippi has seven distinctively different areas. "The Gulf Coast is the Gulf Coast because it is, and the Delta is the Delta because it is," he said. Although we had already mapped out our seven tours when we ran across his remark, we considered it a good omen and a validation for limiting ourselves to writers on or near the tour route. We have included writers of published "literary" works—fiction, memoirs, biography, autobiography, volumes of poetry, and some collected letters.

We are indebted to James B. Lloyd's *Lives of Mississippi Authors, 1817 to 1967* and Elmo Howell's books, *Mississippi Home-Places* (1988), *Mississippi Scenes* (1992), and *Mississippi Back Roads* (1998). The Mississippi Writers Page (www.olemiss.edu) was also a useful source.

We'd like to thank Seetha Srinivasan, director at the University Press of Mississippi, for her guidance. We are grateful to the Mississippi Humanities Council and Delta State University for research support and to the staff members who aided us in our research at the library and historic preservation divisions of the Mississippi Department of Archives and History and at the Eudora Welty Library and other libraries across the state. Collecting photographs was a formidable task, and we thank Elmo Howell, Hunter Cole, Barnard and Richard Trippett, Tommy Covington, William McMullin, Fred Edminston, Elaine Owens, Richard Cawthon, Billy Whittington, Kim Spencer, John Evans, Dr. Nancy Clark, and Georgie Fisher, as well as those who granted permission to reproduce photographs.

We would also like to thank the many individuals who helped us: Dr. Peggy Prenshaw, Dr. Ann Abadie, Mary Hartwell Howorth, Mimi Miller, Tom Spengler, Valerie Boyette, Leila Wynn, Sue Stock, Dorothy Shawhan, and Claiborne Barnwell. Special thanks to the people from all over the state who literally pointed the way when we were lost.

To the traveler, we have made every effort to direct you to some compelling literary sites, but a good map, a good sense of direction, and a good sense of humor will also help.

Touring
Literary Mississippi

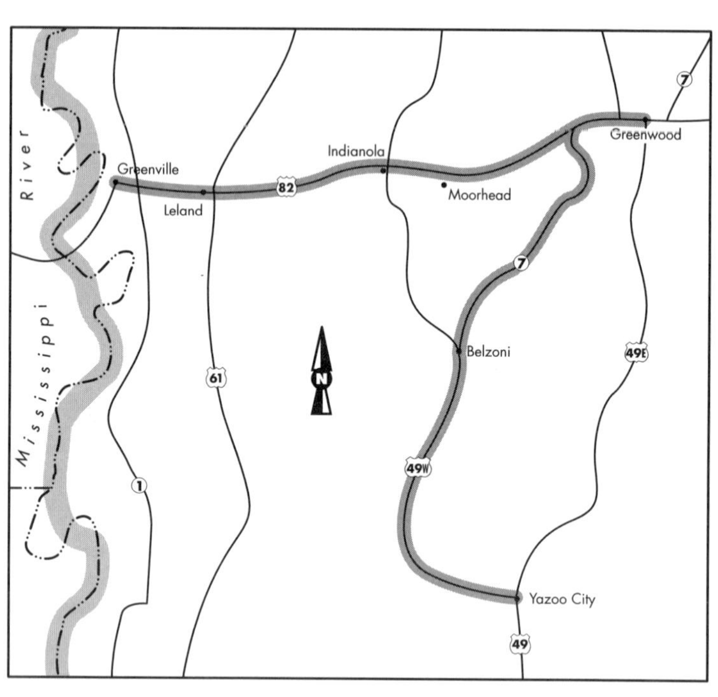

River
Mississippi
Greenville
Leland
Indianola
Moorhead
Greenwood
Belzoni
Yazoo City
82
61
1
7
49W
49E
49
N

Delta Tour

The Delta tour begins in Greenville, follows Highway 82 to Leland, Indianola, Moorhead, and Greenwood, then loops down to Belzoni and ends in Yazoo City.

Greenville

The Mississippi River has shaped the history of Greenville. Beginning in the 1840s, celebrated steamboats such as the *Pargo*, the *Natchez*, the *Robert E. Lee*, and the *Belle of the Bends* made stops in this port city. In Greenville, the river has continued to attract commerce and trade, creating a melting pot of Caucasians, African Americans, Jews, Italians, Irish, Chinese, Syrians, and others.

Incorporated in 1870, the city was named for Revolutionary War general Nathaniel Greene and the county for his friend George Washington. In the nineteenth century the Grand Opera House in this cosmopolitan city was a standard bearer for opera houses built at that time.

Greenville once declared it had "more writers per square foot than any other city of its size," and this claim may still be true.

The energy generated among writers once caused writer Shelby Foote to say that nobody reads books in Greenville because they're too busy writing them. One man, more than any other, nurtured Greenville's rich literary life: William Alexander Percy. The city has also achieved a progressive spirit, largely through the enlightened views of Hodding Carter and his family, who ran the *Delta Democrat Times* for many years.

Among early Greenville writers are James Robertshaw (1846–1913), who wrote two novels, *Volney Randolph* (n.d.) and *Merrivale* (1898), and Ernest D. Elliot (1898–1969), who wrote *Prelude to the Storm* (1942), *Swamp Angel* (1943), and *Scottie's Story* (1953). Maude Leet Prenshaw grew up in Greenville under the influence of William Alexander Percy and was named Mississippi's first poet laureate by Governor Ross Barnett. Among her publications is a sonnet sequence entitled *Resurrexit.* Other Greenville writers include Clarence Brannon, Anne Metcalfe Clark, Mary Berkeley McNeilly Finke, Henry Tillinghast Ireys, Jay Milner, Jane Taylor Overton, Sinclair O. Lewis, and Emma Harrington.

Author and poet L. C. Dorsey (1938) was born in nearby Tribbett, and poet-playwright Ava Haymon (1944) grew up a few miles up the road, in Hollandale. Now residing in Baton Rouge, Haymon has published chapbooks of her poetry including *A Name Gift for Every Child* and *Kitchen Heat.*

Instead of becoming a physician like his father, William Attaway (1911–1986) pursued a writing career so that he could give a voice to other African Americans. Before graduating with a B.A. degree from the University of Illinois, he worked as a laborer, a seaman, and an actor. As a freelance writer, he became part of the Harlem Renaissance. In his second novel, *Blood on the Forge* (1941), published in the same year as William Alexander Percy's *Lanterns on the Levee,* he dramatized the loss of identity southern blacks faced during the Great Migration to northern cities in the early 1900s, a migration he experienced firsthand when his family moved to Chicago. Two facts about Attaway are less well known: he was the first African American to write scripts for television and films, and he composed more than five hundred songs, many of them calypso, for Harry Belafonte and others.

Greenville native Jessie Rosenberg Schell (1941) received her B.A. degree in 1963 and an M.F.A. degree in writing in 1971 from the University of North Carolina. She has written short stories for regional and national magazines such as the *Virginia Quarterly Review* and *The Atlantic Monthly* and a novel called *Sudina* (1967), which was published under her maiden name, Rosenberg, and reprinted in 1978 under her married name.

Born in Vicksburg, D. C. Berry (1942) grew up in Greenville. After receiving a degree from Delta State University and a Ph.D. from the University of Tennessee, Berry began teaching in the English department at the University of Southern Mississippi. He is poetry editor for *Mississippi Review.* His first collection of poems was *Saigon Cemetery* (1972). In 2000, Berry received the Mississippi Institute of Arts and Letters award for poetry.

Angela Jackson (1951) was born in Greenville, the fifth of nine children and the last born in Mississippi. She grew up on Chicago's South Side. She has observed a difference between herself and her siblings born in Chicago and has said she is glad for her rural roots. She was educated at Northwestern University and the University of Chicago. Her collections of poems include *The Greenville Club* (1970) and *Voo Doo/Love Magic* (1974). She has also written fiction and drama. Her play *Comfort Stew* was produced in 1997. She has been praised for her poetic diction and her ear for dialect. She has won many awards including the 1985 American Book Award for *Solo in the Boxcar Third Floor E.*

Approaching Greenville from the west, the tour begins at the home of journalist Hodding Carter.

FELICIANA

1710 Highway 82 West

Hodding Carter was one of the town's most important citizens, not only for the newspaper he started and the books he wrote, but also for the stands he took as a political liberal (see below). Several members of Carter's family have also written books. Betty Werlein Carter (1910–2000) coauthored with her husband *Doomed Road of Empire: The Spanish Trail of Conquest* (1963) and *So Great a Good: A History of the Episcopal Church in Louisiana and of Christ Church Cathedral, 1805–1955* (1955). Son Hodding Carter III (1935) became editor of the *Delta Democrat Times* after his father's death. He wrote the essay collections *The South Strikes Back* (1959) and *The Reagan Years* (1988). His work on the PBS series *Inside Story* earned him three Emmys. Hodding Carter IV writes travel books such as *Westward Whoa: In the Wake of Lewis and Clark* (1994) and *Viking Voyage* (2001).

From Highway 82 West, take a left onto the Broadway Loop. You will pass the visitors' center on your right. Follow the loop to Broadway. The old Percy home was at the intersection of Broadway and Percy on the right.

Site of Percy Home

601 Percy Street

If the Delta, as David Cohn has so famously remarked, begins in the Peabody Hotel in Memphis, then its literary life began in the home of William Alexander Percy (1885–1942), planter, lawyer, and writer. A large, rambling two-story structure in the Greek Revival style, the house was built by Will Percy's grandfather, Colonel William Alexander Percy. Called "the Gray Eagle," the colonel was a leader during the Reconstruction era.

Will's father, LeRoy, was an aristocrat who became a state senator. Will Percy's mother, Camille, was French Catholic. His only sibling, a younger brother, LeRoy, was killed in an accidental shooting by a playmate at age ten.

Percy is best known for his autobiography, *Lanterns on the Levee* (1941). Enormously popular, *Lanterns* was reprinted ten times in its first year. In it, Percy provides a vivid description of the 1927 flood in Greenville. As chair of the flood-relief committee for the Red Cross, he supervised the rescue of sixty thousand people and thirty thousand head of stock. He describes the horror of a dead mule floating through the living room and the serendipity of bootleggers providing rescue in their motorboats free of charge. He comments on sharecropping and class structure.

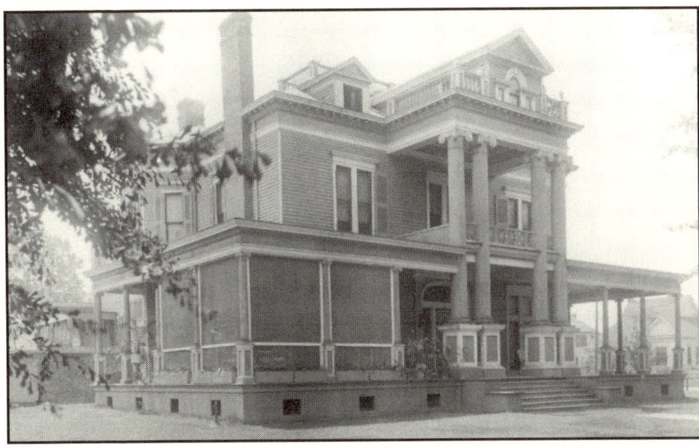

William Alexander Percy home, Greenville

He laments the loss of agrarian values such as moral integrity, kindness, and social conscience in the face of technological progress. He describes dances and other social activities and the idiosyncracies of family members—the genteel aunt, for instance, whose inopportune napping was found to be caused by her secret habit of nipping morphine.

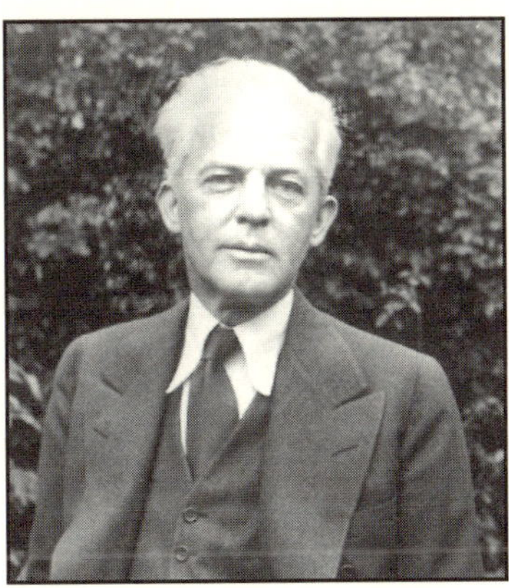

William Alexander Percy

Percy was also a poet who wrote in a distinctly Victorian style. Among his published volumes are *Sappho in Levkas and Other Poems* (1915), *In April Once* (1920), *The Collected Poems of William Alexander Percy* (1943), and *Of Silence and Stars* (1953).

In midlife, after the tragic suicide of cousin LeRoy Pratt Percy of Birmingham and the subsequent death of his wife in a car accident, Percy adopted their offspring, three teenage boys, LeRoy, Phinizy, and Walker. The Percy home was a gathering place for friends of these young boys and a cultural magnet for writers. Local ones included Shelby Foote, David Cohn, Hodding Carter, and William Faulkner, who came to play tennis. From other parts came Roark Bradford, Conrad Aiken, Ruth Draper, Langston

Hughes, Stephen Vincent Benét, Hortense Powdermaker, Stark Young, and Dorothy Parker. Psychiatrist Harry Stack Sullivan came to study race relations in the South. Carl Sandburg visited and played his guitar. Vachel Lindsay came up from Gulf Park (see Long Beach) and recited poems complete with sound effects. A small man, weighing only 110 pounds, with silver hair and grey-blue eyes, Percy greeted them all politely at the front door, perhaps offering them one of his famous mint juleps. (He gives the recipe in *Lanterns on the Levee.*)

After the house was demolished, Shelby Foote, who once spent a week there after being expelled from school, wrote a letter to his friend Walker (collected by Jay Tolson): "You ought to see 601 [Percy Street]—or rather you oughtnt. A skeleton. You can look right through the walls and see where we used to sleep and read, and the fireplaces where the fires were and where Mr. Will used to light his matches, padding around in fuzzy slippers and robe that he couldnt keep the belt tied to."

Walker Percy (1916–1990) was born in Birmingham. His early life was marked by the tragic death of his father by suicide and his mother three years later in a car accident. He and his brothers, LeRoy and Phinizy, were subsequently adopted by Will Percy, their second cousin, whom they always called "Uncle Will." Walker attended Greenville High School where he was befriended by two other young men who would grow up to be writers, Shelby Foote and Charles Bell. He later attended the University of North Carolina where he wrote for the school's *Carolina Magazine* and graduated in 1937.

He intended to become a doctor. He received his M.D. degree from the College of Physicians and Surgeons, Columbia University, with high honors. But while an intern at Bellevue Hospital in New York, he contracted tuberculosis. During his convalescence at a sanatorium on Saranac Lake in the Adirondacks, he began to read widely and deeply, especially the great Russian novelists and philosophers such as Kierkegaard and Heidegger. Like his Uncle Will, he turned to writing.

His first novel, *The Moviegoer* (1961), won the 1962 National Book Award. Subsequent novels followed, to wide acclaim: *The*

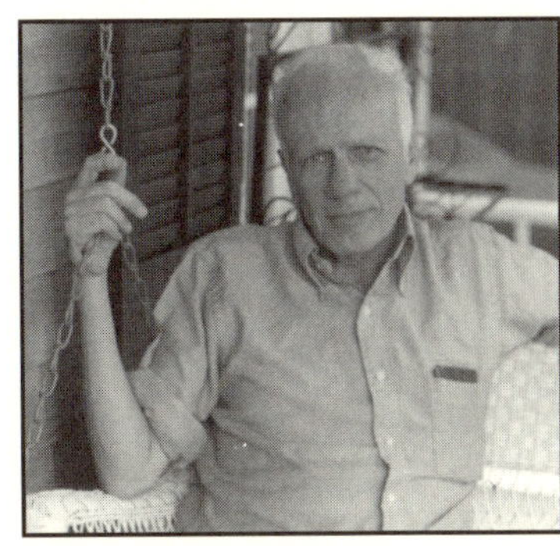

Walker Percy

Last Gentleman (1966), *Love in the Ruins* (1971), *Lancelot* (1977), *The Second Coming* (1980), and *The Thanatos Syndrome* (1987). In addition, he published important philosophical essays and such nonfiction works as *The Message in the Bottle* (1975) and *Lost in the Cosmos* (1983). With these publications, Percy came to be regarded by critics as a writer of major importance. Significant biographies and critical studies have been published about Percy and his writings, including Jay Tolson's *Pilgrim in the Ruins: A Life of Walker Percy* (1992).

A converted Roman Catholic, Percy was married to the former Mary Bernice "Bunt" Townsend. They lived in Covington, Louisiana, and raised two daughters there. His death elicited stirring tributes from other writers. Eudora Welty said his work had "boldness and daring and grace and imagination." His old friend Shelby Foote said, "He belongs with the great Southern writers."

Site for Robertshaw House

Percy Street

Will Percy's relative Sarah Catherine Lee Ferguson (1842–?) and her Rebel husband, General Samuel Wragg Ferguson, lived next door to the Percys for two years in the Robertshaw house built by her father. Kate was the daughter of Eleanor Ware Lee, a poet from Natchez, and aunt of novelist Sarah Ann Ellis. (See Natchez for their biographies.)

In a journal collected in *Samuel Wragg Ferguson*, Kate wrote, "We had a large comfortable frame house, horses, dogs, carriages, and everything to make the home a happy one." The Fergusons and Percys were close. Will Percy's mother had played the piano at their wedding, and one of their daughters was named Percy. But their friendship was marred in 1894 when twenty thousand dollars disappeared while Ferguson was secretary and treasurer of the levee board. Suspicions against him further intensified when he suddenly left town, first going to Charleston, South Carolina, then to Ecuador. In *Lanterns on the Levee*, Will Percy describes Ferguson's return many years later: "A little shabby old man in a gray suit and bright red tie, his white hair untidy, his white beard untrimmed." After greeting him, Will's father, LeRoy, quietly and graciously invited him in to dinner.

Kate was a poet and also wrote a novel called *Cliquot*, published in 1889 by T. B. Peterson & Brothers. One critic described it as a "racy" novel. The subtitle *A Racing Story of Ideal Beauty* raised the question as to whether it was a *racy* novel or a *racing* novel. The answer is—both. Although the novel's protagonist is male, the reader's interest is captivated by the saucy Gwendoline Gwinn, who disguises herself as a male jockey, mounts Cliquot, a racehorse famous for throwing his male riders, and rides him to victory. Other revelations follow. Ferguson cleverly uses the gender reversal to examine "the woman question" brewing at the time.

Continue north on Broadway to Main Street. Take a left on Main.

William Alexander Percy Memorial Library

341 Main Street

The library has a fine display with biographical texts and pictures of Greenville writers. Also of interest is the Hodding Carter room, which contains oral histories and other archival material that reflects the life of the town. Housed here is a bust of William Alexander Percy sculpted by Greenville artist Leon Koury. The sculpture captured the attention of both *Time* and *Life* magazines in 1964. Koury's career in art was initiated and nurtured by William Alexander Percy.

Former Delta Democrat Times Office

201 Main Street

Will Percy, David Cohn, and several other prominent businessmen were responsible for bringing to Greenville newspaperman Hodding Carter (1907–1972). Born in Hammond, Louisiana,

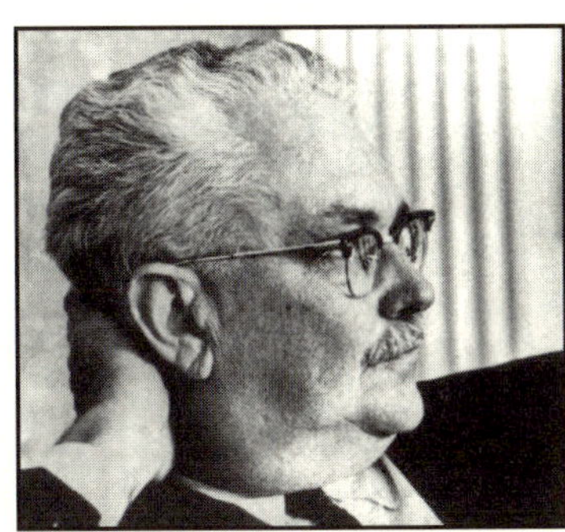
Hodding Carter

Carter graduated from Bowdoin College and studied at the Pulitzer School of Journalism at Columbia University. He worked at the New Orleans *Item-Tribune,* then for the Associated Press in Jackson, Mississippi. Although he was once dismissed from a newspaper for "insubordination" and told he would "never make a good newspaperman," Carter prevailed and went on to win the Pulitzer Prize for journalism in 1946.

In a 1948 issue of *America,* he recalled that, after selling his first story, he telegraphed his beloved Betty Werlein and instructed her to get fitted for a wedding dress because he had sold the story to *American Magazine* for three hundred dollars. Coauthored with Carter Bynum, the story, "Brothers under the Skin," was about two marines in Haiti. With that three hundred dollars and sixty-seven dollars more, Carter started a daily newspaper in Hammond, Louisiana. "Hodding has never been a marine," Betty later admitted, "and we keep telling ourselves that we ought to go to Haiti some time to see what our favorite foreign country is like."

In 1935, Will Percy and others recruited Carter to start a daily newspaper to rival the *Democrat Times.* Before long, Carter had it going and named it the *Delta Democrat Times.* In 1945, Carter published a series of editorials calling for racial, religious, and economic tolerance after the war, the most notable of which was "Go for Broke," in which he urged tolerance for Japanese-Americans. For these editorials, he was awarded the Pulitzer Prize in journalism.

A moderate during the racial turbulence of the fifties and sixties, Carter is credited by many for the progressive spirit of Greenville. But the stands he took were often controversial. For instance, after he editorialized against the newly formed Citizens' Council in 1954, the Mississippi House of Representatives voted a resolution against him. Never one to back away from a fight, Carter printed a counterattack on the front page of his newspaper.

Along with the autobiographical *Where Main Street Meets the River,* Carter wrote many other nonfiction works such as *Southern*

Legacy (1950) and *So the Heffners Left McComb* (1965). He also wrote poetry collected in *The Ballad of Catfoot Grimes* (1964).

Carter's literary leanings were contagious. On his staff were reporter Shelby Foote, who would go on to become a famous novelist and historian, arts columnist Ben Wasson, who would write a novel, and society columnist Louise Crump, who would write two.

• The Levee Press

The newspaper office of the *Delta Democrat Times* provided a location for the Levee Press, Greenville's famous literary press. The originators of this venture were Hodding Carter, Ben Wasson, Kenneth Haxton, and David Cohn. When the problem of naming the press came up, one of them, no one remembers who, nodded towards the river and said the Levee Press, and that was that.

Although short-lived, the press spawned four collector's items, Shelby Foote's *The Merchant of Bristol* (1947), Eudora Welty's *Music from Spain* (1948), William Faulkner's *Notes on a Horsethief* (1950), later part of *A Fable*, and William Alexander Percy's *Of Silence and Stars* (1953). A few months after his *Notes on a Horsethief* was published by Levee Press, Faulkner received the Nobel Prize for literature.

In a lively chapter from *Where Main Street Meets the River*, Carter described a momentous afternoon when Bill Faulkner decided to pay a visit to the Levee Press. Carter said Faulkner was crouched in an awkward half-sitting, half-standing position to sign his books and that his ratio of signed books to beer was "sixty copies per Budweiser." Shelby Foote later described the signing in a letter to Walker Percy. Faulkner told Foote that *Follow Me Down*, just published, was a good book. "And then," Foote wrote, "he looked at me rather piercingly and added: 'Do better next time.'"

Historic Marker at the Levee

"Where Main Street Meets the River"

One of the most significant events in the life of the town was the 1927 flood when the levee broke at Mound Landing near Scott, about fifteen miles north of Greenville. The waters flooded and stood over 2,722,000 acres of Delta land for four months. The flood was the great antagonist in Will Percy's autobiography.

The levee was the subject poet Charles Bell used to win his first literary prize. When he was a child, he participated in a school-run writing contest and was given the topic "The Greatest Hill I Have Known." He was stumped until he saw that with a little literary license the levee qualified as a hill. About that "hill," he found he had much to say, and did, and won the prize.

Beyond the levee, Lake Ferguson is a setting in Ellen Douglas's short story "Hold On," and beyond Lake Ferguson is the Mississippi River, immortalized by great writers from Mark Twain to William Faulkner. Faulkner's *The Old Man* is set during the 1927 flood, its drama derived from Parchman prisoners desperately trying to rescue helpless men, women, children, and livestock.

Turn around and travel east on Main Street over the railroad tracks.

Bass Auditorium

305 South Main Street

Walker Percy, Shelby Foote, and Charles Bell all attended Greenville High School, now Bass Auditorium and Delta Center Stage. Caroline Stern, mentor to Will Percy and others, taught here. A lifetime friendship between Shelby Foote and Walker Percy began in study hall. They both worked on the school newspaper and published poems in the school literary journal, *Pica.* In letters collected by Jay Tolson, Percy claimed that Foote decided to become a writer when he saw students paying Percy fifty cents for every sonnet he wrote for their assignments.

McCormick Book Inn

825 South Main Street

Hugh McCormick runs this comfortable, family-owned bookstore. It houses a fine collection of first editions by Mississippi authors and a postcard collection of buildings no longer standing, such as the Grand Opera House. Ellen Douglas first met fellow writer Willie Morris at a McCormick book signing. In

Remembering Willie, she recalled, "He was having a grand time and he made it an exciting time for everyone."

Greenville Cemetery

South Main Street

The Percy plot is dominated by the life-size bronze statue of Will Percy's father, U.S. senator LeRoy Percy, depicted as a knight draped in heavy mail. It was crafted by the highly regarded American sculptor Malvina Hoffman. The knight's lowered head and sword suggest defeat. Matthew Arnold's poem "The Last Word" is engraved on the back of the statue. Percy devotes a chapter in *Lanterns on the Levee* to the cemetery. Greenville native and writer Beverly Lowry has recalled that in her youth, she would sneak into the cemetery at night to visit the defeated knight with his "gloomy countenance."

From Main, take a left onto Weatherbee.

234 Weatherbee Street

This handsome cottage called "Twin Oaks" was once the home of Louise Eskrigge Crump (1903–1968). Born in Greenville, Mrs. Crump was an energetic and civic-minded journalist who wrote for the *Delta Democrat Times*. Her husband, Brodie, also wrote a column. Mrs. Crump single-handedly started a health campaign to punch holes in used tin cans to prevent mosquitoes from breeding. She published the novel *Helen Templeton's Daughter* (1952) about a plantation family in Washington County in the early nineteenth century. She also wrote a murder mystery set in Greenville, *The Face of Fear* (1954).

Haxton House

410 Weatherbee Street

In 1961, a short story entitled "On the Lake," clearly set in Greenville, appeared in *The New Yorker*. The writer was Ellen Douglas (1921). Knowing no Ellen Douglas, natives speculated about who had written the story, which featured a thinly disguised Lake Ferguson. They finally narrowed the field to two candidates who lived in Greenville: Josephine Haxton and her husband at the time, Kenneth. Hodding Carter was dispatched to make the call to the Haxton residence. One of the Haxtons' three sons answered, and Carter asked, "May I speak to Ellen Douglas?" When the child yelled, "Mama, telephone," Douglas's identity was no longer a secret. "On the Lake" won an O. Henry Prize and later appeared as "Hold On" in *Black Cloud, White Cloud* (1963).

Her friend Charles Bell gave Douglas's manuscript *A Family's Affairs* to his publisher Craig Wiley at Houghton Mifflin. Soon after, Wiley called Douglas to say he wanted to enter it in the twenty-fifth anniversary fellowship competition. After some hesitation on Douglas's part, Wiley told her that the sooner she made up her mind to enter it, the sooner he could tell her she had already won. Since *A Family's Affairs* appeared in 1962, Douglas has published many novels and stories, and won many awards. Her novels include *Where the Dreams Cross* (1968), *Apostles of Light* (1973), *The Rock Cried Out* (1979), and *A Lifetime Burning* (1982). Among her awards are Book-of-the-Month Club Alternate Selection and Mississippi Institute of Arts and Letters Award for Literature. (See Jackson for more about her.)

Kenneth Haxton is Josephine Haxton's former husband and currently resides at this address. A musician and one of the founders of the Greenville Symphony, he was also a cofounder of the Levee Press, and has published a novel, *The Undiscovered Country.*

Under the positive artistic influence of his parents, Kenneth and Josephine, Brooks Haxton became a poet, an impulse that began with protest poetry inspired by Bob Dylan songs in junior high. Haxton studied poetry at Beloit College and Syracuse University. He has taught creative writing at George Mason University, the University of Maryland, Sarah Lawrence College, and Warren Wilson College.

Dominion (1986) is a collection of Brooks Haxton's shorter poems. *Fragments* (2001), a translation of the ancient Greek writings of Heraclitus, was favorably reviewed in *Time* magazine. In 2001, he published a poetry collection entitled *Nakedness, Death, and the Number Zero.*

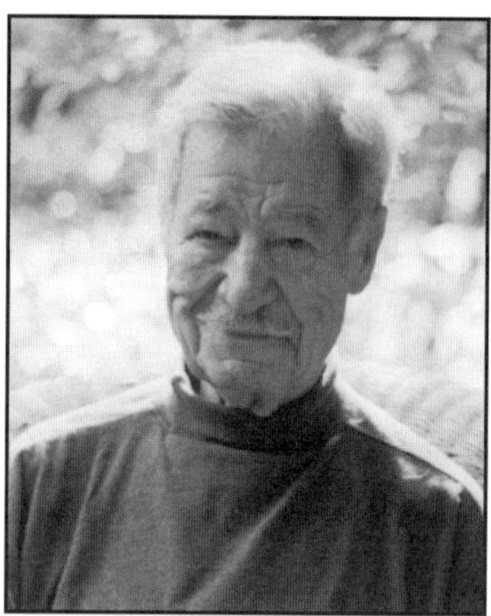
Bern Keating

Return to Main and continue south to Bayou Road.

Keating House

141 Bayou Road

Bern Keating (1915) grew up in Quebec Province, Canada. After serving in the navy during World War II, he came to Greenville with nine hundred dollars he had won in a craps game. He opened a photography studio and set to work as a photojournalist. He was soon swamped, and his wife, Franke, quietly took over as photographer. With him, his daughter Kate Keating (1948–1971) coauthored three travel books for young people on Denmark, France, and Italy.

His articles and stories for such magazines as *Town and Country, Smithsonian, Travel and Leisure, Life, Look,* and *National Geographic* have taken him all over the globe—to Australia, India, the Philippines, and Russia. He has published in a number of genres, including histories for children, among them *Zebulon Pike: Young American's Frontier Scout* (1965), and, for adults, *Life and Death of the Aztec Nation* (1964). He has also written fiction (*The Horse That Won the Civil War*, 1964). With Franke Keating, he published *Mississippi* (1982), a pictoral history of the state.

Bern and Franke Keating continue to live and work together in Greenville. In 1995, the two received the Special Achievement Award from the Mississippi Institute of Arts and Letters.

Return to Main Street. When Main merges with Washington, take the right fork onto Washington.

930 South Washington Avenue

Born and raised in Greenville, Lucile Robinson Finlay (1897–1985) published a book called *The Coat I Wore* (1947) about Mississippi under Spanish rule. She was the first woman to be admitted to the Mississippi Bar Association and was for a time associated in a firm with Charles Bell's father, Judge Percy Bell.

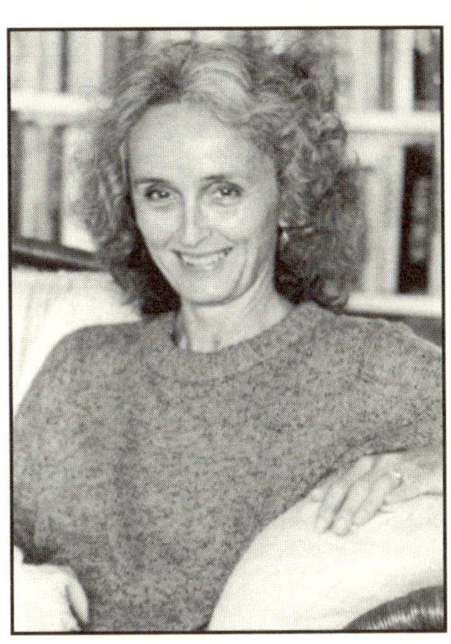
Beverly Lowry

830 South Washington Avenue

Born in Memphis, Beverly Lowry (1938) grew up in Greenville. She attended the University of Mississippi and received a degree from Memphis State University. She moved to New York, then to Texas. Put off by Greenville's worship of its aristocratic "patron saint," William Alexander Percy, she disclaimed Greenville's influence on early novels such as *Come Back, Lolly Ray* (1977), *Emma Blue* (1978), and *Daddy's Girl* (1981). Yet, paradoxically, she was haunted by the knight in the Percy plot of the Greenville cemetery, and he appears in two of her novels. In later interviews, she admitted that Percy's influence was unavoidable.

A more recent novel, *On the Track of Real Desires* (1995), is set in a thinly disguised Greenville. *Crossing Over: A Murder, A Memoir* (1992) is a departure from the early works both in theme and setting. It involves the artistic overlapping of the story of an accused murderer from Houston, Karla Faye Tucker, with a poignant memoir about Lowry's son, Peter, who was killed in an unsolved hit-and-run.

Lowry has won many awards, including the Jesse Jones Award. She has been a recipient of a National Endowment for the Arts Fellowship and a Guggenheim Fellowship. She is past president of the Texas Institute of Letters.

717 South Washington Avenue

Charles Bell (1916) grew up in this red-brick, white-columned home built by his father, Judge Percy Bell. Here young Charles set up his telescope to watch the stars and developed a passion for

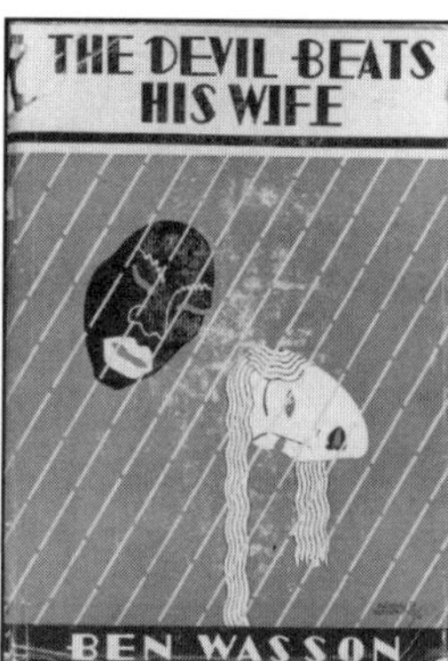

Book jacket, *The Devil Beats His Wife*, by Ben Wasson

astronomy that spilled over into almost every field of study. It led to his "Symbolic History," a multimedia historic study of Western culture, presented in Washington, London, Chicago, and many other cities.

After graduating from the University of Virginia as a Rhodes Scholar in 1936, he went on to receive higher degrees from Oxford University. He has taught English and physics at various colleges and universities. A collection of poems, *Delta Return* (1956), and the novel *The Married Land* (1962) particularly reflect Bell's early years in the Delta.

623 South Washington Avenue

Ben Wasson (1899–1983) lived in this two-story, mission-style house of stucco and red tile, built about 1913 and purchased by the Wassons in 1919.

Wasson met Faulkner on his first day at Ole Miss. Seeing Faulkner for the first time, Wasson asked his companion who he was and was told, "That's Count No 'Count. Tha's what everybody calls him 'cause he ain't any good." Later, Wasson would write a book about Faulkner, *Count No 'Count* (1983).

As a literary agent, he rescued two important literary works from the rejection heap: Erskine Caldwell's *Tobacco Road* and Dashiell Hammett's *The Thin Man.* Wasson was for a time Faulkner's literary agent and edited what would become *Sartoris*, shrewdly cutting away the excess but preserving the now famous "mule passage." Wasson was also writing his own novel at the time, *The Devil Beats His Wife.* Both novels were published in 1929. Wasson was responsible for bringing Faulkner to the Levee Press for publication.

After living in New York and southern California, Wasson returned to Greenville in the late 1940s and began to write an arts column, "The Time Has Come," for the *Delta Democrat Times.* The title was used for a 1982 celebration of Greenville writers.

502 South Washington Avenue

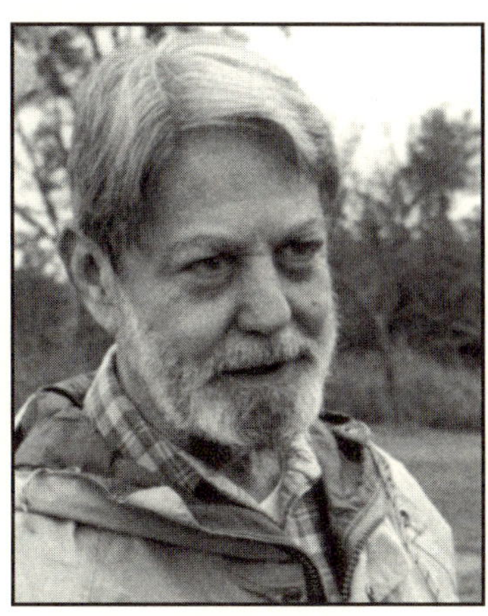
Shelby Foote

Greenville-born Shelby Foote (1916) spent the early years of his life moving with his family where his father's work took them, to Jackson, Vicksburg, Pensacola, and Mobile. After his father's death in 1922, he and his mother returned to Greenville, to this California-style bungalow on Washington Avenue, not far from the Old Sanitarium Hospital where Foote was born.

Foote wrote his first five novels in five years while living at this address. He confessed some discomfort about living with his neighbors when his first novel, *Tournament,* was published in 1949. In a letter collected by Jay Tolson, he remembered that, while getting a haircut in the local barbershop, he overheard a remark made by a woman in the beauty shop next door. "He says it's about his grandfather," she said, "but I knew his grandfather and *he* was a nice man." Other novels include *Follow Me Down* (1950), *Love in a Dry Season* (1951), and *September, September* (1977).

A major achievement for Foote was *The Civil War: A Narrative,* a three-volume history published in 1958, 1963, and 1974. The exhaustive history required twenty years of research yet flows like a good story. "Been going great guns," Foote wrote to Walker Percy, "more than 10,000 words in the past month. Captured Jeff Davis yesterday, locked him up in Ft Monroe today. Now on to Andy Johnson, who looks to me as if he's headed for impeachment. Strike the tent!"

Foote was a popular narrator for the PBS series *The Civil War,* written by Ken Burns. He resides with his wife, Gwyn, in Memphis.

Continue on Washington to Walker Street. At Walker, take a right.

343 Walker Street

David Cohn (1897–1960) was a descendent of Polish Jews who migrated to America in the nineteenth century. After many successful years in the business world (among other jobs he was advertising manager for Sears, Roebuck), Cohn resigned in order to write. He took up residence at Will Percy's home for two years while writing *God Shakes Creation* (1935), a study of Delta blacks in the thirties (expanded in the 1967 book *Where I Was Born and Raised*). In this memoir, Cohn muses on the impossibility of reconciling racial prejudice with democracy. In chapter two, Cohn makes his famous remark: "The Delta begins in the lobby of the Peabody Hotel in Memphis and ends on Catfish Row in Vicksburg."

In articles he wrote for magazines such as *The Atlantic Monthly*, Cohn revealed a serious concern for politics in the Deep South, yet his views were anything but provincial. He wrote the 1952 campaign speech for Adlai Stevenson at Richmond, Virginia, which was a carefully guarded secret until Stevenson himself let it be known. The speech was hailed as a masterful blend of tradition and progress. When asked why he quit a successful career for writing, Cohn replied that writing was similar to duck hunting: Once started, he couldn't seem to stop.

Continue on Walker to Carrie Stern Lane. Take a right onto Carrie Stern, then a left on McAllister.

Carrie Stern School

Highway 82 at McAllister Street

The Carrie Stern School was named for Caroline Stern (1868–1920). Her charming pen-and-ink rendering gives an idea of what her now-razed house on Edison Street looked like. Frequent guests were young protégés Will Percy and David Cohn. At age sixteen, she began teaching at Greenville High School, but she always wanted to paint. After struggling for several years to save money out of her teacher's salary, she attended art school in New York. Upon discovering she had lead poisoning, she had to give up painting.

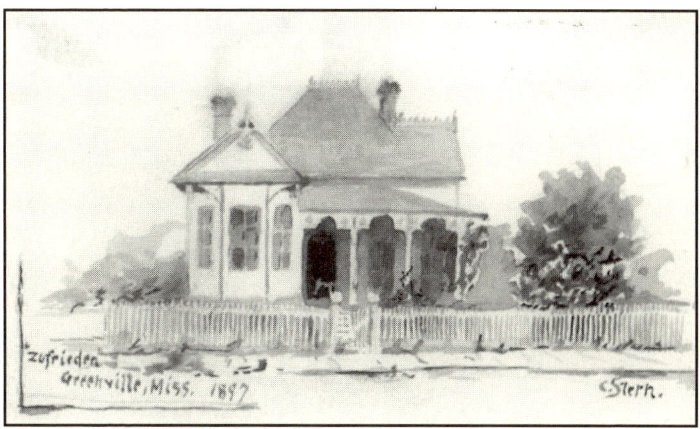

Caroline Stern home, Greenville

She turned to poetry and published a collection called *At the Edge of the World* (1916). Cohn attributed his love for English verse and for the Italian Renaissance to her. Percy pays tribute to her in *Lanterns on the Levee.* "Miss Carrie," he wrote, "had failed in everything—in painting, in poetry, in making money, in winning love, in dying easy. Yet she was one of the few successes I ever knew. I think I learned more from her of what the good life is and of how it may be lived than from almost anyone else."

Go east on Highway 82 to Leland. The Jim Henson Museum is on your left on Highway 82 at Deer Creek.

Leland

Jim Henson Museum

Highway 82

Born in Greenville, Jim Henson (1936–1990) grew up in Leland. He became a famous television writer when he created the Muppets of *Sesame Street.* His life and work are celebrated at the Jim Henson Museum. He received eighteen Emmy awards, seven Grammy awards, and numerous other tributes. He died of pneumonia at the young age of fifty-four.

Leland native Robert Hitt Neill has published a collection of hunting stories, *The Flaming Turkey.* With James Baugh, he wrote a memoir entitled *How to Lose Your Farm and Cope with It in Ten Easy Lessons* (1985).

Continue on Highway 82E to Indianola

Indianola

Originally named Indian Bayou for the slow-moving waters that meander through it, Indianola was also called Eureka and Belengate before its present name was chosen. The town has been a source for two major studies, one sociological—John Dollard's *Caste and Class in a Southern Town* (1937)—and one anthropological—*After Freedom* (1939) by Hortense Powdermaker. Internationally recognized blues artist B. B. King was born on a plantation on the outskirts of town. A major influence on other blues artists, King throws an annual concert every June for fellow Indianolans. A few miles to the north is Drew, home of Archie Manning, the legendary football star who, with his son Peyton, published a sports memoir, *Manning* (2000). Deborah Powell, author of the mystery *Bayou City Secrets* (1991) and others, grew up in nearby Sunflower.

Yarbrough Site

Beaverdam Road

Steve Yarbrough (1956) grew up in a house on Route 2 three or four miles from the Fairview Baptist Church on Beaverdam Road. The house burned down over twenty years ago. His fiction is filled with people like the ones he knew while growing up in Indianola—catfish farmers, bankers, and history teachers. Like the character in "The Tower," his father ran a local television station for many years.

Yarbrough has published two short story collections, *Family Men* (1990) and *Mississippi History* (1994). In 1999, he published his first novel, *Oxygen Man*, which won the Mississippi Author's Award, the California Book Award, and an award from the Mississippi Institute of Arts and Letters. In 1999–2000, he was writer-in-residence at Ole Miss. His second novel, *Visible Spirits*, was published in the spring of 2001. Yarbrough lives with his wife in Fresno, California, where he currently teaches creative writing at the University of California.

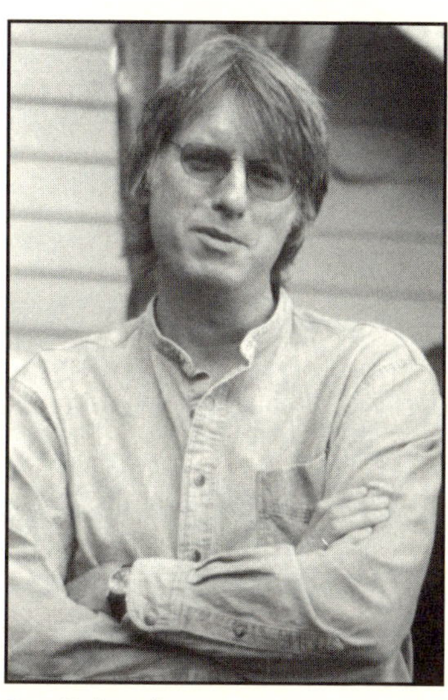

Steve Yarbrough

From Highway 82, go right on Catchings Street. Take a right at the post office onto Percy Street.

208 West Percy Street

This boyhood home of Craig Claiborne was once a boardinghouse run by Claiborne's mother. Two of Mrs. Claiborne's most famous boarders were Hortense Powdermaker and John Dollard.

Craig Claiborne (1920–2000) was born in Sunflower, a town of fewer than five hundred people at the time. The family moved to Indianola in 1924. Claiborne attended Mississippi State College and graduated from the University of Missouri with a degree in journalism. He served in the navy during World War II and the Korean conflict. After studying at École Hôtelière, in Lausanne, Switzerland, he went to work for *Gourmet* magazine. In 1957, he became food editor for the *New York Times*, a position he held until 1971. He is credited with transforming American taste in food. Along with his columns, Claiborne published over a dozen cookbooks including the popular 1961 *New York Times Cookbook*, which sold over a million copies.

Claiborne's most famous meal was a four-thousand-dollar dinner at Chez Denis in Paris in 1975. When American Express auctioned a dinner for two anywhere in the world, Claiborne put in a single bid of three hundred dollars and was amazed to discover he had won. With fellow chef Pierre Franey, he feasted on caviar, foie gras, truffles, quail, oysters, lobster, sweetbreads, charlottes, and pears. In his autobiography, *A Feast Made for Laughter* (1982), Claiborne admitted that the eleven bottles of wine they ordered

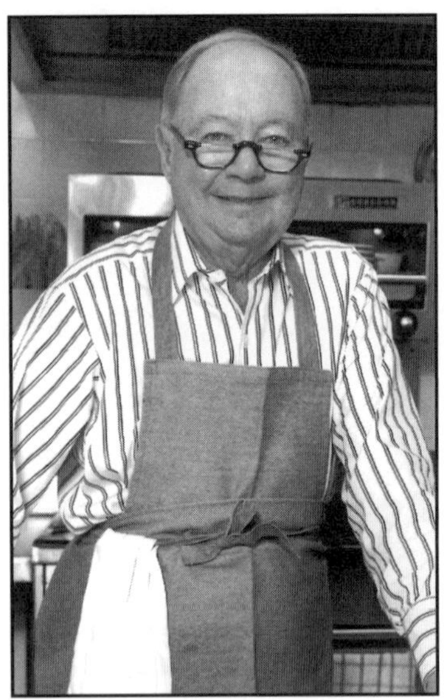
Craig Claiborne

had run up the tab. Among the wines were a 1918 Château Latour, a 1929 Romanée-Conti, and a 1928 Château d'Yquem. And what did the eminent food critic think of the meal? "The food itself was generally exemplary, although there were regrettable lapses . . . ," he wrote.

507 East Percy Street

When Anne Reed Rooth (1933) was growing up, this stucco home on Percy Street was pink and was referred to as "The Pink Palace." Rooth was named Debutante of America in 1951 and in 1952 was chosen Miss Indianola. Her first mystery, *The Ninth Car*, coauthored by James P. White, was published in 1978. Several other mysteries have followed, including *Southern Exposure* (1999), set in the Delta. Ms. Rooth now lives in Dallas, Texas, and Rancho Santa Fe, California.

At East Percy Street's dead end, take a right, then a quick left to Barberry Lane.

101 Barberry Lane

Mary Dubose Garrard (1937) lived briefly in this home built by her parents in 1951 before she went to college. Her sister, Marion Garrard Barnwell, coauthor of this book, grew up here.

Garrard attended Newcomb College and Radcliffe College, and received a Ph.D. from Johns Hopkins University. An eminent art historian and professor at American University in Washington, D.C., she and coauthor Norma Broude have written several significant works on women artists, including *Feminism and Art History* (1982), *The Expanding Discourse* (1992), and *The Power of*

Feminist Art (1994). In *Artemesia Gentileschi* (1989), Garrard rescued from obscurity the life and works of the notable Italian woman artist of the Baroque period.

Return to Percy Street. Go two blocks and take a right at Park Avenue.

207 Park Avenue

Historian, educator, and author, Terry Alford (1945) was born in Mobile, Alabama, and grew up in Indianola. In his biography *Prince Among Slaves* (1977), Alford recounts the story of Abd al Rahman Ibrahima, an African prince who became a slave owned by Thomas Foster of Natchez. A National Endowment for the Humanities fellow, Alford has taught American history at Northern Virginia Community College since 1972.

Continue on Park Avenue to Highway 82. Go right and continue on Highway 82 east to Moorhead.

Moorhead

Turn off Highway 82 into downtown Moorhead on Highway 3 South. Just off Highway 3, the C & G intersects the Southern railroad.

The Yellow Dog Crossing

Two important train rails, the Columbus-Greenville (the Southern) and the Yazoo-Delta (Yellow Dog), intersect at this historic crossing, calling forth the now famous phrase "where the Southern crosses the Dog." Some say the initials Y. D. painted on the engine may have inspired the imaginative nickname Yellow Dog. Others remember a yellow dog that barked at the train. Legend has it that during World War I, homesick soldiers overseas would holler, "Who knows where the Southern crosses the Dog?" and then wait to hear a fellow Mississippian call back, "Moorhead."

The crossing has artistic significance as well. Blues musician W. C. Handy sang about it in "The Yellow Dog Blues." Eudora

Welty wrote about it in the novel *Delta Wedding*. Artist Carroll Cloar captured it in his painting *Where the Southern Crosses the Dog.*

In November of 2000, citizens of Moorhead were outraged when, without notice, the C & G ripped up the spikes, ties, and nails to make repairs. Because the crossing has never been officially declared a Mississippi landmark, its long-range outcome is uncertain.

Continue on Highway 82E to Itta Bena.

Itta Bena

Itta Bena is a Chickasaw name said by locals to mean "home in the woods." It is the home of Mississippi Valley State University.

After passing Mississippi Valley State University on the left, take a right at the sign for Itta Bena. At Schley Street, turn right and continue through town on Schley. Take a right on Cleveland, then an immediate left onto Main Street.

202 Main Street

Born in Jackson, Lewis "Buddy" Nordan (1939) spent his first eighteen months in Forest, Mississippi, then moved with his mother to Itta Bena when his father died. Nordan received a B.A. from Millsaps College, an M.A. from Mississippi State University, and a Ph.D. from Auburn University. Among his honors are the 1997 John Gould Fletcher Award for fiction, the Porter Fund Prize, and the Mississippi Institute of Arts and Letters Award for Fiction.

When he heard Elvis Presley sing "Heartbreak Hotel," Nordan decided he wanted to be a writer, to communicate in words the loneliness, longing, and joy expressed in the song. Music has heavily influenced Nordan's work and runs through nearly all of his fiction, as reflected in such titles as *Music of the Swamp* (1991), *The Sharpshooter Blues* (1995), and *Lightning Song* (1997). Delta landscapes and locales figure prominently as well—country stores, shanties, baptisms, bus stations, swamps, and the "breathy asthma of the compress."

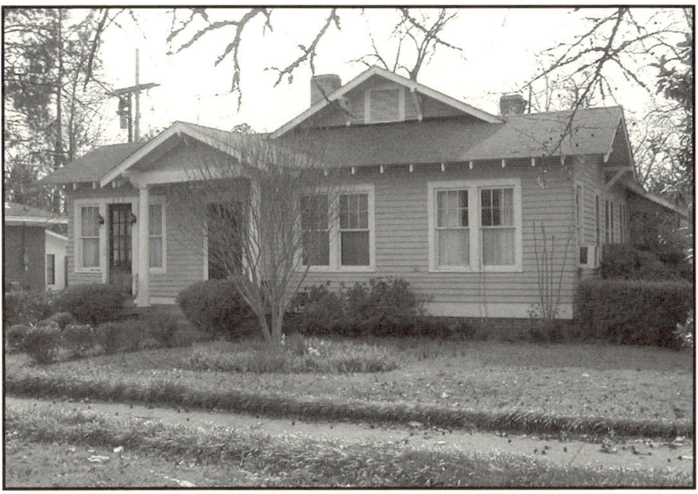

Lewis Nordan's childhood home, Itta Bena

Framed by his salt-and-pepper hair, Nordan's blue eyes reveal both the mischief and sorrow of his fiction. He uses a distinctively Delta brand of zaniness to alleviate stories otherwise full of grief. In *Lightning Song*, for instance, llamas roam the Delta.

Much of Nordan's work is experimental. He often challenges the boundary between "fiction" and "truth," at times using magic realism, and he admits to having "made up" parts of his memoir, *Boy with Loaded Gun* (2000). The author of seven books of fiction, he has taught at the University of Arkansas and currently teaches creative writing at the University of Pittsburgh in Pennsylvania.

Greenwood

Begun as a steamboat landing on the Yazoo River, the town was first named Williams' Landing for settler John Williams, who sold flour, sugar, rice, potatoes, and whiskey off his shanty boat. It was renamed for Greenwood Leflore, the Choctaw chief who became one of the largest landowners in neighboring Carroll County. After the first passenger train came through the town in 1886, Greenwood became known as the "world's largest inland long staple cotton market." The Tallahatchie River on the town's north end was the subject of the song "Ode to Billie Joe," made famous by Greenwood native Bobbie Gentry. Lined with stately oaks, Grand Boulevard is a main artery that stretches from the Tallahatchie to the Yazoo River.

Among Greenwood writers are Ray Locke and Cathy Criss Adams. Greenwood is the birthplace of Jim Fraiser and Donna Tartt. (See Grenada for Tartt's biography.) Mary Jayne Whittington, for many years a contributor to the *Delta Review*, edited with her sister Mabelle Garrard White the letters from their brother Staff Sergeant James Garrard, *Allegiance: World War II Letters Home* (1990).

Memoirist Chalmers Archer, Jr., is from nearby Tchula. John Fraiser Robinson, who collaborated with his friend Eudora Welty on the script for *The Robber Bridegroom* and published stories in *Harper's* and *The New Yorker*, lived on a plantation near Greenwood.

Born in Marshall County and raised in Mt. Pleasant, Tom Person (1900–1976) moved to Greenwood in 1944. Here he befriended a displaced Latvian family, models for the Zarins in his book, *The Land and the Water* (1953). He also wrote a historical novel, *Trouble on the Trace* (1954). Among Person's closest friends in Greenwood were fellow writers Mildred Topp, who lived down the street, and Frank Smith. An avid fisherman, Person wrote books for adolescents, among them *Bar-face* (1953).

Approaching Greenwood from the west, Highway 82 forks as it makes a curve. Take the left fork, which is West Street and becomes Park Avenue. Take Park to Grand Boulevard, take a left, and go over the Tallahatchie River Bridge to Money Road. The former Kimbrough house will be on your right.

Kimbrough House

73000 County Road 518

Mary Craig Kimbrough Sinclair (1882–1961) was born in Greenwood and grew up in this spacious house built about 1905. In 1976, the house was moved to this location from its original site at the corner of River Road and Mulberry Lane by owners Billy and Aubrey Whittington.

In 1900 Craig Kimbrough attended the Gardner School for Young Ladies in New York. There she visited Mrs. Jefferson Davis, who was a neighbor of the Kimbroughs at their summer home at Ashton Hall on the Mississippi sound near Beauvoir. (See Gulfport for more about Ashton Hall.) Young Craig aspired to write a biography of Winnie Davis, "the daughter of the Confederacy." Although she completed the manuscript, she decided it was not objective enough for publication.

While enrolled in a New York school to study writing, she renewed acquaintance with the writer and socialist Upton Sinclair. In the preface to the memorial edition of *Southern Belle*, Sinclair describes himself as "a man who had set out to help in the ending of poverty and war in the world." In 1913 Craig married Sinclair and joined him in his social causes. Among their acquaintances were Albert Einstein, Charlie Chaplin, Theodore Dreiser, and George Bernard Shaw.

In 1913, Upton Sinclair published a book called *Sylvia*, about a southern girlhood, material he clearly "borrowed" from his wife's writings. In the early 1920s, he also privately published a collection of Mrs. Sinclair's poetry called *Sonnets*, by M. C. S., also published in the 1962 edition of *Southern Belle*.

Return to Grand Boulevard. Continue several blocks to Claiborne Street. Take a left on Claiborne.

605 East Claiborne Street

Born in Sidon, Frank Smith (1918–1997) grew up in this home provided through public subscription by Leflore County citizens after the tragic and senseless death of his father, Chief Deputy Frank Smith. In 1926, Deputy Smith stopped to pick up a black hitchhiker named Sylvester Mackey, then hesitated when he thought he recognized the man from the "Wanted" list. Though innocent, Mackey panicked and shot Smith. Before he died the next day, Smith urged fellow deputies to keep their heads, thereby heroically heading off a possible lynching. Mackey went to trial, was found guilty, and was later executed. Young Frank's later political career was shaped by the tragedy.

During World War II, Smith rose to the rank of major and received a Bronze Star. In 1947, he was elected to the Mississippi Senate and became legislative assistant to Senator John Stennis. He later served in the U.S. House of Representatives. In his autobiographies *Congressman from Mississippi* (1964) and *Look Away from Dixie* (1965), Smith wrote about his defeat for reelection in 1962 after he took a stand against segregation.

In *The Yazoo River* (1954), written for the Rivers of America series, Smith provides a rich cultural and geographical history of the region, with stories about local characters such as Mike Hooter, Mildred Maury Humphreys, John Sharp Williams, James K. Vardaman, and W. C. Handy. In columns for the *Clarion-Ledger* from 1985 to 1990, Smith often wrote about Mississippi's legacy of outstanding writers.

Return to Grand Boulevard. Continue over the Yazoo River Bridge. Once you cross the bridge, you are on Fulton Street. The courthouse is on the right. The former Spurrier photography shop is on the left.

109 Fulton Street

Now a real estate company, this office was once Mrs. Spurrier's Photographic Gallery. In 1906, after the death of her husband, Mrs. Spurrier moved to Greenwood from Tennessee, bringing along her nine-year-old daughter, who would grow up to be the writer Mildred Spurrier Topp (1897–1963). Her mother set up a portrait photography shop in the two-story building, rented out the top floor, and lived with her daughter below. Topp used the setting in her best-selling autobiography, *Smile Please* (1948).

A 1917 graduate of the Industrial Institute and College (now Mississippi University for Women), Topp taught English at Greenwood High School and served in the Mississippi legislature from 1932 to 1936. After receiving an M.A. degree at the University of Mississippi, Topp stayed on to teach creative writing for several years.

In 1947, at age fifty, she found a ream of paper in her attic and began writing because she didn't know what else she would do with it. She met fellow Mississippian Ben Ames Williams at a writers' workshop at the University of Colorado, and he helped her publish

Smile Please. Best-seller *In the Pink* (1950) soon followed, with more humorous anecdotes about her childhood years in Greenwood.

Continue through downtown Greenwood on Fulton Street. At Gibbs Street, take a left. The empty lot at 114 East Gibbs was formerly the Holland home.

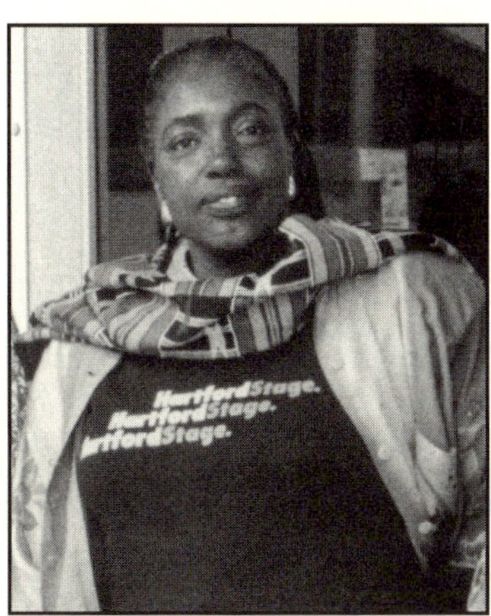

Endesha Ida Mae Holland

Holland Site

114 East Gibbs Street

Playwright Endesha Ida Mae "Cat" Holland was born in Greenwood in 1944 in a section of town called "Gee Pee." The lot where the Holland house once stood is now empty.

Ida and her mother, called Aint Baby, were both named for crusader Ida Wells of Holly Springs. The driving force in her daughter's life, Aint Baby was born on a plantation in Belzoni. Often destitute, she was a laundress and ran a brothel in Greenwood. Although illiterate, she became a midwife through sheer determination. Aint Baby's dramatic acting out, or "play-liking," about events and people—often to hide grief—was a major source for Holland's plays.

Holland's growing-up years were filled with poverty and racism. At age eleven she was raped by the white father of children she was babysitting. Her dead-end life turned around when she gave an impromptu reading of the poem "Casey at the Bat" at Broad Street High School to uproarious applause.

In 1962, Holland was recruited by civil rights activist Bob Moses for the Student Nonviolent Coordinating Committee (SNCC) to help with the voter registration drive in Greenwood. As a field secretary, she was arrested thirteen times and once served thirty-three days in the state penitentiary at Parchman.

In 1965, Holland's home was firebombed by the Ku Klux Klan. Aint Baby Holland died from burns incurred in the bombing. After her mother's death, Holland attended the University of

Minnesota, where she received a B.A. and, in 1985, a Ph.D. In completing these degrees, Holland fulfilled the promise she made to her mother to make something of herself.

Her career as a playwright was launched when she "accidentally" enrolled in a drama class for advanced playwrights. From her assignments, she later developed the plays *From the Mississippi Delta* and *Second Doctor Lady,* performed throughout the United States and England. *Miss Ida B. Wells* (1983) celebrates the nineteenth-century civil rights activist. The mayor of Greenwood declared October 19, 1991, Dr. Endesha Ida Mae "Cat" Holland Day and gave her a key to the city.

Take a right on Carrollton Avenue to Highway 49 East. Go south on 49E past Tchula. Seven miles south of Tchula, take Highway 12 to Belzoni.

Belzoni

Located in the heart of the Delta, Belzoni is the catfish capital of the world. The old depot downtown, renovated by architect John Robbins, is a center for visitors interested in learning about catfish "from pond to plate." Wister Gardens, north of Belzoni, on Highway 7, is also an attraction.

Go east on Highway 12 (also Highway 7) until it becomes First Street. Take a right onto Central Avenue.

Mama's Dream World Museum

307 Central Avenue

Ethel Wright Mohamed (1893–1992) was a folk stitchery artist. At the death of her husband when she was sixty-five, she began capturing in fine stitchery scenes remembered from childhood. She received the Governor's Lifetime Achievement Award in 1978, and her work is reprensented in the Smithsonian Institute. She published an autobiography that comments on her images, *My Life in Pictures* (1976). *Ethel Wright Mohamed* (1984), an overview of her work, was edited by Christine Wilson. For tours, call Carol Ivy at (662) 247-1433.

Take a right on Bowles and a right onto Church.

308 Church Street

George Marion O'Donnell (1914–1962) was born on Silver Home Plantation and spent his early years at Blue Ruin Plantation near Midnight—names that sound straight out of Tennessee Williams plays. He lived at this house on Church Street until he graduated from Belzoni High School in the early 1930s.

While an undergraduate at Vanderbilt, O'Donnell was associated with the Agrarian group and contributed several poems to their Agrarian-Distributist Symposium. In 1940 his poems appeared in *Five Young American Poets*, along with Randall Jarrell's and John Berryman's. One of O'Donnell's poems, "The Hound That Hunts No More," was chosen by the *New York Times* as the best in the collection. As an English professor, he taught in various colleges, among them Louisiana State University, Auburn, Oglethorpe College in Atlanta, and Yale.

His poetry appeared in major journals including *The Southern Review*, *The Sewanee Review*, *The Virginia Quarterly Review*, *Poetry*, and *The New Yorker*. One of his most important literary contributions, a 1939 essay published in the *Kenyon Review* on how to read Faulkner, was considered a turning point in understanding the writer's work.

Witty and urbane, he was a writer's best companion. In an interview with Jane Reid Petty, Eudora Welty recalled his coming to her home in Jackson from the Delta by train and how he'd "regale" her and her friends with stories about other writers. "We'd feel we'd been in the company of the great," she said. "We'd all drink whiskey and then go and help him onto the Pullman as best we could, and he'd go on his way."

While an undergraduate at Louisiana State University, writer Charles East was editor of the student literary magazine, and O'Donnell was the faculty sponsor. The magazine was called—what else?—*Delta*.

In 1962, O'Donnell died at a young forty-eight. His beloved Faulkner died the same year.

Continue on Church Street to Jackson Street. Take a right on Jackson and continue to Highway 49. At Highway 49 turn south to Yazoo City. About a half mile south of Midnight, you will see Blue Run Road on the left, leading to what used to be Blue Ruin Plantation, once the home of George Marion O'Donnell. At some point, "Ruin," an unpleasant word to farmers, was changed to "Run."

Yazoo City

Yazoo City is on the southern cusp of the Delta. In the nineteenth century, the Yazoo River was a detour for steamboats from the Mississippi. Stephen Foster's famous song about the river was originally named "Way Down Upon the Yazoo River" until he learned that the Indian name means "death" or "waters of the dead." The city was named for the river. Ornithologist John J. Audubon, who wrote the famous book *Birds of America*, hunted wild cougar, bear, and deer when this land was a wilderness.

In 1904, a great fire destroyed many homes and buildings, though fortunately many lovely historic churches and houses remain. A legend grew that the fire was set by a witch. It is a story that has been embellished with many tellings, especially with the help of quintessential storyteller and native son Willie Morris.

The town has produced several notable figures including Haley Barbour, once national chairman for the Republican Party, and Mike Espy, the first black congressman since Reconstruction. Comedian Jerry Clower lived here while working for the Mississippi Chemical Corporation. (See Liberty for his biography.) Writers include Zig Ziglar, Rachel Zeller Nelson, James Gilmore Ewing, the Reverend Beverly M. Carradine, poet Jennie Noonan Sheless, memoirist Charles K. Chiplin, historical romance writer Carolyn Martin, poet Claire Feild, and editor Herschel Brickell.

Charlemae Hill Rollins was born here in 1897, although her family soon moved to Holly Springs. Rollins wrote a classic collection of folktales, *Christmas Gif'* (1963), dramatizing Christmas customs of black families. Russian-born writer Yelena Khanga came here in 1991 to research the history of her black American great-grandfather, Hilliard Golden, a former slave, and published *Soul to Soul* (1992), based on her findings.

Ruth Tuttle Williams (1952) attended Yazoo City High School where she was editor of *The Yazooan*. In 1969, one of her editorials caught the eye of Jeff Durstewitz, editor of *Hoofbeats*, the student newspaper at Calhoun High School in Merrick, Long Island. Durstewitz wrote a scathing letter to Tuttle chastising her for the racial problems in the South, particularly in Mississippi. When his indignation precipitated an angry response, letters on the subject of civil rights flew back and forth, with the happy result of greater maturity on both sides. In 2000, these exchanges were collected in a collaborative memoir, *Younger Than That Now.*

Once in Yazoo City, Highway 49 is called Broadway. Head south and take a left off Broadway onto Ward. At Dunn Avenue, jog onto College. After you cross Canal, College will become Grand Avenue.

615 Grand Avenue

Without question, the city's most famous and beloved son is writer Willie Morris (1934–1999). When he died, he was the only writer thus far to lie in state at Mississippi's Old Capitol.

When Willie was six months old, the family moved to Yazoo City from Jackson. They lived in this modest one-story home built by his parents. When Willie was born, most of the town's streets were unpaved, the South was still segregated, and television had yet to be invented.

Both parents provided Willie a rich legacy of statesmen and politicians. His father hailed from Tennessee, where *his* father had served in the U. S. Senate with Cordell Hull. Morris's personal hero was an uncle by marriage, Henry S. Foote, who defeated Jefferson Davis in the race to be governor of Mississippi in 1851. Foote was also a relative of writer Shelby Foote, a connection Morris and Foote delighted in discussing. Morris's mother's family were Harpers from Virginia, relatives of the family who founded Harpers Ferry. Willie's maternal great-grandfather, Major Harper, served in the Mississippi legislature. Somewhat more middle class in their callings, Willie's father, Ray Morris, was a bookkeeper for Cities Service, and his mother gave piano lessons. They raised their only child in a way that proved ideal for the future writer.

The story of Willie Morris's boyhood in Yazoo City, chronicled in his memoirs *North Toward Home* (1967), *Good Old Boy* (1971), and *My Dog Skip* (1995), reads like pages from *Tom Sawyer*. Known for his pranks, Morris has often been described as a cross between Tom Sawyer and Huckleberry Finn. Whether terrifying passersby at the cemetery, calling up the fire station to predict baseball scores previously obtained on an earlier broadcast on short-wave radio, setting up his fox terrier behind the steering wheel of his car to trick people into believing the dog was driving, or simply disguising his voice on the telephone, Willie was an incurable prankster. He loved sports of all kinds and was a sportscaster for the local radio station. He was often seen playing baseball on a back lot with his dog, made famous in the movie *My Dog Skip*.

"This is WAZF, 1230 on your dial in downtown Yazoo City, the Gateway to the Delta," Willie would announce at the radio station high above the Taylor and Roberts Feed and Seed Store on south Main. After school he would work as a disc jockey on a program called *Darkness on the Delta*. He also broadcast football and baseball games.

Away from Mississippi, he was perhaps its best ambassador. Personable and big-hearted, he loved his native state, even as he despised its racism. Once, on a trip to Paris, Morris sought out a fellow writer and Mississippian, the expatriate Richard Wright, who had at one time lived on a tenant farm near Yazoo City. Together, they commiserated over the horrendous racial divisions in their home state. Morris is credited with helping ease Yazoo City into integration by giving talks at both black and white high schools. Race relations were central concerns in his books *The Courting of Marcus Dupree* (1983), *Yazoo* (1991), and *The Ghosts of Medgar Evers* (1998).

On the way to becoming the youngest editor of *Harper's* magazine, he attended the University of Texas on a baseball scholarship, and he was editor of the student newspaper. After graduation, he was honored with a Rhodes Scholarship and studied

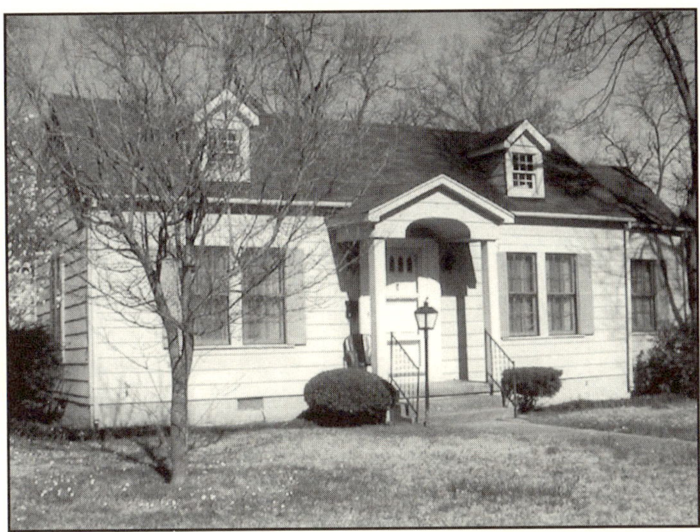

Morris home, Yazoo City

modern history at New College in Oxford, England. Later he was editor of the *Texas Observer.*

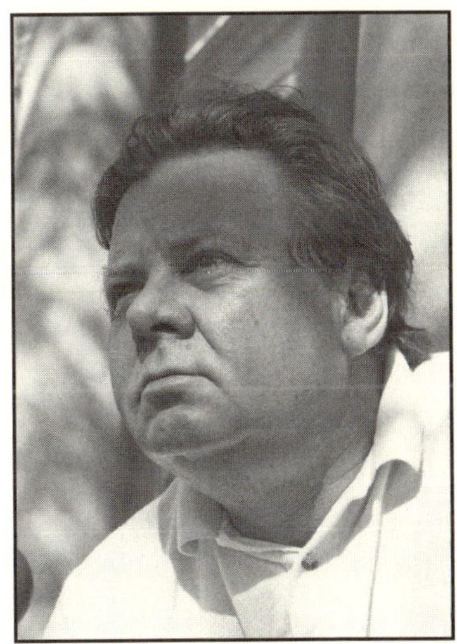

Willie Morris

Under Morris's editorship at *Harper's*, beginning in 1967, the magazine became a forum for some of the most scintillating writing of the late twentieth century. To its pages, he attracted such luminaries as William Styron, Norman Mailer, Joan Didion, and David Halberstam. His vivacity, energy, and unorthodox methods ultimately became too much for the magazine's owners, who had conservative views, and he resigned in 1971.

Morris returned to Mississippi in 1980 as writer-in-residence at Ole Miss where, looking somewhat like a disheveled Dylan Thomas, he taught Donna Tartt, among others, and where he continued to inspire writers, and yes, to play pranks. Morris moved to Jackson when he married book editor JoAnne Shirley Prichard, an Indianola native.

In 2000, a travelogue of essays, *My Mississippi*, was published, having been completed by Morris shortly before his death. The book features photographs by his son, David Rae Morris. Morris's novel *Taps*, which he had worked on over a number of years, was edited by his wife, JoAnne, and published in 2001.

Former Yazoo Herald

1035 Grand Avenue

At age twelve, Willie Morris became a part-time sportswriter for the *Yazoo Herald*. He described even football and baseball games in the well-articulated language that would later make him famous.

Glenwood Cemetery

Grady at Lintonia

Pass the fountain, and stop at the sign that says "Plot 1—Odd Fellows." Willie Morris's grave is about thirty yards from the sign.

- **Grave of Willie Morris**

One of Willie's favorite pranks was scaring passersby in the dark by making wailing sounds on his trumpet, the same trumpet he'd use to play "Taps" for funerals. In *North Toward Home*, Willie called the cemetery "the coolest place in town and in some ways the most sensible."

- **Grave of the Witch of Yazoo**

Second only to Willie Morris in fame, the witch of Yazoo is supposedly buried here. A crotchety old crone who lured fishermen into a house to poison them with arsenic, she threatened to burn the town, causing the city fathers to put a chain around her grave. On May 24, 1904, she broke the chain and burned the town. In 1991, Willie confided to a reporter for the *Clarion-Ledger*, "A lot of people think I invented the witch. The truth is, the witch invented me." Morris is buried *thirteen* paces from the witch's grave. Count them and make of it what you will.

• Grave of Reuben G. Davis

Section 1A, Block B

Born on a plantation in the Delta at Paynes in Tallahatchie County, Reuben G. Davis (1888–1966) is buried here. Davis served as a buck private and went to France in World War I. In 1926, after marrying Helen Dick, the family moved to Carter in Yazoo County. (Helen Dick Davis was the transcriber and editor of Mary Hamilton's memoir, *Trials of the Earth*, published in 1992.)

Davis wrote many short stories which were published in the *Saturday Evening Post* and other magazines. He wrote two novels, *Butcher Bird* (1936) and *Shim* (1953). Set in Tallahatchie County, both novels use effective dialect and are good examples of local color. In his preface to *Shim*, Davis wrote, "I was born on a plantation in the delta section of Mississippi in the days when the timber was virgin, the hunting good, and work was something somebody else did."

Former Yazoo High School

516 East Canal Street

Now the junior high school, the building was Yazoo High School in Willie Morris's day. Most of the building burned, though part of the structure and a statue remain in back. Here the Yazoo Indians played football, their games reported by Willie on the local radio station. By age fourteen Willie was a writer for the school paper, the Yazoo High *Flashlight*, and in his senior year was editor; he was also valedictorian and was voted most likely to succeed.

First Methodist Church

203 North Washington

Willie Morris regularly attended Sunday school and church and a number of times played a king or wise man in pageants. He was an officer in the Methodist Youth Fellowship. Willie's church youth group often sang hymns on the radio and made testimonies on Sunday afternoons, or Willie would play "The Old Rugged Cross" on his trumpet.

His funeral was held here, and was attended by many famous writers, among them William Styron and Winston Groom, as well as by multitudes of friends and admirers. At the end of the service, officiator Will Campbell pointed out that Willie's life had been a speech, a sixty-four-year oration, and suggested that, as with any good speech, applause was in order. The suggestion was met with a thunderous standing ovation.

The Ricks Public Library

332 North Main Street

Built in 1900, the library was a gift made by Mrs. Fanny Jones Ricks. One of the oldest libraries in the state, it was designed by Alfred Zucher of New York in Beaux Arts classical design. Here the young Willie Morris would read *Boys' Life* and other magazines, survey the long rows of books, and wonder what was in them.

Triangle Cultural Center

332 North Main Street

Willie Morris's desk is preserved in this building, formerly the Main Street Elementary School. In fourth grade, the teacher, Miss Abbott, taught Willie and his classmates their lessons and "enough Bible verses to assure their salvation." Under Miss Abbott's supervision, for a six-week stint, Willie had to stay in for two hours after school working long division as punishment for throwing spitballs. In seventh grade, Willie read Eudora Welty's "A Worn Path" and decided to become a writer.

Confederate Monument

332 North Main Street

In *North Toward Home*, Morris writes about this statue of a lady holding the Confederate flag and a soldier with a rifle in one hand reaching for it. He notes the soldier's reluctance, "as if he didn't want to go around all day holding both a flag and a gun, particularly with a ten-inch bayonet attached."

This is the end of the Delta tour.

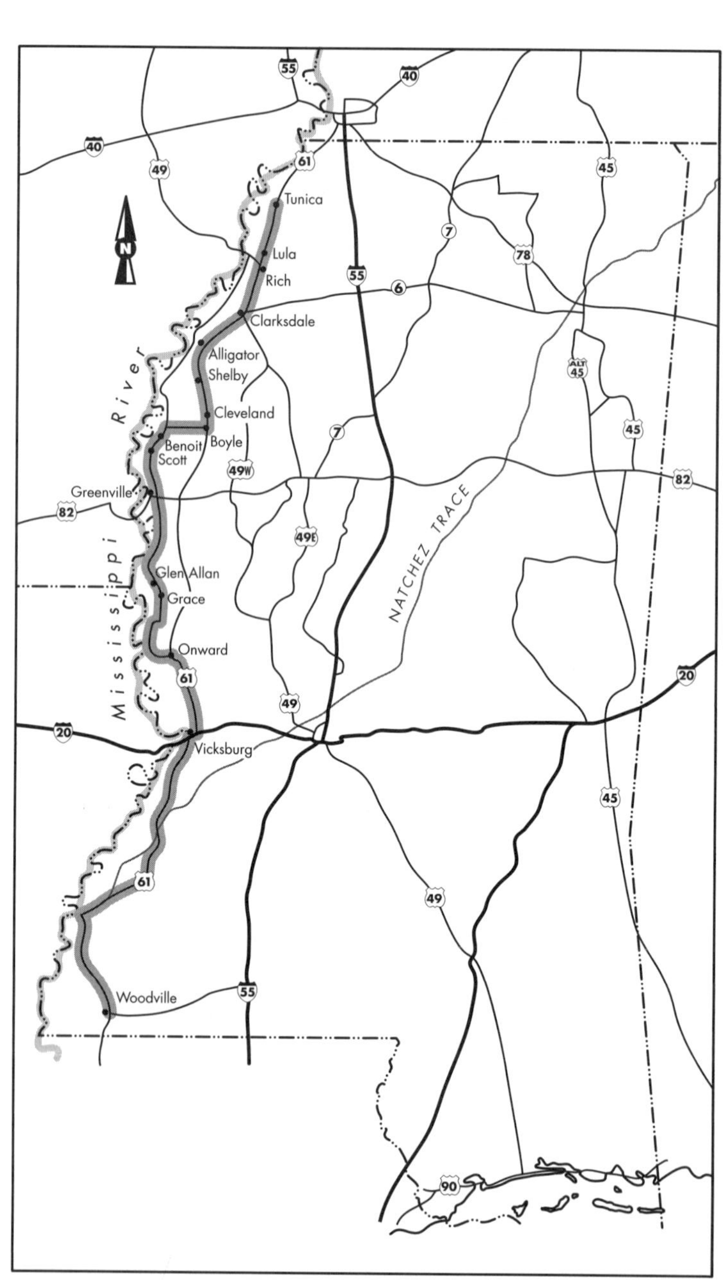

55
40
40
49
61
45
Tunica
7
78
Lula
Rich
55
6
Clarksdale
Alligator
Shelby
ALT 45
River
Cleveland
45
Benoit
Boyle
7
Scott
49W
Greenville
82
82
NATCHEZ TRACE
49E
Mississippi
Glen Allan
Grace
Onward
61
20
49
20
Vicksburg
45
61
49
Woodville
55
90

Highway 61 Tour

The tour begins on Highway 61 in Tunica and continues to Lula-Rich, Clarksdale, Alligator, Shelby, and Cleveland. At Boyle the traveler will detour on Highway 1 to Benoit, Scott, Foote, Glen Allan, and Grace, return to Highway 61 at Onward and continue to Vicksburg and Woodville.

The blues were born in the Mississippi Delta. As early as the 1890s, blues musicians plucked their guitars and sang their songs of oppression, hope, joy, love, or sorrow along Highway 61, long before Bob Dylan wrote a song about it. Originating from field hollers, spirituals, work chants, and slave songs, the blues were shaped by the harsh conditions African Americans suffered while laboring in cotton fields under a relentless sun.

The blues began to flourish when sharecropping, with its relative mobility, replaced the static plantation system and cross-fertilization between musicians became possible. Freedom of movement was itself a celebrated theme, with trains an important symbol as well as a literal means of escape, to Chicago and other places where conditions were perceived as being less harsh. Charley Patton wrote a song called "Peavine Blues" about the

Peavine Railroad that connected Dockery with Cleveland, Boyle, and Rosedale. In "Yellow Dog Blues," W. C. Handy immortalized the railroad crossing at Moorhead where the Southern Railroad crossed the Yazoo-Delta. Mobility brought uprootedness and alienation, and new refrains of loneliness and despair began to touch an appreciative audience, displaced by industrialization.

W. C. Handy, the "Father of the Blues," first heard the strange sounds that would become known as the blues in a train station in Tutwiler in 1903 and soon after received an enthusiastic reception when he repeated them at a white dance in Cleveland. Another early performer was Charley Patton, who grew up on a plantation at Dockery and was a significant force in drawing other musicians to the area, particularly Howlin' Wolf (Chester Burnett) and Robert Johnson.

Some of the world's best-known blues musicians were born near or were associated with Highway 61. They include Big Bill Broonzy (Scott), John Lee Hooker (Clarksdale), Son House (Riverton), Mississippi John Hurt (Teoc), Bukka White (Houston), Arthur "Big Boy" Crudup (Forest), Charley Patton (Edwards), Muddy Waters (Rolling Fork), Howlin' Wolf (Tupelo and Dockery), Son Thomas (Leland), Robert Johnson (Dockery), Mathis James Reed (Dunleith), Sam Chatmon (Hollandale), B. B. King (Indianola), and Willie Dixon (Vicksburg).

The rough, itinerant lifestyle excluded most women, but a few broke through the daunting barriers. Tragically, Bessie Smith, the "Empress of the Blues," was killed in a car accident on Highway 61 en route from Memphis to Clarksdale in 1937.

Tunica

The town was named after the Native Americans of the Tunica tribe who forced Hernando de Soto's expedition to cross the Mississippi River in 1542. It was once the poorest city in the state, but, with the advent of the casino industry in 1992, Tunica now glitters with the gold that de Soto was looking for. The Blue and White Cafe at 1355 Highway 61 features a map of famous blues artists and some fine turnip greens. Mystery writer Charlaine Harris is from Tunica.

Michigan-born writer William Richard Russell (1915) grew up in Tunica, where his parents owned land. He attended Tunica County High School, studied at Indiana University, and graduated from the University of Mississippi. He worked as a clerk in road construction for a while before traveling to Europe and settling in Berlin. His first novel, *Robert Cain* (1942), is set in the fictional Delta town of Newton, Mississippi. His second novel, *A Wind Is Rising* (1946), was published in England and translated into French and Czech. Other novels that followed were *Strayhorn* (1948), published only in England, and *Love Affair* (1956). Russell's novels have been praised for the descriptions of life in small southern towns. He also wrote a three-act play, *Cellar* (1945).

From Highway 61, go west for four blocks on State Route 4, which is also Magnolia Street.

The Tunica Times

991 Magnolia Street

Turner Catledge (1901–1983), author of *My Life and The Times* (1971), was resident editor for the *Tunica Times* for thirteen months after he graduated from Mississippi State College. When publisher Clayton Rand (see Gulfport) began running anti-Klan editorials, the paper folded. Soon after, Catledge moved to Tupelo where he became managing editor for the Tupelo *Journal*. (See Philadelphia.)

Lula-Rich

About twenty miles south of Tunica, take a right at the Helena, Arkansas, exit on Highway 49. Go two miles and turn left on Moon Lake Road. Uncle Henry's is on the left.

Uncle Henry's Place and Inn

5860 Moon Lake Road

Built in 1926 and owned by "Uncle Henry" Trevino since 1946, this restaurant/inn was once a notorious gambling den and dance hall. In the 1930s, a man was shot and killed upstairs. The club was shut down when its patrons learned the gambling franchise had Chicago mob connections. It was reopened as Uncle Henry's.

As "the Moon Lake Casino," it was immortalized in fiction by Eudora Welty and in plays by Tennessee Williams, who came here often as a boy while accompanying his grandfather the Reverend Walter Dakin on parish calls around the county. In *Summer and Smoke*, John Buchanan, Jr., gambles here and dances with Rosa. In *The Glass Menagerie*, Amanda Wingfield's beau is shot and killed after brawling with "that wild Wainwright boy." In *A Streetcar Named Desire*, we learn that the young homosexual husband of Blanche DuBois killed himself just outside the casino.

Friars Point Museum south of Moon Lake is noteworthy. Return to Highway 61. Take a left onto the Lula-Rich Road. Go about a mile.

Harris House and Studio

Lula-Rich Road

When the casinos came to Robinsonville, the little town of Rich was supposed to live up to its name, but unfortunately, the opposite happened and most of the houses here have been abandoned. The now-empty home of Thomas Harris can be identified by its combination of building materials—old brick at one end, painted yellow cypress at the other. Because there were no street addresses when he lived here, Harris would sometimes lean a broom against a tree in the front yard so that interviewers could find him. (A recently placed sign at the house next door says "5 Bridge Street.") Harris fixed up the little red house on the north grounds as a studio, and that is where he wrote *Black Sunday* (1975) and *Red Dragon* (1981).

Thomas Harris (1940) was born in Jackson, Tennessee. His father was an electrical engineer and his mother a high school biology and chemistry teacher. The family moved back to his father's hometown of Rich in the 1940s. As a child, Harris did not request toys for Christmas; he wanted only books and lots of them.

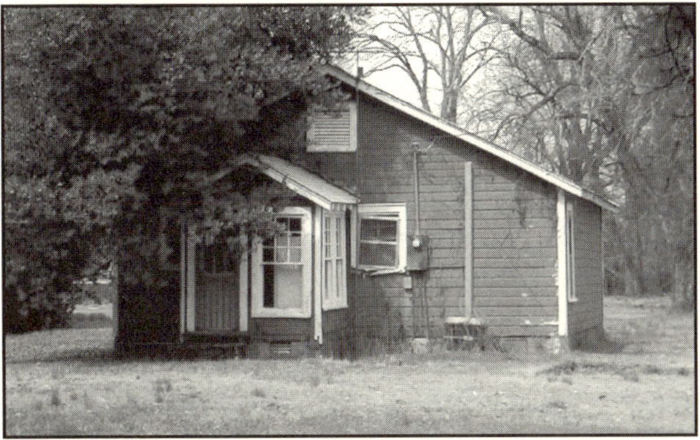

Thomas Harris studio, Lula-Rich

After traveling in Europe, Harris went to work for the Associated Press in New York. After hours, he and two other reporters on the staff concocted the idea for *Black Sunday*. Although the three of them split the advance, it was Harris who finished the book, coming home to Rich to do so.

Harris gained notoriety when his best-selling novel *The Silence of the Lambs* became a thriller movie starring Anthony Hopkins as a cannibalistic psychopath. To the delight of Harris fans, Hannibal Lector returned in a 1999 sequel, *Hannibal*. The initial printing was 1.2 million copies.

Despite the Porsche and the Jaguar he drives, Harris claims he has a modest lifestyle. He divides his time between his homes on Long Island and in Miami. He no longer gives interviews or signs books. His friend Floyd Shaman, a sculptor from Cleveland, Mississippi, told *Washington Post* correspondent Linton Weeks about visiting the elusive Harris at his Sag Harbor home on Long Island. What did his friend, a renowned chef, serve for dinner? *Homo sapiens* fricassee? No. They feasted on squash blossoms Harris had laboriously scoured with pipe cleaners to get the bees out. "He's always thinking about strange things," Shaman said.

At the first sign for Jonestown, take a left onto an asphalt road (Highway 316). Go two miles. Rosebud Plantation, with its three wide porches and deep pink shutters, is on your left.

Rosebud Plantation

Highway 316

Pulitzer Prize–winning writer Richard Ford owned Rosebud Plantation and lived here with his wife, Kristina, from 1985 to 1987. It was a time when Ford felt the need to reconnect with his Mississippi roots. Asked how he felt being back in his home state, Ford once replied that, if anything, he felt a little too comfortable. (See Jackson for his biography.)

Clarksdale

Clarksdale is known as a town of three rivers, the Sunflower, the Tallahatchie, and the nearby Mississippi. In 1848, John Clark, a planter from Philadelphia, Pennsylvania, brother-in-law of Governor Alcorn, bought land abandoned by the Choctaw Indians around Friars Point and named it Clarksdale. In October every year a Tennessee Williams festival is held, and plays are performed on the porches of the lovely antebellum homes. The Sunflower River Blues Festival is held the first weekend in August. The Delta Blues Museum at 14 Delta Avenue houses videotapes, slide-and-sound programs, photographs, recordings, books, performances, memorabilia, archives, and other sources of information about the blues and about Mississippi and its writers. With a partner, actor Morgan Freeman recently opened a restaurant here called Madidi's and a blues bar, Ground Zero.

Literary writers include Jim Collum from nearby Belem and memoirists Perrian Conerly, who wrote *Backseat Quarterback* (1963) about her husband, Charles Conerly, and Aaron Henry who (with Constance Curry) wrote *The Fire Ever Burning* (2000).

Lamar Fontaine (1829–1921) was born in Texas but settled in Coahoma County after the Civil War. His memoir *My Life and Lectures* (1908) reads like a fabulous tale, and the reader is hard pressed to know what to believe. He describes being captured by Comanches as a child, walking over 750 miles to see his mother, being wounded sixty-seven times during the Civil War, and killing sixty Yankees in sixty minutes in the presence of General Lee. One critic called the memoir a cross between Texas bragging and a dime novel, with travelogues and a captivity narrative thrown in. A diehard Confederate and white supremacist, he wrote a series of pamphlets praising the Ku Klux Klan. He also wrote *Outlines of Southern History* (1909), *A Short Discourse on the Causes of the Lincoln Invasion and Bloody Conquest of the South* (1909), and a second memoir, *Prison Life of Major Lamar Fontaine* (1910).

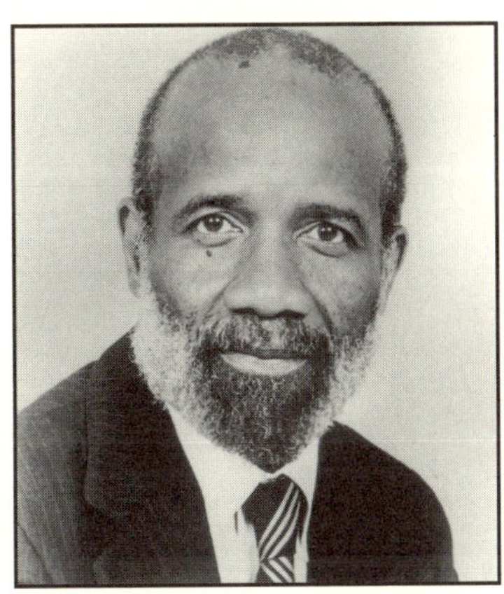
Lerone Bennett

Son of a chauffeur and cook, Lerone Bennett (1928) was born in Clarksdale, but lived here only a few months before his family moved to Jackson. By age twelve, he was performing in his own Duke Bennett's Band, playing both clarinet and sax. He might have been a musician but believed his journalistic talents would be more lucrative. "As a little boy," he said in his valedictory speech, "I knew if I could become a master of words, if I could understand Mississippi, I could make a ladder to climb out of the prison I was in." His grandmother knew it too, as she watched him reading obsessively from discarded newspapers.

He received his first paid editorial assignment in junior high when he was asked to write about returning to school after the summer. He was named editor of Lanier High School's newspaper and yearbook. He was ten or eleven when he wrote his first article for the *Mississippi Enterprise* and soon after wrote for the *Jackson Advocate* as well.

He graduated from Morehouse College in Atlanta in 1949 and became a reporter for *Atlanta Daily World*. In 1978, he won the Literature Award given by the American Academy of Arts and Letters. A historian, critic, poet, essayist, and writer of short stories, he is author of eight books, including *Before the Mayflower* (1962), considered one of the bibles of black history, and *What Manner of Man: A Biography of Martin Luther King Jr.* (1964). As senior editor of *Ebony,* he covered the freedom movement of the sixties. He now resides in Chicago.

The Old St. George Rectory

106 Sharkey Avenue

The old rectory has been restored and is now used as a church office, but it was once a residence of Thomas Lanier "Tennessee" Williams (1911–1983), born in Columbus to Edwina and Cornelius Coffin (C. C.) Williams. (See Columbus for more on Tennessee Williams's early life.) As a clothing salesman, C. C. traveled a great deal, so Edwina resided with her parents, the Reverend and Mrs. Walter Dakin, while rearing her children, first in Columbus and later in Clarksdale. Here they lived frugally but well in a friendly town full of flowers and parks. Next door, a Mrs. Maggie Wingfield kept a collection of glass animals in her window, a source for Williams's most famous play, *The Glass Menagerie* (1945).

For nearly ten formative and influential years for the future playwright, Tom and his sister, Rose (brother Dakin was born later), lived at the rectory in Clarksdale, a happy situation for Edwina, who enjoyed playing cards and singing in the choir, as well as for the children, content at home with their nurse, Ozzie, who filled their days with imaginative stories. Tom too would tell stories, usually with animals as characters, another source for Amanda's glass animal collection in *The Glass Menagerie.*

Well-read, aristocratic, and kind, Reverend Dakin was an important influence. The high ritual of the Episcopal service and his grandfather's sermons were young Tom's first taste of the drama that would one day make him famous. He often accompanied "Grandfads" on his visits to the sick and dying and learned firsthand about trouble and sorrow, which were to be so much a part of his plays.

Tom was a sickly child and at age five nearly died from an illness thought to be diphtheria; later, he was also diagnosed with Bright's disease. He remembered with pleasure his mother devotedly reading to him from Dickens, Thackeray, and Shakespeare, although it was his father's approval he would seek throughout his life. He was named for his paternal grandfather, Thomas Lanier Williams II, who depleted the family's fortune by running unsuccessfully for governor. Tom's admiration for his Tennessee forebears inspired him to take the nickname "Tennessee." Williams was also related to the American poets Tristram Coffin and Sidney Lanier.

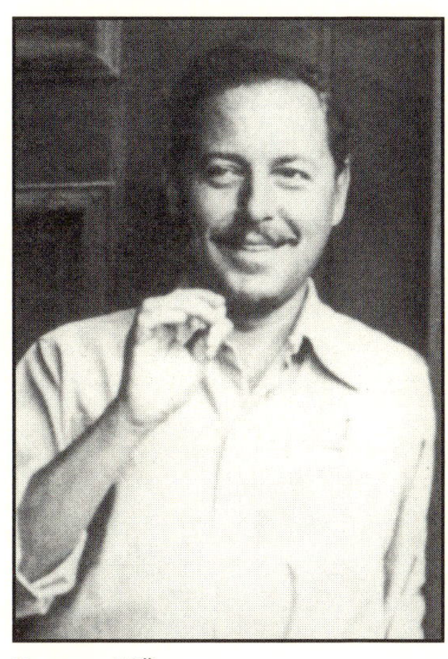
Tennessee Williams

In 1914, when his father went to work for the International Shoe Company in St. Louis, he took his family with him, ending Tom's idyllic childhood at the rectory. Tom returned to Clarksdale for the school year of 1920–1921 and again in 1928 when he came back to join his grandfather's European tour for members of his parish. A farewell party was given the group by Mrs. Maggie Wingfield, whose name was soon to become famous in *The Glass Menagerie* and *Cat on a Hot Tin Roof.* According to the *Clarksdale Press Register,* "[T]he hospitality [was] marked with charm and distinction, and sustained Mrs. Wingfield's well-known reputation as a most gracious hostess."

Tennessee Williams's first produced play, *The Glass Menagerie* (1945), his most autobiographical work, was hailed with great critical acclaim. *A Streetcar Named Desire* (1947) soon followed and won the Pulitzer Prize. His creative outpouring continued, and soon another Pulitzer Prize was awarded for *Cat on a Hot Tin Roof* (1955). Many of his plays gained further popularity when they were made into movies; these include *Cat on a Hot Tin Roof, The Night of the Iguana, The Rose Tattoo, Suddenly Last Summer,* and *Summer and Smoke.* The films featured famous movie actors and actresses of the day such as Elizabeth Taylor, Anna Magnani, Paul Newman, and Burl Ives.

Although Williams's first plays were considered superior in many ways to his later ones, there is no question about the greatness of his stature as an American playwright. Among his contributions to the field of drama are the psychological depth of his characters, his innovative use of symbol, his experimentations with narrators and flashbacks, and the lyrical beauty of his language.

When Williams died, his brother, Dakin, made the decision to have him buried in St. Louis with his mother at the historic Calvary Cemetery, despite Williams's wishes to be put out to sea at Key West.

Although he did not live at the rectory in Clarksdale, Dakin Williams should be mentioned here since he has written extensively about his brother's formative years at the rectory in such works as *His Brother's Keeper: The Life and Murder of Tennessee Williams* (2000), a self-published memoir in which he contends that his brother was murdered and names the killers. Other self-published books include *The Bar Bizarre* (n.d.) and *Tennessee Williams: An Intimate Biography*, with Shepherd Mead (1983).

Tennessee Williams Park

Polly Place at Court Street

The statue of an angel, the signature set piece from *Summer and Smoke*, was placed in this park named for the playwright.

Cutrer Mansion

109 Clark Street

This eighty-three-year-old Italian Renaissance villa of eight thousand square feet was built by J. W. Cutrer and his wife, Blanche, daughter of Clarksdale founder John Clark. Blanche was the inspiration for Blanche DuBois in *A Streetcar Named Desire* by Tennessee Williams, and the Cutrers were a source for the aristocratic Cutreres in his *Orpheus Descending*. In 1999, when it became known that St. Elizabeth's Catholic Church, which owned the mansion, planned to raze it for future expansion of their school, the building was bought through the joint efforts of businessman Jon Levingston, Delta State University, and Coahoma Community College, the plan being to keep the famous literary site intact and use it as an educational facility.

Historic Marker Celebrating the Life of W. C. Handy

313 Issaquena Avenue

Born in a log cabin in Florence, Alabama, near the Mississippi line, W. C. Handy (1873–1958) came to Clarksdale in 1903 to teach members of the Negro Knights of Pythias Band. He stayed here until 1905. "Memphis Blues," for which he was paid only seventy-five dollars, was written while he was in Clarksdale.

As the story was told in his autobiography, *Father of the Blues* (1970), Handy first heard the strange new music in a deserted train station in Tutwiler. Because his train would be nine hours late, Handy sat down and listened as a black man dressed in ragged clothes pressed a knife against the strings of his guitar to produce a wailing sound. "Goin' where the Southern cross the Dog," the hobo sang, referring to the famous crossing of two railroad lines at Moorhead. Then he picked up the refrain on the guitar. Later at a white dance in Cleveland, when a competing band threatened to upstage him, Handy resorted to the primitive music he'd heard in the train station. Soon silver coins rained onto the stage, and Handy knew he had something. The music he played would become known as the blues, and he would be acclaimed as its founder.

Northeast Corner of Riverside Avenue and West Second Street

A historic marker memorializes the life of Louise Moss Montgomery, "Poet Laureate of Mississippi, 1973–1978." Inscribed is a verse from one of her poems:

Spirit on high, come down, come down
And rest Thy hand upon this town
And let Thy love flow full and free
Through human vessels just like me.

434 West Second Street

A native of Dyersburg, Tennessee, Louise Moss Montgomery (1892–1978) and her banker husband, Robert, raised their three children in Clarksdale. They lived for a time in this two-story house.

For years, the family lived in a boardinghouse without a kitchen, so that Mrs. Montgomery could concentrate on her poetry. Her lyric verse, with close observations about the domestic life she avoided, is collected in *Songs for Soldiers* (n.d.), *Village Vignettes* (1949), *Trail of Years* (n.d.), and *Soul Stirrings* (1976). She also wrote a weekly column for the *Clarksdale Press Register* for over thirty years and in the 1959 school year taught German and French at Delta State University. In 1973, she was named poet laureate of Mississippi, a title she kept until her death.

Alligator

The son of a Baptist preacher, Jack Butler (1944) spent his first eight years in a house in the middle of a Delta cotton field. The family moved around a lot, to Newton and Glen Allan, among other places, before settling in Clinton, where Butler graduated from high school in 1962.

Now living in Arkansas, Butler says his fiction is influenced by the King James Bible and by science fiction. His first novel, *Jujitsu for Christ* (1986), was set in Jackson in the 1960s, while his second, *Nightshade* (1989), was set on the southern hemisphere of Mars. Butler commented that the two cultures are equally strange.

Shelby

103 Spruce Street

Charles East (1924) was born in Shelby and grew up in Cleveland. He attended Louisiana State University; while a student there, he was the editor of the student literary magazine. The faculty advisor for the magazine was another Mississippian, in fact another Deltan, George Marion O'Donnell. Unsurprisingly, the magazine was named *Delta.*

East served as director of the Louisiana State University Press from 1970 to 1975. A freelance writer, he has written books about Louisiana and edited *The Civil War Diary of Sarah Morgan* (1991). He has published two collections of short stories, *Where the Music Was* (1965) and *Distant Friends and Intimate Strangers* (1996). Many of his stories are set in the Delta. East has indicated that two main influences on his fiction are his grandmother, who had a natural storytelling bent, and the small-town world in which he grew up.

Cleveland

The town was named for President Grover Cleveland. It was an important crossing for the Peavine Railroad, celebrated in a song by Charley Patton. In the early days, railroads provided crucial transportation from the sawmills to the Sunflower River. On Cotton Row, where planters marketed their cotton, great fortunes were made or lost.

Cleveland is the home of Delta State University, founded as a teachers' college in 1924. Two forward-thinking citizens, Judge Lucy Howorth and her brother-in-law Audley Shands, are credited with its inception. Cleveland's proposal won out over Moorhead when its proponents promised to tear down a building in Cleveland known as the "Honky Tonk."

Among Cleveland writers are William L. Nugent, William Hays, and James Tomek. Keith Frazier Somerville edited *Dear Boys,* a collection of letters to soldiers overseas during World War I. From the area are poet besmilr brigham (Pace), L. C. Dorsey (Tribbett), and poet/memoirist John Milton Wesley (Ruleville).

Poet Carolyn Elkins (1950) was born in Toledo, Ohio. She teaches in the Division of Languages and Literature at Delta State University. She has received a Pushcart Prize nomination for her poetry and has won the poetry slam at the Wildacres Writers' Workshop for several years running. Her poetry has appeared in numerous journals including *Tar River Poetry, New Delta Review,* and *Asheville Poetry Review.* Two collections of her poems, *Coriolis Forces* and *Daedalus Rising,* were published by Palanquin Press in 2000 and Emrys Press in 2002, respectively.

Born in Light, Arkansas, poet Terry Everett (1940) has retired from teaching in the Division of Languages and Literature at Delta State University. Everett's poems have appeared in *Jabberwok, The Researcher,* and *Tapestry,* among others. With Mary Anne Ross, he published a collection of poems, *The Work of Two Hands* (1992). With Mary Anne Ross and James Tomek, he published poems in *Windows After Matisse* (1998).

From Highway 61, go right on Highway 8. Take a left on Fifth Avenue. On both sides, you will see the campus of Delta State University.

400 Fifth Avenue

Born near Goodman, Wirt Williams (1921) was reared in Cleveland. His father was on the staff at Delta State Teachers' College, and Williams himself matriculated at Delta State at a young fifteen and graduated in 1940. From a family of teachers and scholars, Williams attended graduate school at Louisiana State University, where he studied under Robert Penn Warren and Cleanth Brooks. He became a prize-winning reporter for the Shreveport *Times,* then the New Orleans *Item.* In 1949, he was nominated for the Pulitzer Prize for his vigorous research and aggressive coverage of political corruption and racketeering within the state of Louisiana.

Upon receiving a Ph.D. from the University of Iowa in 1953, he published a critical work on Hemingway, *The Tragic Art of Ernest Hemingway* (1981). Although he never met Hemingway, he corresponded with the writer for ten years. As one critic noted, the similarities between Williams and Hemingway are interesting: both went to war and wrote about it, both were journalists, both were boxers, and both created wounded male characters in their fiction. Three of Williams's novels—*The Enemy* (1951), *Ada Dallas* (1959), and *The Far Side* (1972)—were nominated for a Pulitzer Prize.

From Fifth Avenue, go a half block, take a left onto College Avenue, and continue to Leflore Avenue. Take a left on Leflore.

217 South Leflore Avenue

Dorothy Shawhan (1942) was born in Tupelo and grew up in Verona. She teaches in the Division of Languages and Literature at Delta State University. Author of numerous short stories, she published a novel, *Lizzie* (1995), about a Mississippi governor's daughter who becomes involved in politics in the 1920s and daringly starts a newspaper. With Dr. Martha Swain, Shawhan has written a forthcoming biography of Cleveland native Judge Lucy Howorth, leader in the national women's movement during the New Deal.

Continue two blocks on Leflore. Take a right onto Court Street. In the next block, you will see the courthouse and a historical marker for W. C. Handy.

Bolivar County Courthouse

Court Street

On the grounds of the courthouse is a marker for W. C. Handy, dedicated in 1998. Handy often played for the Bogue Phalia Outing Club of Cleveland and first played the blues at a white dance here to lure his audience away from a rival band.

Continue east on Court across the Peavine Railroad tracks. Take a left onto Sharpe Avenue through downtown Cleveland. Take a right on Highway 8 and return to Highway 61. Go south on 61 for three miles to Boyle. At Boyle, go west on Highway 446 through the Dahomey Wildlife Refuge to Highway 1. Turn south on Highway 1 to Benoit. Take Highway 448 and drive about three-quarters of a mile east of Benoit. The Burrus House is set off the highway in a grove of trees on the left.

Benoit

The Burrus House

Highway 448

Now owned by the Bolivar County Historical Society, the Burrus house is also known as "the Baby Doll House"; it was the setting for the 1956 film *Baby Doll*, starring Carroll Baker and Karl Malden, which was an adaptation of the Tennessee Williams play *Twenty-seven Wagon Loads of Cotton* (1946). About a provocative child bride, the steamy drama challenged standards of decency at the time. The film version, which was directed by Elia Kazan, was condemned by the Legion of Decency. Another of Williams's one-act plays, *The Long Story Cut Short*, was also adapted and filmed here.

Built for Judge John Burrus and his wife, Louise, the house has a long history. Construction on the two-story mansion was begun in 1857 or 1858 and was completed by 1860, with materials regionally made. It escaped burning during the Civil War because Judge Burrus had known the Yankee commander while attending the University of Virginia. The house was used as a Confederate hospital during the Civil War. Jubal Early, a disgraced Confederate general, took refuge here. Legend has it that John Wilkes Booth hid here after shooting President Lincoln.

Return to Highway 1 south to Scott.

Scott

Big Bill Broonzy (1890?–1958) was one of the earliest known blues artists. His exact birthdate is unknown because, when asked, he gave varying answers. In 1956, he published his memoirs, *Big Bill Blues*, as told to Yannick Bruynoghe. Broonzy's life of hardship working in the cotton fields was made bearable through his musical talent, which he discovered when he made a fiddle out of a cigar box at age ten. From the Mississippi Delta, he migrated to the coal mines of Kentucky, then to Chicago. His astonishing success reached its pinnacle in 1930 when he appeared at Carnegie Hall.

South of Scott is the Winterville Mounds Museum (ceremonial Native American mounds from a.d. 1,000). About twenty-five miles south of Greenville, turn west off Highway 1 onto Lake Washington Road (to Chatham).

Foote

Mount Holly

Highway 1

This Italianate mansion, with fourteen-foot ceilings, was built in the 1850s from slave-made bricks. Shelby Foote's great-grandfather, Hezekiah William Foote, bought the house in the 1880s. After his death, his son Huger Lee Foote (Shelby's grandfather) lived here. Shelby Foote used Huger Lee as a model for his character Hugh Bart, the protagonist in his first novel, *Tournament* (1949). In the novel, Mount Holly is called Solitaire Plantation.

Continue on Lake Washington Road to Glen Allan.

Glen Allan

Glen Allan is a town of only a few hundred people on the western edge of the state, twenty-seven miles from Greenville. With the publication of his first book, *Once Upon a Time When We Were Colored* (1989), Clifton Taulbert made his hometown famous. You can get a good plate lunch at J. P.'s, owned by James and Carrie Pigg.

From Eighth Street, turn east onto South Street in downtown Glen Allan. On your right you will see Loving Healing Center, a church started by Taulbert's mother. On the left, at the corner of Jennings Road and South Street is Moore Street Elementary School, which Taulbert attended. Off South Street at the end of Jennings Road is Ma Ponk's house, where Taulbert grew up.

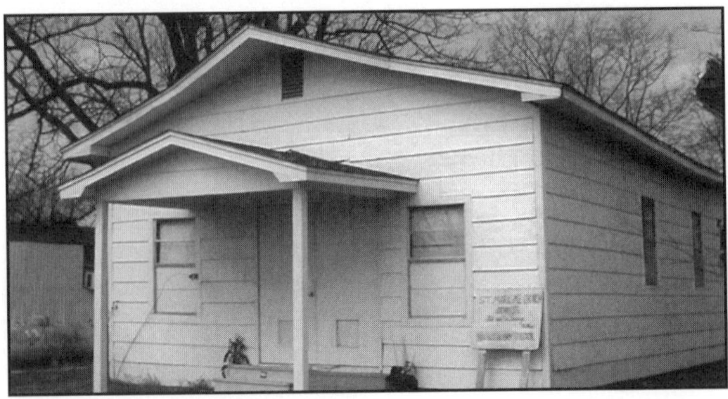

St. Mark MB Church, Glen Allan

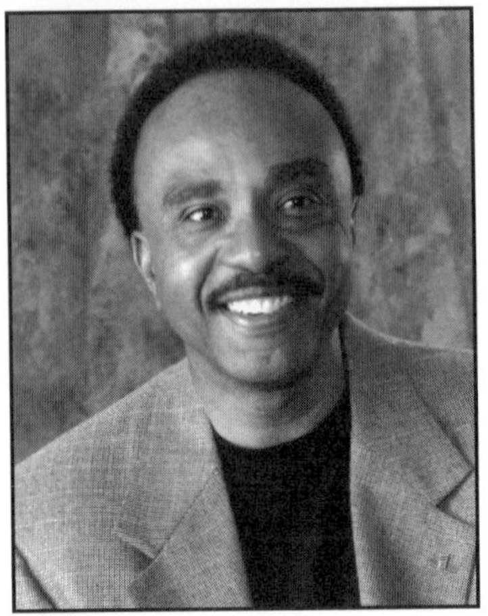

Clifton Taulbert

St. Mark MB Church

South Street

When Clifton Taulbert (1945) was growing up in Glen Allan, the town was strictly segregated. In his memoirs, Taulbert remembers the positive influence of family, faith, and community despite poverty and the cruelty of segregation. St. Mark MB Church, pictured here, was Taulbert's church.

Taulbert was raised by his great-grandfather, whom he called Poppa Young. After Young's death, Ma Ponk, Taulbert's great-aunt, took over. A sharecropper named Louis Fields befriended Taulbert as a teenager and encouraged him to be anything he wanted to be. What Taulbert wanted to be was a writer, a dream that came true upon the 1989 publication of his memoir *Once Upon a Time When We Were Colored.* Several other books followed, all celebrating values learned in a loving community. *Eight Habits of the Heart* was published in 1999.

Continue on Highway 1 to Grace. Although the house no longer stands, the intrepid traveler can turn right at Grace Road, continue about 3 1/2 miles, and then, just after crossing Steele's Bayou, turn left on Hopedale

Road to see the site of Hopedale Plantation. A garage apartment and a yard full of daffodils in the spring mark the spot.

Grace

Hopedale Plantation

Born in Vicksburg, Ellen Gilchrist (1935) grew up at Hopedale on Steele's Bayou in Issaquena County. The cypress house was designed and built by Gilchrist's grandfather Alford on the mounds of the Cherokees. As a child, Gilchrist walked to the nearby store, ready to put her nickel in the slot machine, ready to curse if she lost it. Between trips to the store, she'd put her ear to the ground and listen, hoping to hear what was going on in China.

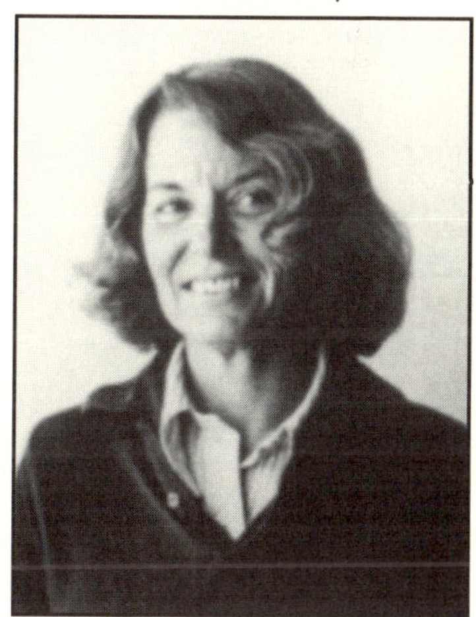

Ellen Gilchrist

During World War II, German prisoners of war worked in these fields. The same war took the family away from Mississippi to Illinois, Indiana, and Kentucky, where Gilchrist's father built military training airports. But Gilchrist spent every summer at Hopedale, and it figures prominently in her fiction. In her short story "Revenge," set on Steele's Bayou in Issaquena County during World War II, Rhoda's brother and cousins exclude her as they prepare for the Olympics, a choice they will later regret as indicated by the title. A spunky redhead, Rhoda appears in stories collected in such works as *In the Land of Dreamy Dreams* (1981) and *Victory Over Japan* (1985). The latter received the National Book Award. In her novel *The Annunciation* (1983), the central character, Amanda, grows up on a plantation similar to Hopedale.

At thirteen, Gilchrist wrote a column called "Chit and Chat About This and That" for a Franklin, Kentucky, newspaper. She also began to write poetry. In 1966, she attended Millsaps College to study creative writing under Eudora Welty, then went on to receive a B.A. degree in philosophy. After graduate work at the University of Arkansas under Mississippian James Whitehead, she published a collection of poems, *The Land Surveyor's Daughter* (1979).

Her comments from journal entries, essays, and *Morning Edition* for National Public Radio from 1984 to 1986 have been collected in *Falling through Space* (1987). Many of the stories in *The Cabal and Other Stories* (2000) are set in Jackson. Gilchrist now lives in Ocean Springs, Mississippi, and Fayetteville, Arkansas, in a home built in the mid-1970s by architect E. Fay Jones.

From Grace, continue on Highway 1 to Mayersville. Rejoin Highway 61 at Rolling Fork. Then onward to Onward.

Onward

The historical marker here commemorates the Great Bear Hunt when President Theodore Roosevelt paid a visit in 1902. The Onward store has photographs of the now-famous hunt. Among Roosevelt's companions were Huger Lee Foote, grandfather of writer Shelby Foote, John McIlhenny, who founded the Tabasco Company in New Iberia, Louisiana, and John M. Parker, who later became governor of Louisiana. Their guide was African American Holt Collier, reputed to have shot over sixteen hundred bears.

Wanting to provide the president a productive hunt, Collier lassoed a bear, then tied it to an oak tree so that Roosevelt could shoot it. Trained in the aristocratic sportsman tradition, Roosevelt considered such an act unsportsmanlike and refused to shoot.

The next day a cartoon by Clifford Berryman appeared in the *Washington Post* depicting Roosevelt's refusal and running the caption "Drawing the Line in Mississippi." Its double meaning was not lost on anybody familiar with Roosevelt's outspokenness against lynchings of African Americans in the South.

Soon after, to commemorate the event, a toy teddy bear was invented, brainchild of toy store owners Rose and Morris Michtom. By 1907 nearly a million teddy bears had been sold. As one writer put it, "The teddy bear turned out to be the biggest trophy ever bagged by the most renowned big-game hunter ever to occupy the White House." Needless to say, it was inspiration for a host of stories.

Vicksburg

This beautiful city built on bluffs overlooking the Mississippi River suffered one of the longest sieges in U.S. military history while Confederate soldiers struggled to maintain control of the Mississippi River during the Civil War. The siege lasted forty-seven days. Today Vicksburg is full of reminders of those days. The eighteen-hundred-acre National Military Park contains thousands of monuments to Union and Confederate soldiers. Today, the phoenix city offers spring and fall pilgrimages of magnificent homes that escaped the war's destruction as well as others built later.

Notable writers from Vicksburg include Earle Basinsky, Virginia Harrell, Joan Henderson, Gordon A. Cotton, Julius E. Thompson, Ann Odene Smith, Otto Salassi, and Ellis Nassour. Poet D. C. Berry (see Greenville) and fiction writer Ellen Gilchrist (see Grace) were born here. William Ferris (see Oxford) grew up on a farm near Vicksburg.

Born in Vicksburg, Julius E. Thompson (1946) graduated from high school in Natchez. He is a professor of African and Afro-American Studies at the State University of New York at Albany. He has published *Hopes Tied Up in Promise* (1970), *Blues Said: Walk On* (1977), and a biography, *Hiram R. Revels, 1827–1901* (1982). He also writes poetry.

Originally from Germany, Rabbi Herman Bien (1831–1895) was called "Rabbi-Poet," though he was both a novelist and a poet. He settled in Vicksburg in 1883 and wrote the novel *Ben Beor* (1891), a Jewish version of *Ben Hur*, describing a wandering anti-Semite who died just as the Declaration of Independence was adopted. The novel was so popular it went into a second printing. Rabbi Bien also wrote a collection of poems called *Oriental Legends* (n.d.) and a dramatic piece called *Tragedy of Samson* (n.d.).

Mary Loughborough (1836–1887) published her "Letters of Trial and Travel" in *My Cave Life in Vicksburg* (1864). In the first chapter, she describes setting out from Jackson to Vicksburg, expecting to have a pleasant visit with friends while her husband, a Confederate soldier, served in the army. On her arrival, she noticed through a window a piano in a sitting room with its corner blasted off. Thus she learned of the Federal siege. Along with her daughter and servant, she quickly retreated to one of the caves dug by ex-slaves for fees sometimes as high as fifty dollars. Believing her cave safe because it faced away from the river, she was horrified when Yankees began to shoot at its entrance. In her diary she wrote, "Really, was there to be no mental rest for the women of Vicksburg?"

In Vicksburg, Highway 61 joins I-20. Continue on I-20 to Indiana Avenue, exit 3. Continue on Indiana and it will merge with Confederate Avenue. From Confederate, take a right on Mulvihill Street.

1306 Mulvihill Street

Born in Yazoo City, Harris Dickson (1868–1946) grew up in Meridian and Vicksburg. In 1908, Dickson built this splendid home, then surrounded by a pasture and stables, and lived here until his death. In 1894, he received his law degree from Columbian College (now George Washington University), and, after serving as private secretary for a Louisiana congressman, began to practice law in Vicksburg. He briefly served as municipal court judge.

He wrote his first novel, *The Black Wolf's Breed* (1899), while waiting for clients at his law office. On a whim, he stuck the manuscript in with other legal correspondence he was sending to Bobbs-Merrill and was amazed to learn of its acceptance for publication. He wrote scores of short stories, as well as nonfiction works and ten well-received historical novels. *The Black Wolf's Breed* is a suspenseful historical romance, set during the French colonization of Louisiana. *The Ravenals* (1905) is set in Natchez and Vicksburg.

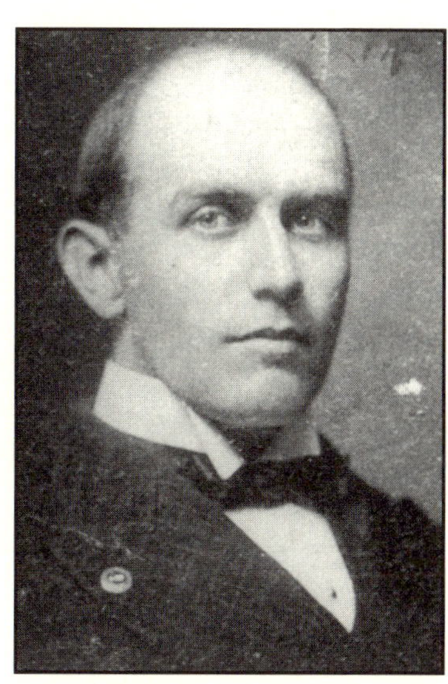
Harris Dickson

Dickson's popular black character, Old Reliable, regularly appeared in the *Saturday Evening Post* stories and in several novels. A mouthpiece for Dickson's satire of both whites and blacks, Old Reliable has been compared to George Washington Harris's Sut Lovingood and Joel Chandler Harris's Uncle Remus. After making a trip to Africa to further his understanding of its people and their culture, Dickson published *Old Reliable in Africa* (1920).

Some of Dickson's best works were the short stories that appeared in the *Saturday Evening Post* during the 1920s. His worst was a nonfiction article he wrote defending the racist views of Governor James K. Vardaman. He also wrote *Old-Fashioned Senator* (1925), a biography of John Sharp Williams. His views of the sharecropper system expressed in *The Story of King Cotton* (1937) are now considered sentimental.

Return to Confederate Avenue. Take a left on Hall's Ferry Road and merge onto Cherry Street going north. Take a right onto Magnolia Street.

Myrlie Evers-Williams Site

Magnolia Street

Myrlie Beasley Evers-Williams (1933) was born in Vicksburg and raised on this street by her paternal grandmother, Annie McCain Beasley. An old city directory cites 1426 for the house number, but the numbers have changed since then. In her memoir *Watch Me Fly* (1999), Evers-Williams states that because her mother was only sixteen when she gave birth, Annie Beasley came over and announced, "I'm taking the baby." Thus, for the first ten

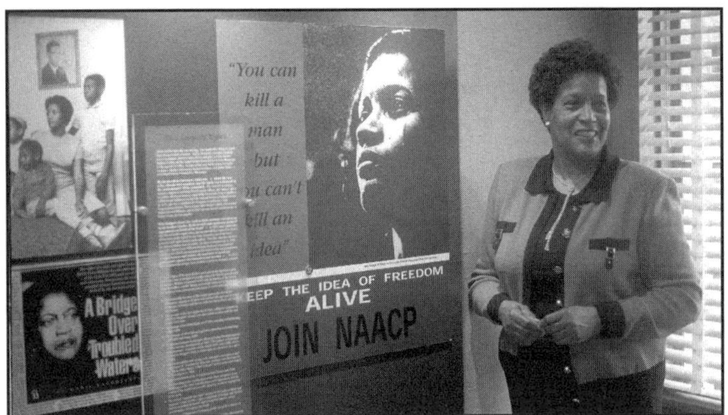

Myrlie Evers-Williams

years of her life, Evers-Williams lived with her grandmother in a modest whitewashed house on this steep hill.

On her first day on campus at Alcorn A&M in Lorman, Myrlie met civil rights activist Medgar Evers. A courtship began after Evers stood outside her window listening while she practiced her piano.

In her memoir *For Us, the Living* (1967), she describes a protected early life and the security she lost when she married Evers, for he was eight years older and determined to challenge Jim Crow laws. In 1963, while field secretary for the NAACP, Evers was assassinated by Byron De La Beckwith at his home on Guynes Street (now Margaret Walker Alexander Drive) in Jackson. Myrlie and her children heard the shots and ran out to see Evers's blood-spattered body. In Eudora Welty's story "Where Is the Voice Coming From?," Welty accurately imagined Evers's assassin *before* he was identified. Two mistrials made up of all-white juries followed Beckwith's arrest.

The loss of her husband devastated Evers-Williams and her children, emotionally and financially. Nevertheless, as she writes in *Watch Me Fly*, she continued on. In an autobiographical piece for Brian Lanker's *I Dream a World*, she states that, from the beginning, Medgar had prepared her for the possibility of his assassination and wanted her "not only to survive but to be able to live and achieve without him."

She did just that. She went on to become development director at Claremont College. She served as the first black woman commissioner on the Los Angeles Board of Public Works. She became spokesperson for the NAACP and, in 1995, was elected its president. She married Walter E. Williams, who joined her in keeping Medgar Evers's memory alive and who supported her hope that Evers's assassin would one day be brought to justice.

In 1994, that hope was realized. Upon new evidence presented by Bobby DeLaughter, who had been assistant district attorney at the time, Byron De La Beckwith was retried and found guilty of the murder of Medgar Evers. Sentenced to life in prison, Beckwith died of a heart attack in 2001. In the same year, Darrell Kenyatta Evers, the oldest son who had witnessed his father's brutal death, died at the young age of forty-seven.

Return to Cherry Street. Continue to the corner of Cherry and Crawford.

The Balfour House

1002 Crawford Street

This brick mansion was built in about 1835 in the Federal style. It was bought by Dr. and Mrs. William T. Balfour in 1850. It was restored and since 1981 has been featured on the Vicksburg Pilgrimage Blue Tour.

Mrs. Balfour kept a diary during the siege of Vicksburg which has been donated to the Mississippi Department of Archives and History for preservation. The diary begins with the chilling announcement that interrupted the Balfours' Christmas ball in 1862: Federal troops had been spotted heading downriver. A Confederate officer declared the ball over; the men bowed to their partners, and galloped away to meet the enemy. In that first skirmish, two thousand Yankees were killed.

Rather than resort to cave life as many other civilians did, Mrs. Balfour stayed in the underground quarters of this house, subsisting with her family on cornbread, bacon, and peas. Her mules were sacrificed to feed Confederate soldiers, and her cows provided milk for General Lee and his staff. In one of her diary entries she complained about the shelling going on all around her and instructed a servant to "go tell General Grant not to shoot these shells so near here that they might break some of my flower pots." In June of 1863, the Balfour home became headquarters for a Yankee general.

Old Courthouse Museum

1008 Cherry Street

In 1882, at the height of the arts and crafts movement, British writer Oscar Wilde made a lecture tour of the South. In Vicksburg, he gave a speech praising the region. "This part of America," he extolled, "should be essentially the land of art, the home of song, and the cradle of beauty of all this broad continent." (See Biloxi for more about his visit.)

Continue to the corner of Cherry and First East Street.

McNutt House

815 First East Street

Governor Alexander McNutt (1802–1848) built this house circa 1829 in the style of the saltbox types he had known while growing up in Rockbridge County, Virginia. The burial site for a Confederate soldier, the house survived the Civil War with little damage and now belongs to the Vicksburg Foundation for Historic Preservation.

After running unsuccessfully for governor against Henry S. Foote (relative of both Willie Morris and Shelby Foote), McNutt was implicated in the murder of his law partner, a planter named Cameron. Many people believed the accusation was political sabotage made by the Foote camp. McNutt later became governor (1838–1842) and married Cameron's widow. While governor, he entertained Andrew Jackson on Jackson's only visit to the capital city named for him.

McNutt's literary career began with sketches he wrote for the *Spirit of the Times* (1844–1847) under the pen name "The Turkey Runner." His Chunkey and Jem stories depict country boys based on real ones who ran his plantation in the Delta. In the stories, the boys hunt in the lush, abundant forests of the Delta before the Civil War. With the publication of these stories, McNutt claimed an important place in the tradition of the literature of the Old Southwest. He is buried in historic Greenwood Cemetery in Jackson.

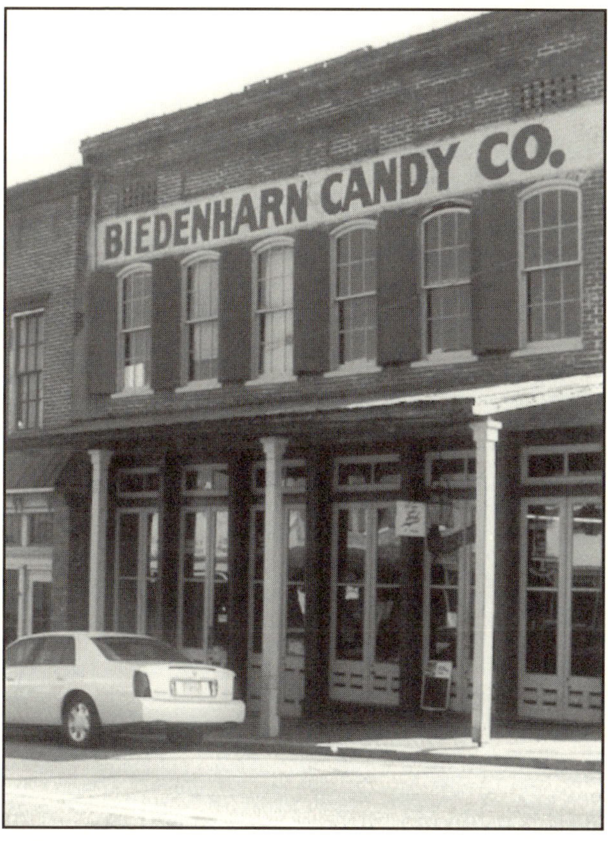

Biedenharn Museum, Vicksburg

Take a left on First East to Washington Street.

Biedenharn Museum of Coca-Cola Memorabilia

1107 Washington Street

Here in 1894 Joseph Biedenharn dreamed up the idea of bottling the popular cola soda, making a vast market possible for the first time. His daughter Emy-Lou Biedenharn (1902–1984) wrote a memoir about her father, *Biedenharn Heritage: 1852–1952*, in which she describes how her father got into business because of his father's urgings: "Son, go into the nickel business. Everybody's got a nickel. People will spend a nickel, but they will hold onto a dime." Emy-Lou Biedenharn was a contralto opera singer. There is also a Biedenharn Museum and Gardens in Monroe, Louisiana, operated by the Emy-Lou Biedenharn Foundation.

Woodville

The houses and even the trees, which are adorned with Spanish moss, show a definite Louisiana influence on the town of Woodville. The Jefferson Davis Oak planted on the lawn of the courthouse square commemorates the life of the president of the Confederacy and is registered with the American Live Oak Society.

Drive one mile east of Woodville to Rosemont, Jefferson Davis's boyhood home, just off Highway 61 on Highway 24. The house is open Monday–Friday, 10–5, March 1–December 15.

Rosemont

Highway 24

This modest one-and-a-half-story house was the Davis family residence after they moved here from Kentucky in 1810. It is the only home built by the Davises that survives. Originally situated on a 270-acre farm, the house was first called Poplar Grove, then changed to Rosemont in honor of Mrs. Davis's rose garden.

The house was restored in 1970 and opened to the public in 1971. It still contains a four-poster bed, several family portraits, and other Davis furnishings. In 1973, the first Davis family reunion was held here on June 3, Jefferson Davis's birthday. Five generations of Davises are buried in the cemetery behind the house.

After the war, Jefferson Davis wrote his memoirs, *The Rise and Fall of the Confederacy* (1881). Varina Davis wrote a two-volume biography of her husband, *Jefferson Davis, Ex-President of the Confederate States of America* (1890). (See Biloxi for their biographies.)

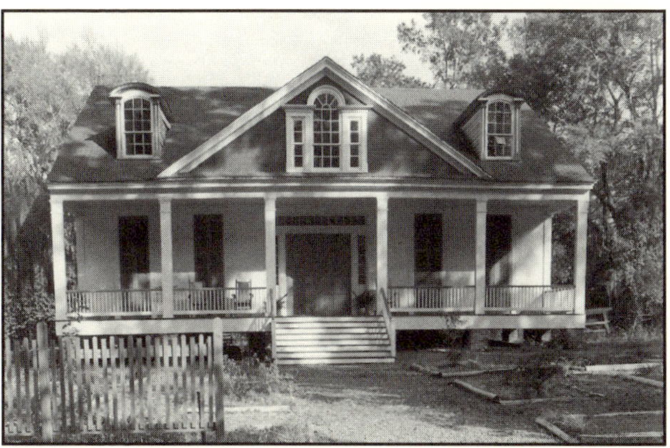

Rosemont, Woodville

Historic Marker for Fort Adams

Main Street

Only a store, a post office, and a picturesque Catholic church remain to indicate the existence of historic Fort Adams; therefore, its historic marker is here in Woodville. The fort was abandoned in 1803 after the Louisiana Purchase made it unnecessary.

The fort acquired literary distinction through Edward Everett Hale's novel *Man Without a Country* (1863) in which the protagonist, Philip Nolan, asks to be buried at Fort Adams and requests never again to hear his country's name. To honor the request, the marker simply states that the character Philip Nolan was stationed at Fort Adams. The novel was propagandistic, designed to frighten southern states out of secession. Hale named his character after a real Philip Nolan, probably because he was a friend to Aaron Burr, the secessionist who attempted to found his own empire in the region in 1807. To make it up to the real Nolan, who was a patriot, Hale wrote a subsequent novel, *Philip Nolan's Friends* (1876).

From the intersection of highways 61 and 24 in Woodville, go south on 61 about a half mile. Turn left on the Woodville/Jackson, Louisiana road. Continue about one mile to the sign for Bowling Green. The site is less than a half mile farther. At a clearing, the columns can be seen over a barbed-wire fence.

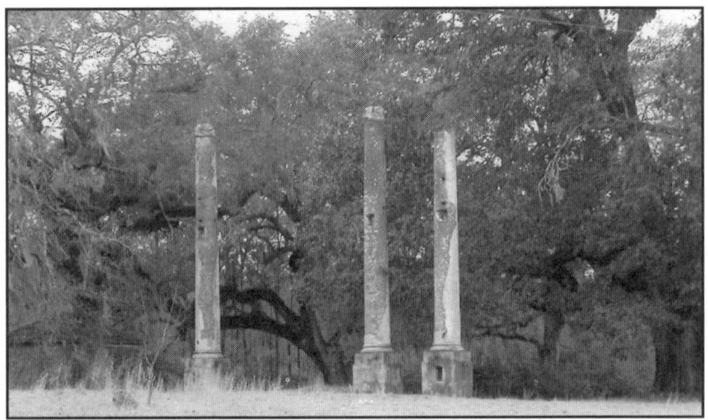

Site of McGehee House, Bowling Green

Site of McGehee House

Bowling Green

Only three columns remain of the house that was built in 1831 by Judge Edward McGehee, the uncle of writer Stark Young. McGehee once owned a plantation of several thousand acres and nearly a thousand slaves. The house contained a library of more than nine thousand volumes. It was burned by Federal troops on October 6, 1864. At the judge's request, the columns were left standing as a warning against senseless destruction.

Stark Young (1881–1963) uses the conflagration in the novel *So Red the Rose* (1934), set during the Civil War, where a mansion is "sacked and burned" by a company "colored, and mostly full of grog." The burning is used symbolically in other works such as *The Pavilion* (1951) to show the senselessness of war.

Wall House

Richland Plantation

Four miles east of Fort Adams is Richland Plantation. The two-story house is deteriorating and no longer open to the public. It is important because Evans Wall (1888–1963) was born on the cotton plantation, and lived and wrote in the house built by his grandfather in about 1760 when it was still Spanish territory. Wall's fiction draws on the unique history of Wilkinson County, which was ruled by three great empires, France, England, and Spain.

Wall's heritage is impressive, with predecessors that include a duke, colonels, captains, commanders, and surgeons, many of whom are included in Burke's Peerage. He had a varied career, first as a psychology student at Louisiana State University, then as a deckhand, railroad worker, farm laborer, newspaper reporter, soldier, and deputy sheriff. He also managed his river plantation, comprising eleven thousand acres.

Wall was the author of seven novels; his most important work is perhaps *The No-Nation Girl* (1929), which was nominated for the Pulitzer Prize. The novel takes up the delicate subject of interracial relationships.

After his first marriage was dissolved, Wall married poet Mary Claire Berthelot, who founded the Louisiana State Poetry Society. Wall's autobiography, *Better After Death,* remains unpublished, his novels are out of print, and many articles and stories remain uncollected.

This is the end of the Highway 61 tour. Continue across the Louisiana state line to Audubon country or catch the I-55 tour.

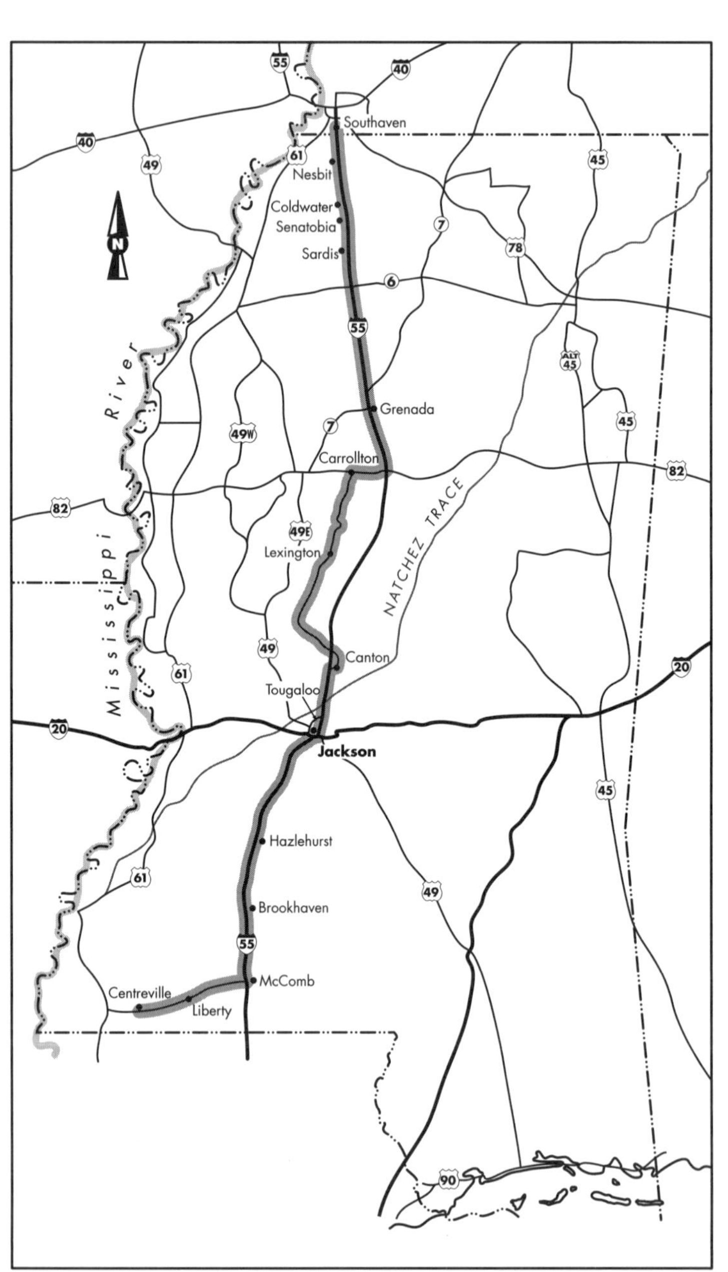

Southaven
Nesbit
Coldwater
Senatobia
Sardis
Grenada
Carrollton
Lexington
Canton
Tougaloo
Jackson
Hazlehurst
Brookhaven
McComb
Centreville
Liberty
Mississippi River
NATCHEZ TRACE
N

I-55 Tour

The I-55 tour goes nearly the entire length of the state, starting in Southaven and continuing through Nesbit, Coldwater, Senatobia, Sardis, and Grenada before meandering off to Carrollton and Lexington. The traveler returns to I-55 at Canton and continues to Tougaloo, Jackson, Hazlehurst, Brookhaven, and McComb. At McComb, the tour leaves I-55 to follow Highway 24 to Liberty and Centreville.

Southaven

Southaven is a prosperous suburb of Memphis. It was once home to the world-famous suspense writer John Grisham (see Oxford). Grisham grew up here and later returned to practice law after graduating from Ole Miss.

Site of Malone House

5618 Malone Road

A poet and judge, Walter Malone (1866–1915) was born in a large, white, two-story home acquired by his father in 1859. The house no longer exists, and the neighborhood is now filled with fashionable homes, newly built.

Among Malone's distinguished family members were his father, who served as a physician in the war with Mexico, his uncle, who died at the Alamo, and his brother James, mayor of Memphis, historian, and author of *The Chicasaw Nation* (1922), a definitive work.

The youngest of twelve children, Malone subsidized publication of his first volume of poetry at age sixteen by selling newspaper subscriptions. *Claribel and Other Poems* (1882) led the way for him to receive a grant to attend Ole Miss. In addition to being a judge on the Shelby County circuit court, during his lifetime he published ten more books of verse and a collection of short stories, *The Coming of the King* (1897). He wrote a 630-page poem, "Desoto," described by one critic as one of the most ambitious of American poems. He is best known for a very short poem, "Opportunity," often quoted in sermons and graduation speeches and set to music by W. C. Handy ("And every day I stand outside your door, / And bid you wake, and rise to fight and win.")

Nesbit

A resident of Nesbit, Claude Wilkinson (1959) taught at Ole Miss as part of the John and Renée Grisham Visiting Writer Series, the first poet to do so. A graduate of Ole Miss, Wilkinson attended graduate school at McNeese State University in Lake Charles, Louisiana, and at the University of Memphis. In 1998, he published a critically acclaimed collection of poems, *Reading the Earth*, which won the Naomi Long Madgett Poetry Award. He was the recipient of the Whiting Writer's Award, which annually honors the ten most promising writers in the United States. The collection *Joy in the Mourning* is in progress. In addition to writing poetry, Wilkinson is a gifted visual artist and literary critic.

Coldwater

Historian, biographer, teacher, and editor, Dumas Malone (1892–1986) was born in Coldwater and lived here a year before

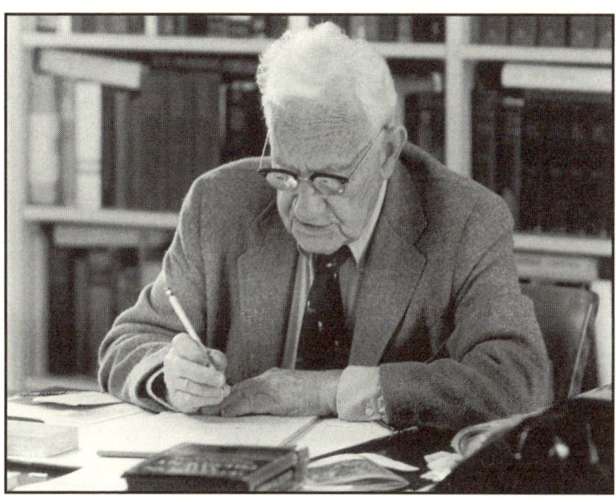

Dumas Malone

his father, a Methodist minister, was sent to a new pastorate. When the Arkabutla Dam was built, Coldwater had to be moved from the banks of the Coldwater River to higher ground. The Malone house and many others were flooded and lost in the process.

The family also lived in Minter City and Oxford before moving to Georgia when Dumas was ten. Dumas's brother, Kemp, was born in Mississippi in 1899, and he too became an author, a professor at Johns Hopkins University, and a noted authority on American speech.

Dumas Malone was educated at Emory and Yale, taking a doctorate from Yale in 1923. After serving as a second lieutenant with the Marine Corps in World War I, he taught history at Columbia, Yale, and the University of Virginia, where he knew Faulkner. He was married to the former Elisabeth Gifford of Cape Cod.

He was a renowned scholar. In 1929, he served on the editorial staff of the monumental *Dictionary of American Biography*, now a standard reference tool. He became its editor in chief in 1931. He spent nearly forty years writing his five-volume history of Thomas Jefferson, *Jefferson and His Time* (1948–1974), which won the Pulitzer Prize in history in 1975. Both the dictionary and the history were considered milestones in scholarly work in America.

Although nearly blind in his later years, he continued his research. He died in Charlottesville at age ninety-four and was buried in the University of Virginia cemetery.

Senatobia

Among writers from Senatobia are Judy Lane Vernon and mystery writer Benjamin Hawkins Dean. It is the birthplace of Herschel Brickell, prominent editor and book columnist during the twenties and thirties for the *O. Henry Memorial Prize Short Stories* and the New York *Evening Post.* John Osier (1938), author of *Covenant at Coldwater* (1983), *Rankin: Enemy of the State* (1986), and *Edge* (1989), lives here and teaches at Northwest Community College.

Once you're in Senatobia, follow the signs to Highway 51. Drive south on Highway 51 and go three or four miles, to the sign that says "Ed Nelson, Private Driveway." The house is set back about a mile from the sign.

The McGehee House

Highway 51

In 1857, Stark Young's great-grandfather, Hugh McGehee, built this stately home with massive columns. A story goes that one of the owners, Caroline McGehee, put a sign at the gate that said "Bad Dog. Worse Old Maid."

The house figures prominently in Young's fiction. It was the setting for his first novel, *Heaven Trees* (1926), and appears in other novels as well. The family graveyard nearby appears in *The Pavilion* (1951). Young is buried in Friendship Cemetery in Como. (See Oxford for Young's biography.)

Sardis

The waters of Sardis Lake were a source of pleasure for Nobel Prize winner William Faulkner. With friends Hugh Evans and

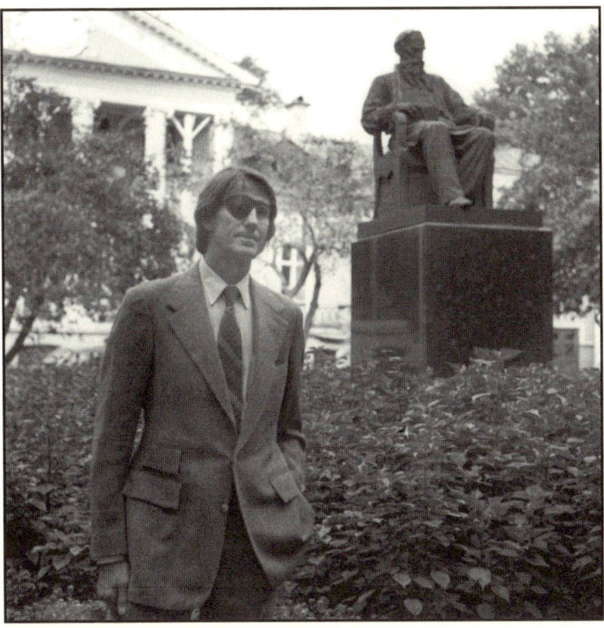

James Seay

Ross Brown, Faulkner built a houseboat with which to navigate the lake. On the vessel, he inscribed: "Out of Confusion by Boundless Hope: Conceived in a Canadian Club bottle She was born A.D. 15th August 1947 by uproarious Caesarian Section in prone positon with her bottom upward in Evans's back yard. . . ." Faulkner's fascination with seafaring vessels at Sardis Lake continued, and he bought a sailboat, *The Ring Dove*, three years later. One of his passengers was Eudora Welty, up from Jackson to visit her friend Miss Ella Somerville. The writers reported a quiet afternoon, both talkwise and weatherwise. Writers from the area include Robert H. Crozier and John Nixon, Jr., from nearby Batesville.

Poet James Seay (1939) is from Panola County. His father was a fiction writer who published the novel *Swamp Water* (n.d.) and others. Seay received his B.A. degree from the University of Mississippi and his M.A. degree from the University of Virginia. He has published four collections of poetry, *Let Not Your Hart* (1970), *Water Tables* (1974), *The Light as They Found It* (1990), and *Open Field Understory* (1997). He coauthored the documentary film *In the Blood.*

He won the Emily Clark Balch Prize and a 1998 award from the American Academy of Arts and Letters. He was included in an exhibit of poetry at the Centre Cultural Americain in Paris. In 1987, he was selected to be part of a delegation of Mississippi writers invited to the Soviet Union. Seay has directed the creative writing program at the University of North Carolina at Chapel Hill.

Grenada

Incorporated in 1836, Grenada was the offspring of a "marriage" between two warring frontier towns, Tullahoma and Pittsburgh. The neutral zone was called Rabbittrack. When Pittsburgh was granted the post office, indignant Tullahomans sneaked across Rabbittrack in the middle of the night, wedged skids under the post office building, and hauled it over to their side. Upon discovering the heist, Pittsburghers armed themselves with slaves, ropes, and mules, and slid the post office, still on its skids, back to their side, delayed but undeterred by a steep incline.

A free-for-all ensued. The fracas subsided only when a peace-loving preacher named Reverend Lucas called out, "Desist! Unhappy men." Shamed, the brawlers agreed to a peaceful settlement, and Reverend Lucas arranged a wedding ceremony with the cooperation of a real flesh-and-blood couple to symbolize the union of the two towns. The result of the merger was named Grenada, a Native American word meaning "united" or "married." Rabbittrack was renamed Line Street and has become one of Grenada's prized streets, lined with antebellum homes.

Among writers from the area are early-twentieth-century travel writer Neill James and contemporary poet Rebecca Hood-Adams. Writer David Donald is from nearby Goodman.

Gloria Norris (1937), from nearby Holcombe, now lives in New York City. She graduated magna cum laude from the University of Southern Mississippi and received an M.A. degree from Ohio State University. She has served as editor in chief of the Book-of-the-Month Club. In 1983, Norris was named one of "America's 100 Most Important Women" by *Ladies' Home Journal.*

Three of her short stories, "When the Lord Calls," "Revive Us Again," and "Holding On," collected in *Three Stories* (1986), won O. Henry Prize awards. A novel, *Looking for Bobby*, was published in 1986. Norris was editor of *The Seasons of Women: An Anthology* (1996), a collection of personal essays, memoirs, and stories exploring the wit and wisdom of American women.

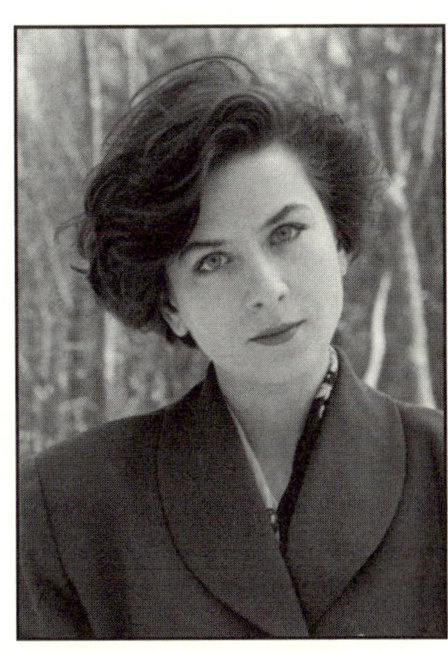
Donna Tartt

In the seventh grade, Otis Williams (1939) began writing blues songs, which he later developed into poetry. He was educated at Jackson State University, Morgan State College, and the University of Maryland. Once a singer with the Temptations, he now directs the Nyumburu Cultural Center at the University of Maryland's College Park campus and teaches courses in blues and jazz. He has published three volumes of poetry, *The Natural Truth* (n.d.), *Hootchie Kootchie Man* (n.d.), and *The Blues Is Darker than Blue* (n.d.).

43 College Boulevard

Born in Greenwood, Donna Tartt (1963) grew up in Grenada. This home, usually referred to as the old Gore family home, was bought by Tartt's mother, Tay Tartt Weatherall. Tartt wrote her first poem at age five and published her first sonnet in a Mississippi literary review at age thirteen. Tartt, who in casual conversation might quote from Thomas Aquinas, Cardinal Newman, the Buddha, or Plato, was once a cheerleader at Grenada's Kirk Academy.

Tartt went on to Ole Miss where she received support from Willie Morris, who pronounced her a genius. With the encouragement of Morris and of Barry Hannah, she transferred to Bennington College in Vermont, where she began her novel *The Secret History*.

After a bidding war with other publishers, Knopf paid an astounding $450,000 to publish *The Secret History* (1992). The novel, which took Tartt eight years to write, is a chilling story about a murder at fictional Hamden College in Vermont. When the advance copies of readers' editions ran out, Knopf had to print an unheard-of second run before the book's release. *The Secret History* stayed on the best-seller list for thirteen weeks.

Like two of her characters in *The Secret History,* Tartt's father once owned a service station and her mother was a secretary. But very little else shows up from her youth in Grenada. Tartt has said that a more important influence was *Blood in the Parlor,* a collection of Victorian murder stories.

At Winona, exit onto Highway 82W. Go about ten miles; then take a right on Highway 17 to downtown Carrollton.

Carrollton

Listed on the National Register of Historic Places, Carrollton, built around a courthouse square, is one of the oldest Mississippi towns. Many of the houses were built in the nineteenth century by James Clark Harris, the architect for Malmaison in Teoc. He also built the Captain Ray House on Washington Street used in the 1969 film *The Reivers,* which was adapted from the William Faulkner novel. (One of the streets is named "Reivers" in tribute to the movie.) Carrollton has produced a writer with an international reputation, Elizabeth Spencer.

Poet Lawrence Olson, Jr. (1918), lived just up the street from the Spencers, who were distant cousins, in an antebellum home. He published a volume of poetry, *The Cranes on Dying River* (1947), and two books on Japan.

Malmaison, in nearby Teoc, was the home of Greenwood Leflore. Only one-quarter Choctaw himself, Leflore represented the Choctaw Nation at the Treaty of Dancing Rabbit Creek and won for them what came to be seen as empty concessions by the government. Spurned by the Choctaws after the treaty, Leflore became a prominent member of white planter society. In 1942, Malmaison was set on fire and burned to the ground.

From the courthouse square, go west on Washington Street to College and turn right.

1010 College Street

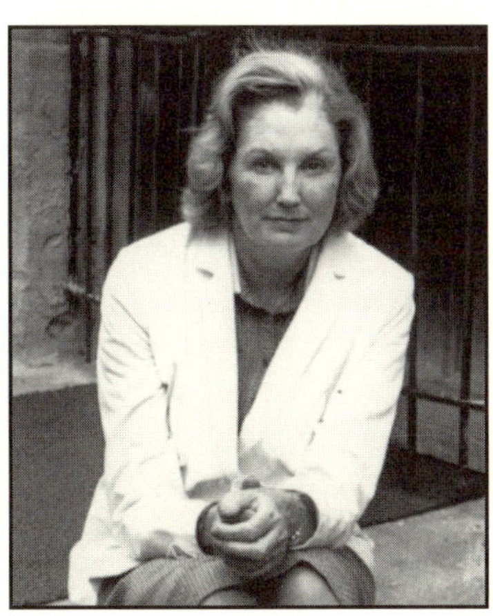
Elizabeth Spencer

Meeting her for the first time, one might imagine that Elizabeth Spencer (1921) grew up urban and cosmopolitan. She is tall and thin, with sophisticated looks that belie the country life she knew as a child. Yet much of her fiction is drawn from her Carrollton background.

Both sides of Spencer's family have lived in Carroll County since the 1830s. Her ancestry is rich with military heroes. Her father's father, Elijah Harrison Spencer, fought in the Civil War. Her maternal grandfather McCain tried unsuccessfully to volunteer for the Civil War at age fourteen. (John McCain, the Republican senator from Arizona who made a presidential bid in 2000, is descended from these McCains.)

As related in her memoir, *Landscapes of the Heart* (1998), Spencer grew up to love the sound of words. The McCains were book lovers who talked about characters as if they were part of the family. "It was a shame," they might say of *Les Miserables*, "that Fantine had to sell her teeth." Her mother's library included Latin and Greek, Dante, Melville, Hawthorne, Poe, and the New England poets.

Sick a lot as a child, Elizabeth would have her mother read to her from Greek and Roman myths, the Arthurian legends, and the Bible. As soon as she could write, young Lizzie began to write stories, mostly to entertain herself. One can picture the skinny seven-year-old, shinnying up a tree, tablet in hand, writing an adventure story about the North Pole that would later become a Christmas gift for her parents.

Despite frequent illnesses, young Elizabeth was active. When not tagging along after her brother, who was seven years older, she hunted with her father or fished with people living on the place. She grew up to be a horsewoman, learning to ride in small increments, first a donkey, then ponies, and finally horses. By horse, she would ride thirteen miles to visit a favorite uncle, Joseph Pinckney McCain, and his wife, Esther, at Teoc, or Teoc Tillila, Choctaw for "tall pines," property the McCain family had bought in the early 1800s.

Also in small increments, Spencer began slowly to leave Carrollton. She attended Belhaven College in Jackson, where, in her senior year, she asked Eudora Welty, who lived on Pinehurst across the street, to come and speak to the creative writing class. Spencer went on to graduate school at Vanderbilt in Nashville. Later, after a short stint teaching in Mississippi, she traveled to Italy on a Guggenheim Fellowship. In 1956, she married John Arthur Rusher of Cornwall, England, and they moved to Montreal, Canada, a place so foreign to her it has not yet appeared in her fiction. The Rushers later settled in Chapel Hill, North Carolina.

Her first novel, *Fire in the Morning* (1948), is set in a small town like Carrollton. Her second novel, *This Crooked Way* (1952), is about the Delta's early settlers, history she learned while riding the crops with her uncle Joseph at Teoc. While in Italy, she wrote her third novel, *The Voice at the Back Door* (1956), also set in Mississippi.

After the first three novels, Mississippi was not a setting for a long time. *Light in the Piazza* (1960), a best seller made into a movie by MGM, was set in Italy. Though it took only a month to write, it is her best-known work.

After moving to Chapel Hill, she returned to a Mississippi setting for the play *For Lease or Sale* about a large, antebellum home that the owners are forced to sell to make way for progress, a plot influenced by her knowledge of the historic homes of Carrollton. In 1968, she published a collection set in Mississippi, *Ship Island and Other Stories.* A novel, *Night Travelers,* set in North Carolina, was published in 1991. *The Southern Woman: New and Selected Fiction* (2001) is a collection of several previously published stories and six new ones.

Continue south on Highway 17 to downtown Lexington.

Lexington

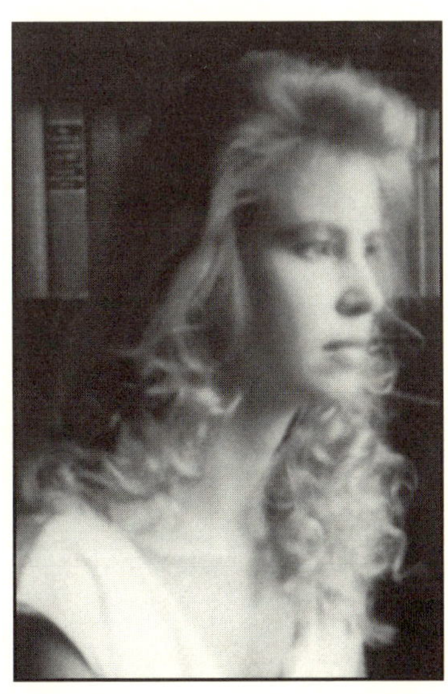

Melany Neilson

Lexington's historic town square features an attractive courthouse with a distinctive clock tower. This town was the home of newspaper-woman Hazel Brannon Smith, who won the Pulitzer Prize in 1964 for her editorials urging racial moderation. Jonathan Henderson Brooks (1905–1945) was born in Lexington. (See Corinth for his biography.) Novelists Billy Ellis and Joe Berman are also from Lexington.

Neilson House

304 Carrollton Street

Melany Neilson (1958) grew up on a farm in Ebernezer before the family moved to a stately, columned mansion near the center of town. (Misfortune struck the home when a fire destroyed the roof in the late nineties.) In 1982, Neilson went to work for Robert Clark, Mississippi's first black state representative since Reconstruction. In her memoir *Even Mississippi* (1989), she describes how she began to identify with victims of discrimination while at Ole Miss when, because of her liberal views, she was not invited to join her mother's sorority. She records reactions to her political activism, particularly her father's, whose views changed from segregationist to moderate. She goes on to describe Clark's defeat in his bid for a seat in the United States Congress.

Even Mississippi was nominated for the Pulitzer Prize and won several awards including the Gustavas Myers Outstanding Book on Human Rights and the Lillian Smith Award. With her husband, lawyer Fred Slabach, and their twin boys, Neilson is now a resident of Long Beach, California. In 2001, she published her first novel, *Persia Cafe*.

Oak Hill

315 North Street

This two-story columned mansion set back on a hill surrounded by trees once belonged to Governor Edmond Favor Noel (1856–1927). In 1912, after serving his term as governor, Noel and his wife moved to this home, which they named Oak Hill. When the house was sold to new owners in 1990, seven diaries were discovered, five written by the governor and two by his wife. The unpublished diaries reported on the daily life of the Noels and the people they saw while he was governor, including President Teddy Roosevelt, in Mississippi for a bear hunt in 1905.

Return to I-55 on Highway 17 south. At Canton, take exit 119. Take a left onto West Peace Street. Continue for about two miles; then take a left on Union.

Canton

Called the "City of Lights," Canton was the setting for Beth Henley's play *The Wake of Jamey Foster.* Parts of the movie versions of John Grisham's *A Time to Kill*, Willie Morris's *My Dog Skip*, and *O Brother, Where Art Thou?* were filmed here. Writers from Canton include Kathleen Schad and memoirist Flonzie Brown.

Reformist Belle Kearney (1863–1939) was born near Canton in the southwest corner of Madison County. In her autobiography, *A Slaveholder's Daughter* (1900), she describes the horrific effects of the Civil War on the daily life of her family. She depicts her life as a determined activist and speaker for reform movements such as temperance and women's rights. *A Slaveholder's Daughter* went through eleven editions. Kearney edited a biography, *Mama Flower* (1918), about Flora Mann Jones, a philanthropist for whom the town of Flora was named. In

1921, she published a novel progressive in its day, *Conqueror or Conquered: Or, the Sex Challenge Answered*, in which she promotes sex education to prevent sex-related problems such as venereal disease. In 1923, she became the first southern woman to be elected to the state senate, an office she held for two terms.

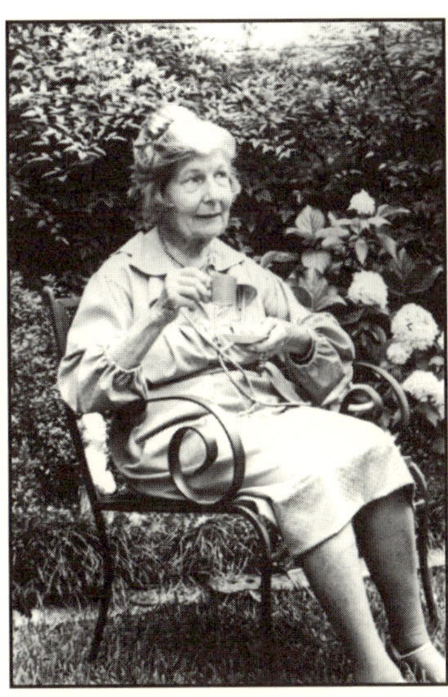

Hosford Fontaine

Allison's Wells School of Arts and Crafts

Trolio Hotel on the Square

Allison's Wells was discovered as a mineral spa as early as 1899. Before it burned, the original structure was located off U.S. Highway 51 ten miles north of Canton just across from Gray Center, an Episcopal retreat. With blessings from the Fontaine family, the spirit of Allison's Wells continues in this location. Over the years it has served as a center for artists, artisans such as potters and weavers, and writers.

Memoirist Hosford Latimer Fontaine inherited the mineral spa, the waters of which were thought to heal a variety of ailments, from her grandparents. Fontaine transformed it into an arts colony, which she directed from 1948 until it burned in 1963. At Allison's Wells, artists studied under Karl Wolfe, Andrew Bucci, and others, and writers gathered for celebrations and readings. Among writers who came were Elizabeth Bowen, Charlotte Capers, and John Faulkner. A dinner party was thrown for Eudora Welty in honor of the publication of her novella *The Ponder Heart.*

Politicians like Bilbo, Vardaman, and John Sharp Williams often spent the day. In her reminiscences, writer and archivist Charlotte Capers recalled that Allison's Wells was a place where the plumbing was "independent," where two sets of newlyweds could find themselves mistakenly assigned to the same room, and where newcomers might find themselves darning linen or shelling peas.

Tougaloo

Poet Carol Cox (1946) lives in the community of Tougaloo. She and her husband, Fletcher, moved to a home near the college in 1972, to make their living as woodworkers. Cox has published two collections of poems, *Woodworking and Places Near By* (1979) and *The Water in the Pearl* (1982).

The community is centered around historic Tougaloo College, founded in 1869 by the American Missionary Association. The college provided refuge for such civil rights activists as Anne Moody (see Centreville), a student during the civil rights strife of the sixties. Pulitzer Prize–winning author Alice Walker (see Jackson) was writer-in-residence in the late sixties. Other writers associated with Tougaloo College are poets Jerry Ward (see Moss Point), Melvin Turner, Jonathan Brooks, John Milton Wesley, and Virgia Brocks-Shedd.

Jackson

The history of Jackson began in 1819 when George Poindexter became the second governor of Mississippi. Through his efforts, twenty thousand dollars was appropriated by the U.S. Congress to buy land from the Choctaws. The Treaty of Doak's Stand came about the following year. Negotiated by Gen. Andrew Jackson and Maj. Gen. Thomas Hinds, it allowed the Choctaws to be paid a grand total of $4,675 for 5 ½ million acres, of which Hinds County was a small part.

For years the capital was moved back and forth between Natchez and Washington, and even once to Columbia, before a trading post, LeFleur's Bluff, was chosen for its "healthful air" and renamed Jackson in honor of Andrew Jackson. On Thomas Jefferson's recommendation, the city was laid out in a checkerboard pattern, with alternate squares designated for public lands. Four times during the Civil War, Jackson was invaded by Federal troops. Burned by the Yankees, it became known as "Chimneyville."

But the culture itself prevailed. The Edwards House was a first-class hotel. A theatre was founded as early as the 1830s, and the Century Theatre featured such top-notch entertainers as Sothern and Marlowe and John Drew Barrymore and his niece Ethel.

Today Jackson is host to major art exhibitions. Every four years the city sponsors the International Ballet Competition. It is the home of New Stage Theatre, a hockey team, a symphony, an opera company, an annual bicycle race, a zoo, a natural science museum, the Smith Robertson and Old Capitol museums, art galleries, and a craftsmen's guild.

Pulitzer Prize winner Eudora Welty (see below) was a lifelong resident of Jackson. Other writers associated with the city are Elizabeth Spencer and Ellen Douglas. Jackson is the setting for *The Cabal and Other Stories* by Ellen Gilchrist (see Grace).

Among nineteenth-century writers from the area was memoirist Susan Dabney Smedes, who lived on Burleigh Plantation near Raymond. Born near Jackson on his grandfather's eighty-eight-acre farm in Hinds County, novelist and biographer John A. Williams grew up in Syracuse, New York. Williams's works include *The Angry Ones* (1960) and a biography of Richard Wright for children, *The Most Native of Sons* (1970). Jim Majure, author of *The Delta Triangle* (1995) and *Reluctant Reunion* (1997), lived outside Jackson.

Stuart Stevens has written travel books, scripts for television programs such as *Northern Exposure* and *I'll Fly Away*, and a political novel, *Scorched Earth* (1994). Mystery writers include Louisa Dixon, Karen Young, Carolyn Haines, and Jim Fraiser. Several writers who were born elsewhere have spent time in Jackson; these include geologist, naturalist, and novelist Rick Bass, Lerone Bennett (see Clarksdale), and Cid Ricketts Sumner (see Brookhaven). Clinton-born poet Sterling Plumpp finished high school here (see Clinton). Novelist Amy Gutman, founder-director of the Mississippi Teacher Corps, was for a time a reporter for a Jackson newspaper.

Jacksonians who have written autobiographies include artist Karl Wolfe (*Mississippi Artist: A Self-Portrait*, 1979), Edward Cohen (*The Peddler's Grandson: Growing Up Jewish in Mississippi*, 1999), and longtime teacher of music Lehman Engel, who wrote a reminiscence of his years in the American theatre. Poets associated with the city include Aleda Shirley, John Stone, Deborah Grison, Greg Miller, Frances Blissard Boeckman, and John Freeman.

Other writers associated with Jackson are Bill Fitzhugh, James H. Meredith, Randall Alan Brieger, Martha Smith Mabey, Henry Tim Chambers, Lottie Boggan, Ann Williams, Terri Herrington, Ralph Cheo Thurman, Renee Easterling, Rae Hederman, Claire King Sargent, C. Terry Cline, Jr., Judith Paige Mitchell, Bobby DeLaughter, and Patti Carr Black (coauthor of this book).

Writers in nearby areas include Brandon's Neil McGaughey, Lorraine Carroll, John Little, Scott Brunner, and Rick Guy. Historical novelist Anne Carsley and Robert L. Long are from Ridgeland. Others include Charles Wilson from Pearl, Lawrence C. Jones from rural Hinds County, and Phil Hardwick from Flora. Memoirist and poet Frankye V. Regis, author of *Dancing With Granny: Selective Memories of Mississippi* (2001), is from near Pocahontas.

Samuel A. Beadle (1859–1937) was born a slave and became a poet. He grew up near Atlanta and later came to Hinds County as a public school teacher. In 1884, against great odds, he taught himself law with the help of a Jackson lawyer and was admitted to the bar. He practiced with his partner, Perry Howard, national committeeman of the Republican Party.

Beadle and his first wife, Aurelia Thomas, had six children. After her death, he married Maggie Williams of Jackson. Around age thirty, Beadle began to write poetry, producing three volumes, *Sketches of Life in Dixie* (1899), *Adam Shuffler* (1901), *Lyrics of the Underworld* (1912), and possibly a fourth called *Fragments.* One reviewer noted that Beadle's poetry was traditional in many ways but progressive in its insistence on Negro rights.

Katherine Bellamann (1877–1956) was born in Carthage, but moved to Jackson in 1944 after the death of her husband, Henry Bellamann, with whom she collaborated on several books. One critic noted that she was overshadowed by her husband's talent and should have been recognized as an artist in her own right. She published two novels, *My Husband's Friends* (1931) and *Parris Mitchell of Kings Row* (1940), and a collection of poems, *Two Sides of a Poem* (1955). The Bellamanns' papers are housed in Special Collections at the University of Mississippi.

Nash Burger (1908) was born in Jackson and attended Jefferson Davis School and Central High School. (He and Eudora Welty were classmates.) After attending the University of the South and the University of Virginia, he headed the department of English in the Jackson school system. He was also editor of the Historical Records Survey and first historiographer of the Episcopal Diocese of Mississippi. He wrote reviews for the *New York Times Book Review* and later moved to New York City to become its editor.

With John K. Bettersworth, he wrote *South of Appomattox* (1959), which features ten biographies of notable southerners (including Jefferson Davis, Robert E. Lee, and Nathan Bedford Forrest) during and after the Civil War. In 1967, he published *Confederate Spy*, a biography of Rose O'Neale Greenhow.

Patrick D. Smith (1927) was born in nearby Mendenhall and grew up in D'Lo. He received a B.A. degree from Hinds Community College and an M.A. degree from Ole Miss. Now a resident of Merritt Island, Florida, he has served as director of college relations for Hinds Community College, the University of Mississippi, and Brevard Community College in Cocoa, Florida.

Among his novels are *The River Is Home* (1953), which won the Gold Medal of the International Mark Twain Society and the Canadian Fiction Award. Three of Smith's novels, *Forever Island* (1973), *Angel City* (1978), and *A Land Remembered* (1984), were nominated for the Pulitzer Prize. *Angel City* was produced as a CBS movie.

In 1985, he was nominated for the Nobel Prize for literature by the Cape Canaveral branch of the National League of American Pen Women. Noted in the nomination were Smith's efforts to raise concern for animals and the environment. In 2001 he was presented with the first Lifetime Achievement Award in Literature by the Lee County Library of Fort Myers, Florida. He was the 1999 inductee in the Florida Artists Hall of Fame.

Born in Jackson, Mildred D. Taylor (1943) moved with her family to Toledo, Ohio, in an attempt to escape racial discrimation. After graduating from the University of Toledo, Taylor served in the Peace Corps in Ethiopia. She then studied journalism at the University of Colorado.

In her acceptance speech for the Newbery Award, she said her writing was impelled by the need to tell stories from a black world that had not been fully described, a world of "strong fathers and concerned mothers." She also remembers the parents and grandparents who were forerunners for the civil rights movement of the fifties and sixties, and their struggles were the foundation of her trilogy, *Song of the Trees* (1975), *Roll of Thunder, Hear My Cry* (1976), and *Let the Circle Be Unbroken* (1981). *Roll of Thunder* was made into a movie scripted by Mississippian Thomas Hal Phillips and starring another Mississippian, Morgan Freeman. In 1988, Taylor's book *The Friendship* won the Coretta Scott King Award.

From I-55, take exit 100 to Northside Drive. Proceed west on Northside. Take a right onto State Street, then another right on Broadmoor and a left onto Woodmont Drive.

4886 Woodmont Drive

Born in St. Louis, poet James Whitehead (1936) settled with his family in Jackson after World War II. Whitehead attended Liberty Grove Elementary School and Bailey Junior High School. He played football for Central High School and received a four-year football scholarship to Vanderbilt.

As an undergraduate, he was in the preordination program of the Presbyterian Church and intended to become a preacher. But after delivering a sermon in iambic pentameter, he surmised that a truer calling was to be a poet and teacher. He went on to receive B.A. and M.A. degrees from Vanderbilt University and an M.F.A. from the University of Iowa.

Although he admits he once foolishly ran off with a country band led by Tom T. Hall while on a sabbatical made possible by a Guggenheim Fellowship, his poetry was anything but diminished by the experience. His collections of poems include *Domains* (1966), *Local Men* (1979), and *Actual Size* (1985). *Joiner* (1971), a novel about the struggles of a football hero, was all set to go to the printer when Whitehead changed his mind about the ending. He wrote the last four pages while lying on his publisher's floor.

A big man (six feet, six inches) with a big appetite for living, loving, and writing, Whitehead discovered his distinctive style in an early poem, "Delta Farmer in a Wet Summer" ("By God, we raised some handsome bales and hell/Then went to New Orleans as usual").

Whitehead has served as director of the creative writing program at the University of Arkansas in Fayetteville. He and his wife, Guendaline Graeber from Yazoo City, have seven children (among them a set of triplets), and nine grandchildren.

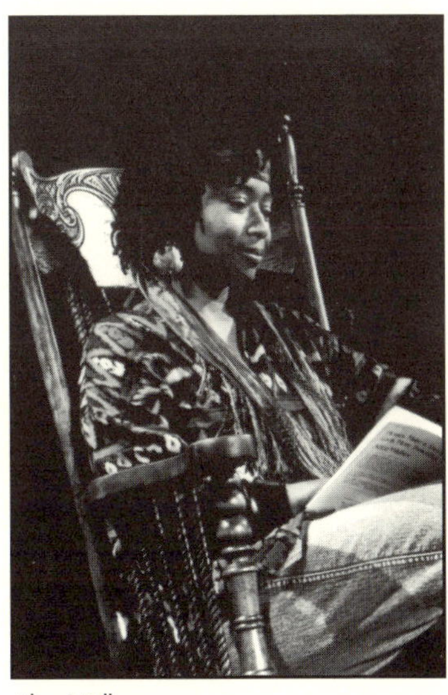

Alice Walker

Return to Northside Drive. At Britton Avenue, take a left. Take another left onto Rockdale Drive.

1443 Rockdale Drive

Born in Eatonton, Georgia, to sharecropper parents, Alice Walker (1944) was one of eight children. She was educated at Spelman College in Atlanta and at Sarah Lawrence College. Knowing no one, she came to Mississippi in 1966 to work for the Headstart program and the voter registration drive. She was soon befriended by a distant cousin, the writer Margaret Walker Alexander. She taught with Alexander at Jackson State University for a time and was writer-in-residence at Tougaloo College in 1969–1970. In 1967, she married Mel Leventhal, a civil rights lawyer.

Walker's first poems were marked by her civil rights experiences. In the novel *Meridian* (1976), the protagonist participates in a voter registration drive in a Deep South town.

Walker is a profound and prolific writer of novels, short stories, poetry, and essays. Her poetry collections include *Revolutionary Petunias* (1974). She is best known for the Pulitzer

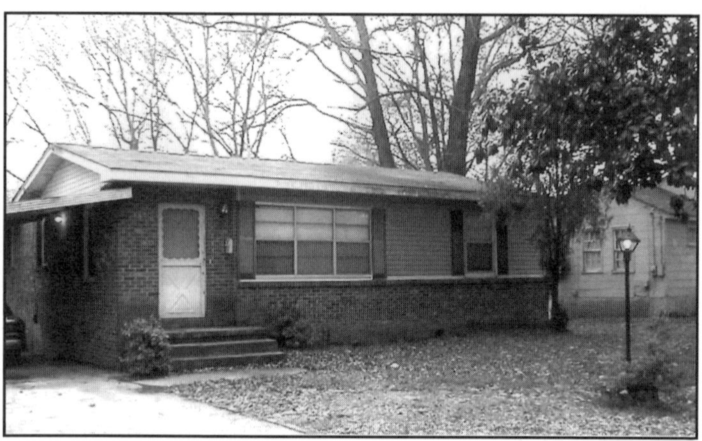

Walker/Leventhal home, Jackson

Prize–winning novel *The Color Purple* (1982), which was made into a movie starring native Mississippian Oprah Winfrey.

In her recent autobiography, *The Way Forward Is with a Broken Heart* (2000), Walker reminisces about living in Jackson on "R Street" with Mel Leventhal, from whom she is now divorced, and about the impending birth of their child. She recalls her neighbors, a tree she planted, and the way the house looked then. "R Street" is clearly meant to refer to Rockdale.

Return to Northside Drive. Turn left onto Highway 49 (Medgar Evers Boulevard). At the stoplight with the Chevron station, take a left onto Ridgeway Drive. Take an immediate right on Missouri Street and then an immediate left on Margaret Walker Alexander Drive.

Walker House

2205 Margaret Walker Alexander Drive

On this street named for her stands the house where Margaret Walker Alexander (1915–1998) lived. Civil rights leader Medgar Evers was living on this street when he was assassinated at his home.

Walker was born in Birmingham, Alabama, the precocious daughter of a music teacher and a minister. Her father, from the British West Indies, for a time attended Tuskegee Institute. When he became a minister in the Methodist Episcopal Church, the family moved to various places in the South, among them Meridian and New Orleans.

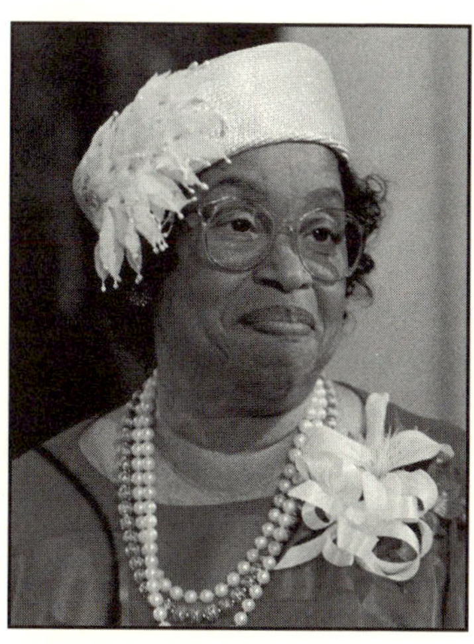
Margaret Walker Alexander

At New Orleans University (now Dillard University), Walker met the poet Langston Hughes, who read her poems and encouraged her. They became lifetime friends. Walker graduated from Northwestern University in Chicago at age twenty with a B.A. in English, and subsequently taught there. In 1940, she received a master's degree from the University of Iowa.

She was hired by the WPA in Chicago and joined the Chicago Writers' Project. When she met writer Richard Wright in this group, another lifelong friendship was forged. She would later write *The Daemonic Genius of Richard Wright* (1987).

In 1934, Walker published her first poem, "I Want to Write," in *The Crisis*. In 1942, a collection of poems, *For My People*, was published as a volume in the Yale Series of Younger Poets. In his foreword, Stephen Vincent Benét expressed admiration for all the anonymous voices she raises. In these verses, many of them ballads, she revives and passes on great folklore characters such as Stagolee, Poppa Chicken, and Big John Henry. In 1966, after ten years of research, her novel, *Jubilee*, was published. It is an account of the Civil War as told from the point of view of a black family. The protagonist, Vyry, is based on Walker's great-grandmother.

In 1943, Walker married Firnist James Alexander and with him had four children. For over thirty years, she taught English at Jackson State University. She also served as Director of the Institute for the Study of the History, Life and Culture of Black People, later renamed for her. The Margaret Walker Alexander Library was named for her as well. She died in Jackson at age eighty-three.

Return to Highway 49. Continue through several stoplights to Woodrow Wilson Drive, a five-way intersection. Take a left onto Woodrow Wilson.

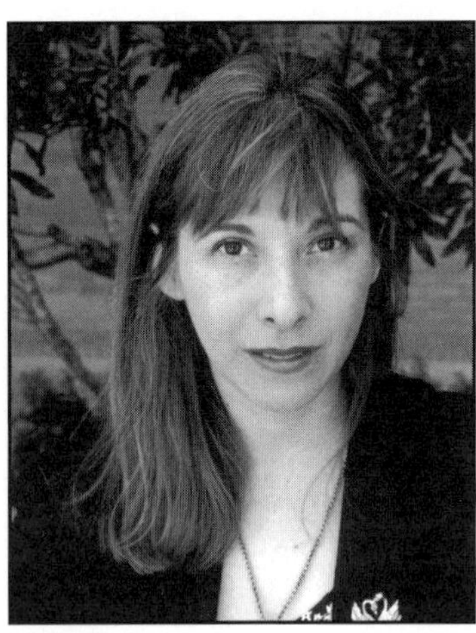

Beth Henley

Go through several intersections to State Street. Take a left on State until it divides. Take the right fork, which is Old Canton Road. Continue on Old Canton through several lights to Avondale Drive. Take a left on Avondale.

835 Avondale

Pulitzer Prize–winning playwright Beth Henley (1952) moved with her family to this house after her fourth-grade year at Duling Elementary School. She went to Bailey Junior High School and Murrah High School before leaving Mississippi to attend Southern Methodist University in Dallas and to study theatre arts for a year in graduate school at the University of Illinois. Her mother, Lydy Caldwell, still resides in this house.

Henley's interest in playwriting was encouraged by her mother, who has acted locally for many years. Henley remembered seeing her mother, who was preparing for the role of Laura in *The Glass Menagerie* for a community theatre production, limping around in the grocery store, buying only foods she thought Laura would buy. Henley's father was an attorney and a Mississippi state senator. When young Beth broke her arm during one of her father's campaigns, her mother nudged her to "play up the arm, kid." In such works as *Crimes of the Heart* and *The Miss Firecracker Contest*, Henley has drawn on her father's native Hazlehurst and her mother's native Brookhaven for material.

In college, Henley wrote a one-act comedy, *Am I Blue*, staged her senior year at S.M.U. In 1976, she moved to Los Angeles, hoping to act in movies or television. In 1978, while waiting for an acting job to materialize, she wrote a screenplay entitled *The Moonwatcher*. Having decided that waiting for a part in a McDonald's commercial was a waste of life, she was soon hard at work writing *Crimes of the Heart* (1981), inspired by a near-tragedy when her grandfather was lost for three days in the woods of Hazlehurst. *Crimes of the Heart* won the 1981 Pulitzer Prize for drama. In 1986, it was made into a hit movie starring Sissy Spacek, Jessica Lange, and Diane Keaton. The actresses soon learned that the best model to imitate if they wanted to convey the idioms and idiosyncrasies of their southern characters was Henley herself.

She has had several plays produced off-Broadway, including *Family Week* in 1999. She has also written scripts for television and movies, including *Nobody's Fool* with Paul Newman. Henley lives in California with her young son, Patrick.

Return to Old Canton Road and merge into State Street. As you continue on State, you will cross Woodrow Wilson and pass Millsaps College, alma mater of many fine writers, including Lewis Nordan. Continue on State Street for several blocks to Pinehurst Street. Take a left on Pinehurst.

Welty House

1119 Pinehurst Street

Here for many years lived Jackson's most famous writer, Eudora Welty (1909–2001). The family lived on Congress Street before moving to this brick-and-stucco Tudor-style home in 1923. The Mississippi Department of Archives and History is in the process of restoring the gardens of camellias, roses, and perennials originally planted by Welty's mother. Across the street at Belhaven College, students practicing their piano were an inspiration for Welty's story "June Recital."

Welty's autobiography, *One Writer's Beginnings* (1983), reveals the main sources of her talent but little about her personal life, for, as she said many times, one need not know the writer's life to understand the work. Yet she has also acknowledged that much of the background for her 1972 Pulitzer Prize–winning novel, *The Optimist's Daughter*, is autobiographical. Welty's mother, Chestina, came from West Virginia, as did the mother of the novel's central character, Laurel McKelva Hand. Welty's father, Christian, was from Ohio, as was Laurel's father.

The foresighted Mr. Welty, who became president of Lamar Life Insurance Company in Jackson, enlisted a Texas architect for the Lamar Life building, whose design of thirteen stories provided Jackson with its first skyscraper. The same architect would soon design the Pinehurst home. Mr. Welty is believed to have had the

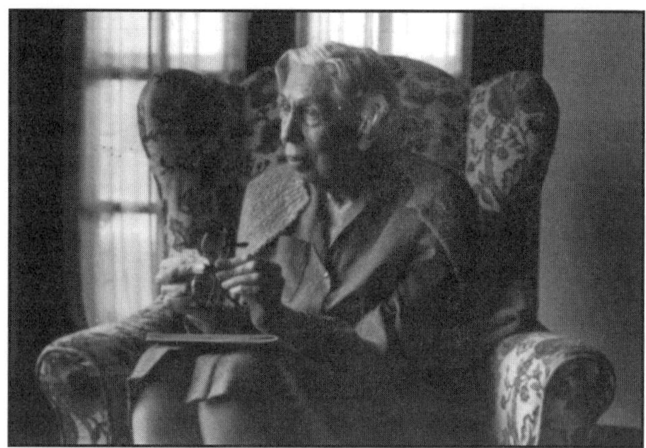

Eudora Welty

first Dictaphone in Jackson and one of the first automobiles. He gave his daughter her first typewriter, a red Royal Portable, when she went off to the University of Wisconsin in 1927.

At age five, Welty attended Davis School where she proved her ability to spell all the counties in Mississippi correctly, including Oktibbeha and Issaquena. At twelve, she won twenty-five dollars in the Jackie Mackie Jingle contest. After attending Central High School in Jackson, she went to Mississippi State College for Women and later graduated from the University of Wisconsin. She attended the Columbia University School of Business for postgraduate work in advertising. In 1931, when her father became ill and subsequently died of leukemia, she returned to Jackson, where she was, as she put it, "locally underfoot."

Welty had a wide range of interests. She once worked at WJDX radio station in the clock tower of Lamar Life, her father's building. At various times, she was an advertising copy writer and the writer of a society column for a Jackson newspaper. During the depression, she worked as publicity agent for the WPA. On her own time she took pictures of rural Mississippians at political rallies and hog killings, honing her observation skills and learning to "part a curtain." Her photographs were later collected in *One Time, One Place* (1978). In 1944 she lived in New York City and wrote book reviews for the *New York Times* under the pseudonym Michael Ravenna, taken when one of the editors questioned whether a woman could review books about war. She was

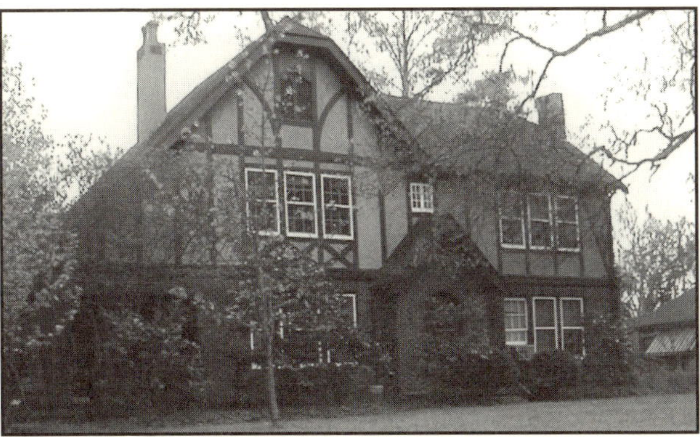

Welty home, Pinehurst Street, Jackson

a persuasive essayist. In "Must the Novelist Crusade?," written in response to the question of whether she should take up the cause of civil rights in her writing, she argued that "[t]here is absolutely everything in great fiction but a clear answer."

Upon publication of "Death of a Traveling Salesman" in *Manuscript* (1936), her career as a writer was launched. Author of over thirty-two books, she is considered a master craftsman of the short story. Her stories "A Worn Path," "Powerhouse," and "Why I Live at the P.O." have appeared in hundreds of anthologies. Welty's ability to convince came from her remarkable aptitude for seeing and hearing, traits developed at an early age in Jackson, as she watched and listened to her family and their friends. Her works evoke what she called "sense of place." Broad comedy enlivens the pages of *The Ponder Heart* (1954) and many other works.

Welty received many prizes and awards, including the 1973 Pulitzer Prize for fiction for *The Optimist's Daughter*, several O. Henry Prize awards, the Gold Medal for Fiction given by the National Institute of Arts and Letters, and the French Legion of Honor medal. She was writer-in-residence at Smith College and Millsaps College, among other places. In 1972, Eudora Welty Day was held in Jackson. She was inducted into the National Women's Hall of Fame in Seneca Falls, New York. She twice received the Freedom Medal of Honor, once from President Carter and once from President Reagan. Every year, a symposium is held in her name at Mississippi University for Women. Countless arts festivals, film festivals, and seminars have been named in her honor.

In 1999, she became the first living writer to be published in the prestigious Library of America series.

1607 Pinehurst Street

Hubert Creekmore (1907–1966) was born in Water Valley to the lawyer son of a planter family. The family moved to Jackson in the mid-twenties. After graduating from the University of Mississippi, he studied playwriting at Yale. He returned to Jackson in the 1930s while working for the Mississippi Highway Department. In Jackson, he founded the *Southern Review.* His sister Mittie Elizabeth Creekmore was married to Walter Welty, Eudora's brother. With Welty, Creekmore helped organize a night-blooming cereus club, a fine excuse for parties and gatherings. After serving in the navy, Creekmore moved to New York City.

Creekmore started writing poetry in high school. His first volume of poetry, *Personal Sun,* was published in 1940. His three novels, all set in Mississippi and dealing with its social conditions, are *The Chain in the Heart* (1953), *The Fingers of Night* (1946), and *The Welcome* (1948). Creekmore also reviewed books for the *New York Times.* He died in a taxi in New York City on his way to the airport en route to Spain.

Continue east on Pinehurst and turn right onto St. Ann Street.

Haxton House

1225 St. Ann Street

Josephine Haxton, whose pen name is Ellen Douglas, has lived here for a number of years. In this house, she composed *Truth: Four Stories I Am Finally Old Enough to Tell* (1998). Although she has labelled the work "fiction," she admits that many of the details are based on events and incidents involving her Natchez family. Douglas has conducted writing workshops at the Sewanee Writers' Conference and elsewhere around the country. She has been writer-in-residence at Millsaps College, Hollins College, and the University of Iowa. In 1999, the University Press of Mississippi Bookfriends sponsored the Ellen Douglas Symposium at the Old Capitol in Jackson; the event was a celebration and discussion of Douglas's life and work by scholars, writers, and family. (See Greenville for more about Douglas.)

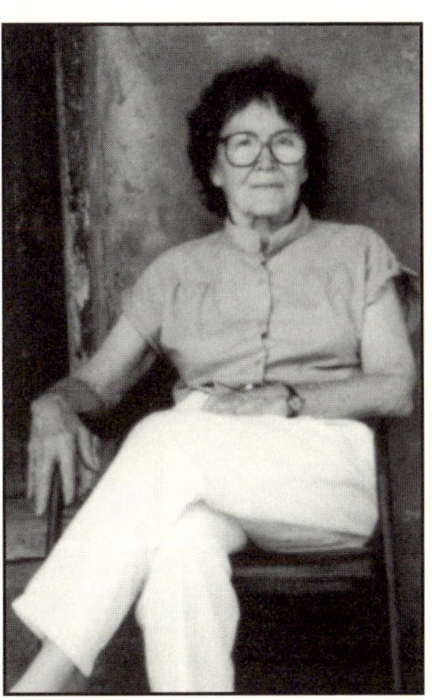

Ellen Douglas

Return to State Street and go south.

903 North State Street

Born and raised in Jackson, Turner Cassity (1929) lived for a time in an apartment at this address. His mother was a violinist and a charter member of the Jackson Symphony. Inspired by family members who worked in sawmills as well as by those who were musicians, he has written poems on a variety of subjects, including music and the natural world. He graduated from Millsaps College and studied under the poet Yvor Winters at Stanford University. Upon receiving a graduate degree in library science, he went to work as a librarian at the Jackson Municipal Library.

A few years later, he got the opportunity to work in the Transvaal Provincial Library in Pretoria and Johannesburg, South Africa, a move that greatly enriched his poetry and gave him a taste for travel to Europe and Asia as well as to Africa. He was for many years a librarian at Emory University in Atlanta.

His lyric poetry about far-flung places has been called "epigrammatic" and "neo-classical." Among his collections of poems are *Black for Beautiful* (1975) and *The Defense of the Sugar Islands* (1980).

Continue south on State Street to Greenbrook Flowers on the right.

Greenbrook Flowers

705 North State Street

Charlotte Capers (1913–1996) was born in Columbia, Tennessee, but grew up in Jackson in this late-Victorian frame house,

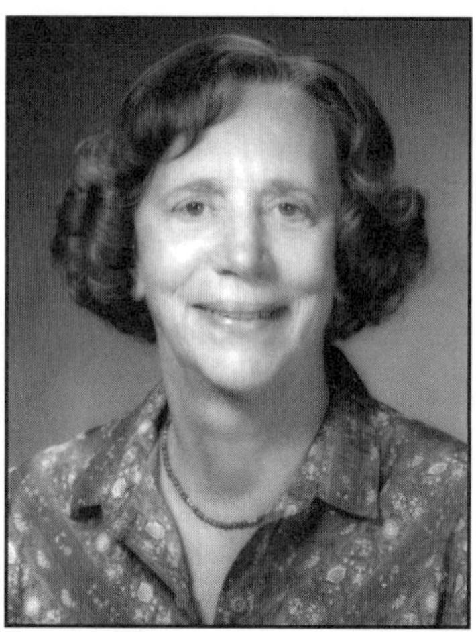
Charlotte Capers

now Greenbrook Flowers. Built between 1895 and 1897, the house was acquired by St. Andrew's Cathedral when Capers's father, Dr. Walter B. Capers, was called to the Episcopal priesthood in 1919. As a child, Charlotte loved the scaled-to-size swinging doors for the dogs and her bathtub shaped like a gondola and mounted on iron paws. In a 1982 Junior League publication, *Jackson Landmarks*, she recalled that while living here even the depression was fun; it was a time when she might be summoned as a witness for impromptu weddings or when tramps might drop in for birthday parties.

After graduating from Ole Miss, Capers came back to Jackson and lived on Poplar Boulevard. She was director of the Mississippi Department of Archives and History for fourteen years and an officer of the Mississippi Historical Society, serving as its president from 1974 to 1975. The Mississippi legislature named the state archives and history building for her.

The spirited pieces she wrote for a Sunday newspaper column called "Miss Quote" were later collected by friends at the archives department and published as *The Capers Papers* (1982). The introduction was written by her friend Eudora Welty.

Turn right on George Street at Greenbrook Flowers. Jog left on President Street and make a quick right to continue on George Street.

George Street Grocery

416 George Street

Eudora Welty remarked that life in Jackson when she was growing up was just right for children; it was a place where the blackberry lady and the watermelon man were familiar and predictable. In her essay "The Little Store," she describes being sent on errands

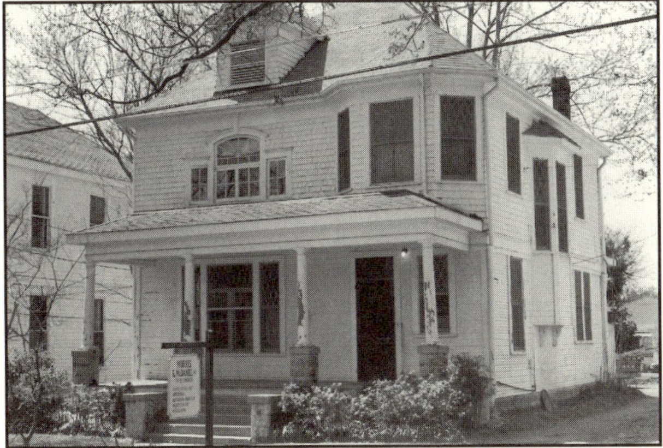

Welty home, North Congress Street, Jackson

to the neighborhood store and the wondrous happenings along the way: seeing the Monkey Man, avoiding the grade school principal who might come out and challenge her to spell "oblige" (missed on that week's spelling test), or making up a poem about a boy named Lindsey who "went to heaven with the influinzy." Once inside the store, she luxuriated in the "tangible smells" of dill-pickle brine and licorice while deciding what to spend her nickel on.

Turn around and go $^{1}/_{2}$ block to Congress Street going north.

741 North Congress Street

Here Eudora Welty and her two younger brothers, Walter and Edward, spent the first few years of their lives. When the house once caught on fire, Welty's mother threw a complete set of Charles Dickens's novels out the window, tossing all twenty-four volumes down one by one to her husband, who was waiting below to receive them. In 1979, the house was bought for commercial use and renovated.

736 North Congress Street

Pulitzer Prize winner Richard Ford (1944) was born in Jackson. Just before his birth, his father, Parker Carrol Ford, a traveling

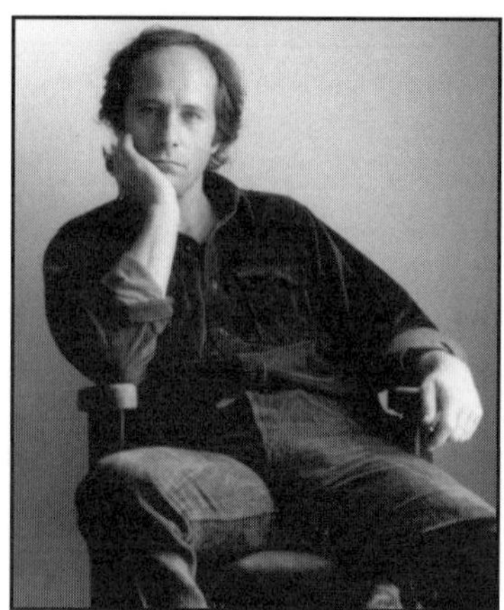

Richard Ford

salesman for Faultless Starch, decided to move from his native Little Rock, Arkansas, to Jackson, in the middle of his sales district. Years before, Eudora Welty had spent her early childhood in a house across the street. Like Welty, Ford attended nearby Davis School, where he had many of the same teachers.

When Ford was eight, his father suffered a heart attack, and the family moved back to Little Rock for a short time, to the Marion Hotel, which was run by his grandfather, Ben Shelley. When Ford was sixteen, his father had another heart attack, this one fatal. Ford has reported that, after his father's death, adolescent pranks with his buddies, such as stealing and eating watermelons from garbage cans, stopped, and he began to take his life seriously.

After graduating from Murrah High School in Jackson, he attended Michigan State University for a time, intending to become a hotel manager like his grandfather. He changed his mind and transferred to Washington University in St. Louis to study law. While there, he realized his deep desire to be a writer. He transferred to the University of California at Irvine and earned an M.F.A. degree. He married Kristina Hensley, a city planner, and they moved to Chicago. Soon after, he received a fellowship from the University of Michigan.

Transience is a familiar condition for the Fords. They have lived in many places, including New York, Boston, Montana, and New Orleans. In 1985, the Fords moved to Coahoma County, Mississippi, and lived for two years at Rosebud Plantation in a home once owned by Governor Alcorn (see Lula-Rich).

Ford has written about his early struggles to get published. His first short stories were repeatedly rejected over a period of nine years before his first novel, *A Piece of My Heart* (1976), was published. He was awarded the Pulitzer Prize for his 1995 novel *Independence Day*, the fourth Mississippi writer, following Faulkner, Welty, and Henley, to win the esteemed literary prize.

Independence Day also won the PEN/Faulkner Award, the first novel ever to win both prizes. He has received many other honors, including awards from the American Academy of Arts and Letters and the Mississippi Institute of Arts and Letters.

Ford denies any southern strains in his writing. Critics have placed his work in the tradition of Raymond Carver, Tom McGuane, Jim Harrison, and Frederick Exley, its tough, masculine style containing echoes of Hemingway. An indebtedness to Walker Percy is also apparent in his fiction.

From Congress Street take a left on Barksdale and another left on N. West Street to the cemetery entrance at the corner.

Greenwood Cemetery

North West Street at George Street

In 1823, land was granted for this cemetery, one of Jackson's oldest landmarks. Seven Mississippi governors and four supreme court justices are buried here. Among the writers whose graves are here are Alexander McNutt, Mississippi governor from 1838 to 1842, James D. Lynch, secretary of state during the Reconstruction era, Congressman John R. Lynch (see Natchez), Bishop Charles Betts Galloway, and Eudora Welty.

Take a left on Lamar Street. Take a right on High Street. The entrance to the museum is on your left.

Smith Robertson Museum and Cultural Center

528 Bloom Street

Richard Wright (1908–1960) is one of Mississippi's most famous native sons. Born in Roxie near Natchez to a sickly mother and a sharecropper father who soon deserted the family, he lived for a time in Jackson, in a house no longer standing, and attended school at Smith Robertson, the first Jackson public school for African American children. A mural of him was painted by Belhaven art major Lawrence Quinn on the outside of the Smith Robertson Community Center Building.

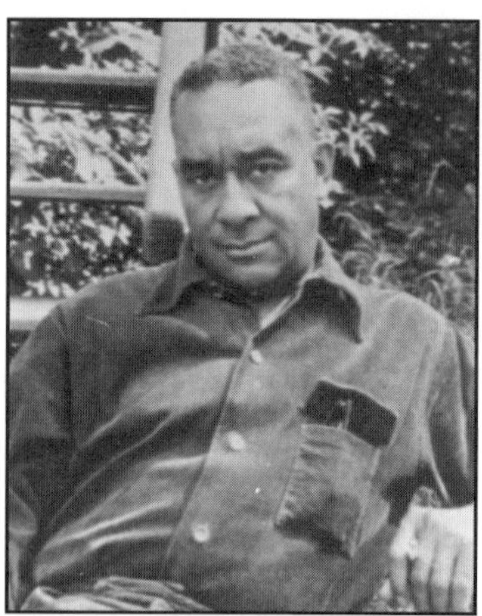
Richard Wright

As described in his memoir *Black Boy* (1945), Wright's early years were harsh. Yet despite interruptions in his schooling as he was passed from relative to relative, Wright graduated from ninth grade at Smith Robertson first in his class and gave the graduation speech. When he was fifteen, he published his first story, "The Voodoo of Hell's Half Acre," in a local black newspaper. From an early age, he read everything he could get his hands on, from Edgar Lee Masters to Nietzsche.

Wright's life can be viewed as a series of attempts to escape racism; he went first from Jackson to Memphis, then to Chicago and New York, and finally to Paris as an expatriate. While in Chicago, he joined the Communist Party and soon relocated to New York to become the Harlem editor of the *Daily Worker*. In 1944, he broke his ties with the Communist Party, a decision he explains in the 1944 essay "I Tried to Be a Communist." After the failure of his first marriage to Dhima Meadman, Wright married Ellen Poplar. They had two daughters.

One critic described Wright as the best-known black writer in the world and hailed *Native Son* (1940) as "the most significant black novel ever published." He wrote many other novels, including *The Outsider* (1953), *White Man, Listen!* (1957), and *The Long Dream* (1958).

Wright died in Paris in 1960 at the young age of fifty-two. A copy of *Black Boy* was cremated with him in the Paris Columbarium.

Go east on High Street to State Street. Turn right on State, then right on Yazoo Street. The Galloway House and church are on the corner of Congress and Yazoo.

The Galloway House

304 North Congress Street

This Second Empire–style Victorian house, now a law office, was built in 1889 for Charles Betts Galloway (1849–1909). Bishop Galloway was called by one critic "one of the most remarkable men of the post–Civil War South." At age thirty-six, he was the youngest person to be elected bishop of the Methodist Episcopal Church, South. Born in Kosciusko, he resided primarily in Jackson and Vicksburg.

When he and his wife contracted yellow fever during the 1878 epidemic, a Jackson newspaper carried his obituary, but fortunately, as with Mark Twain, the news of his death was greatly exaggerated. He went on to become editor of the *New Orleans Christian Advocate*, and once entered a newspaper debate with Jefferson Davis over prohibition. (He was for it; Davis opposed it.)

As a scholar, he published articles on Aaron Burr, Lorenzo Dow, and others. In 1908, he published a well-respected biography, *Jefferson Davis: A Judicial Estimate.* He wrote books on religion and temperance and was an early advocate of equal protection and education for blacks.

305 North Congress

Galloway Memorial United Methodist Church

This church, in Neoclassical Revival style of brick and sandstone, was built in 1915. It was erected on the site of the first Methodist Church built in Jackson in the 1830s. Designed by Reuben H. Hunt of Chattanooga, Tennessee, it was named for Bishop Galloway.

Take a left on Congress Street to Pascagoula Street. At Pascagoula, take a left onto State Street. Directly ahead is the Mississippi Department of Archives and History. (For parking, take a right on Amite Street.)

Mississippi Department of Archives and History

100 South State Street

The second-oldest state archives department in the country, the Mississippi Department of Archives and History houses papers of Eudora Welty, William Alexander Percy, Ellen Douglas, and Rebecca Hill, among others. Its main library has a portrait of Eudora Welty painted by Mildred Wolfe. It also contains eighteen hundred private collections, including the diary of Emma Balfour. The Old Capitol Museum next door often features books by Mississippi writers.

Eudora Welty Library

300 North State Street

As a young child living on Congress Street, Eudora Welty was allowed to walk to the nearby Andrew Carnegie Library at the corner of Congress and Mississippi streets. She would sometimes take a shortcut and *glide* on her roller skates across the marble floors of the state capitol. An insatiable reader, she was crushed when she learned that she would be allowed to check out only two books at a time.

By the time the library was moved around the corner to North State and Yazoo streets in 1954, Welty had published four short-story collections, a novel, and two novellas. In 1986, the library was moved to its present location and fittingly renamed the Eudora Welty Library. At its west end, the library houses a Mississippi room with a fine display of photographs, books, and biographies of Mississippi writers.

Continue north on State Street, then east on High Street to return to I-55.

Hazlehurst

The last spike for the Great Northern Railway was driven here in 1868. Poet William Lowenkemp was born in Hazlehurst, and surrealist poet/novelist Charles Henri Ford (see Columbus) lived here for a time in the family-owned Ford Hotel. Built by Ford's grandfather, the hotel burned after World War I. Blues legend Robert Johnson was born in 1912 near Hazlehurst and raised in Commerce, a sharecroppers' settlement.

Take the north exit off I-55. At the underpass, take a left and continue to a four-way stop, which is the intersection of highways 51 and 28. Take a right onto Highway 51 and go south. Highway 51 becomes Extension Street.

333 South Extension Street

Built in 1925, this Colonial-style mansion was the home of the W. S. Henleys, grandparents of playwright Beth Henley (see Jackson). Henley visited often. Hazlehurst was the setting for Henley's *Crimes of the Heart*, and the kitchen of this house was an inspiration.

Brookhaven

A town filled with lovely old homes, Brookhaven has several literary ties. The writer Charles Henri Ford (see Columbus) was born here; the family home, no longer standing, was across from the First Presbyterian Church. Other writers associated with Brookhaven include Carroll Case, James E. Alford, Charles Thornton, and Royce Hart. Thomas Jefferson Young lived in nearby Oma.

Cid Ricketts Sumner (1890–1970) was born in Brookhaven. The family moved to Jackson when her father accepted a teaching position at Millsaps College. Sumner received a B.S. degree from Millsaps and a master's degree from Columbia University. She was enrolled as a medical student at Cornell University before she married one of her professors, James B. Sumner, who received the Nobel Prize in chemistry in 1946. The Sumners, who were later divorced, had four children. Sumner's cousin was writer Berry Morgan, to whom she paid extended visits at Albena Plantation in Port Gibson.

Before taking up a writing career, Sumner taught English and French. She was employed in a munitions plant during World War II. In launching her writing career, she promised herself she would write thirty-nine stories, at which time, if none had been published, she would quit. She didn't have to. She hit the jackpot when story number thirty-six was accepted for publication.

She is best known for the novels that were turned into the sentimental Tammy movies starring Debbie Reynolds; they were based on her *Tammy out of Time* (1948) and *Tammy in Rome* (1965). Much of the depth of these books, in which many of the female characters are strong, capable women, was lost in the Hollywood versions.

Sumner's life ended violently and tragically when she was killed by her own grandson. She was eighty years old.

Take the Highway 550 exit at Brookhaven. It will become Congress Street. Take Congress to Jackson and take a right. Whitworth College will be on your right.

Whitworth College

South Jackson, Monticello, and Cherokee Streets

Founded in 1858, Whitworth Female College served as an educational institution until 1984. Writer Martha Lacy Hall was a student here, and Tallulah Ragsdale taught English for many years (see below). Plans are under way to open an arts school on the site of the former college.

At West Chippewa, take a right.

Becker House

507 West Chippewa

This is the former home of Mr. and Mrs. M. G. Becker, maternal grandparents of Beth Henley. Henley spent a lot of time here when she was growing up.

Return to Jackson Street and go south to Natchez Avenue. Take a right on Natchez. The Hardy House is in the curve.

205 Natchez Avenue

Born at the beginning of the Civil War, Tallulah Ragsdale (1862–1953) would never know her father, a Confederate soldier who died four months after her birth. At his death, mother and baby daughter moved from Cedar Hall in Lawrence (now Lincoln) County to live with Mrs. Ragsdale's sister, Ella Hooker Hardy, in a house Mr. Hardy built in 1872.

After graduating from Brookhaven's Whitworth College in 1878, Ragsdale taught English there for a while, then went to New York to act on the stage. After a modest success in Tom Taylor's *The Fool's Revenge*, she returned to Brookhaven, settled in this house, resumed teaching, and began to write poetry and novels.

Although her novels have been described as conventional, sentimental, and melodramatic, they present themes ahead of their time. In the 1893 novel *A Shadow's Shadow*, the female protagonist is torn between a career and marriage. In *Miss Dulcie from Dixie* (1917), women's roles are explored in more depth. At one point, the female protagonist laments, "Oh, I wish I wore pants, and didn't have any sex reputation to live up, or down, to!" The novel was made into a film that opened in 1919, starring Gladys Leslie. In *Next-Besters* (1920), reconciliation between North and South, a theme introduced in earlier novels, is given fuller exploration. Ragsdale's poems were collected in *If I See Green* (1929).

Return to I-55 and continue on to McComb.

McComb

Writers associated with McComb include Allie Bellue Rueff, playwright and poet Charles Braxton, and novelist Ernest Herndon. Hodding Carter (see Greenville) wrote *So the Heffners Left McComb* (1965) about the civil rights struggles that took place here.

Martha Lacy Hall (1923) was born in nearby Magnolia, in a house at 411 Clarke Avenue, razed in the late 1970s. Her father was a newspaperman, and other members of her family wrote as well. After attending Whitworth College and Millsaps College, Hall worked as an editor for Louisiana State University Press, editing over a hundred books, including John Kennedy Toole's *A Confederacy of Dunces*. She also worked as an editor for the Mississippi Art Association in Jackson until her husband, an electrical engineer, was transferred to Baton Rouge.

When Hall began to write fiction, she recalled her early years in Magnolia—the church socials, the Sunday dinners, the conversations. The town of Magnolia became Sweet Bay in her stories. About her stories, writer Walker Percy, noting their deceptive calm, said, "As peaceful as Main Street in Magnolia, Mississippi, on a Sunday afternoon, lurk the secret and sometimes terrible motions of the human heart." Her stories are collected in *Call It Living* (1983), *Music Lesson* (1984), and *The Apple-Green Triumph* (1990).

Just south of McComb, take Highway 24 west to Liberty.

Liberty

On Liberty's courthouse square, Mississippi's first Confederate monument was erected in 1871. Tichenor's Antiseptic and Gale Borden's condensed milk were first manufactured here. Opera star Jennie Lynn once sang in the old Railford Building.

Willoughby (Rose Budd Stevens) House

7506 Highway 24

This is the last home of Mamie Willoughby (1915–1996). A little shed near the house still bears the pen name she used as a columnist for local newspapers for over fifty years—Rose Budd Stevens. Her first column was written for the *Gloster Wilk-Amite Record* in 1947. Her colorful and zestful pieces about daily life on a farm have been collected in *Along the RFD* (1987) and *Sweetly Be!* (1990). To capture the various human conditions, she fictionalized her husband, family, and friends, then described everything about their rural lives, from the making of lye hominy to the effort to understand a man who didn't get out of bed for forty years. Several installments concerned the loss of her good scissors, which were necessary for making slingshots, cutting the mule's tail, and trimming the cat's whiskers.

Continue on Highway 24 to the sign on the right for East Fork Baptist Church. Take Amazing Grace Lane on the right.

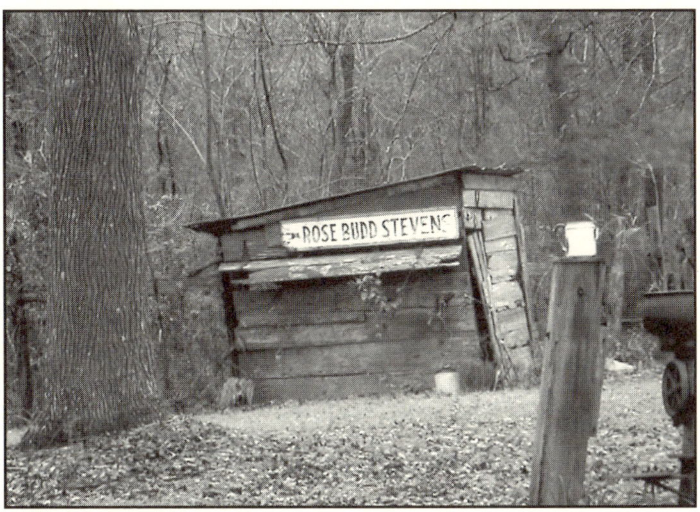

Stevens shed, Liberty

Clower House

Amazing Grace Lane

This is the contemporary brick home of comedian Jerry Clower (1926–1998). The lane was named in honor of Clower's religious views, and his gate is adorned with a large "C."

After serving in the navy during World War II, Clower attended Southwest Mississippi Junior College and graduated from Mississippi State College with a degree in agriculture. He served as lay minister and deacon for many years at East Fork Baptist Church. He and his wife, Homerline Wells, his childhood sweetheart, had four children.

Clower began developing homespun stories about growing up in Liberty while traveling around the state as a fertilizer salesman for Mississippi Chemical Corporation in Yazoo City. Soon he achieved acclaim for his salesmanship, and he became a popular banquet speaker for the company. He was persuaded to record his stories for a local label in 1971. Told in exaggerated vernacular and peppered with his Christian convictions, stories such as "Bully Has Done Flung a Cravin' on Me," "Sittin' Up with the Dead," "Bird Huntin' at Uncle Versie's," and others gained a national audience. They soon became so popular that, in 1970,

Clower made a comedy album which sold more than five hundred thousand copies within a month. Many others followed, including best sellers *Ain't God Good?* (1975) and *Stories from Home* (1992).

Next door to Clower's home is a museum with memorabilia. Museum hours are Monday–Friday, 8–3.

Continue on East Fork Baptist Road to the church, less than a mile off Highway 24.

East Fork Baptist Church

From the fold of this rural church came two famous members, writer Will Campbell and comedian Jerry Clower. In 1985, on the occasion of the church's 175th anniversary, the two men returned home to celebrate and reminisce. Campbell recalled teaching Clower, who married Campbell's first cousin, how to tie a necktie. Clower was in the congregation when Campbell was ordained. While Clower remained true to the faith of his fathers, Campbell split from organized religion early in his career.

Return to Highway 24. From the East Fork turnoff, Will Campbell's house is the second house on the left.

6188 Highway 24

Preacher/writer/activist Will Campbell (1919) was born in this modest cottage built by his father. He grew up in a family of six on a small cotton farm during the depression. He attended East Fork School and East Fork Baptist Church. At sixteen, after borrowing a friend's black hat two sizes too big, he took over the pulpit at the graduation practice as a prank. The usurpation might have been disastrous, but his diminutive stature and big hat were so funny that his audience—including the principal—broke out in thunderous laughter. After that, he began preaching in earnest, practicing by sermonizing to the backside of his horse while plowing a field. Soon he grew into the role of preacher, and the black hat became his trademark. He is the prototype for Reverend Will B. Dunn in the comic strip "Kudzu," created by Mississippian Doug Marlette.

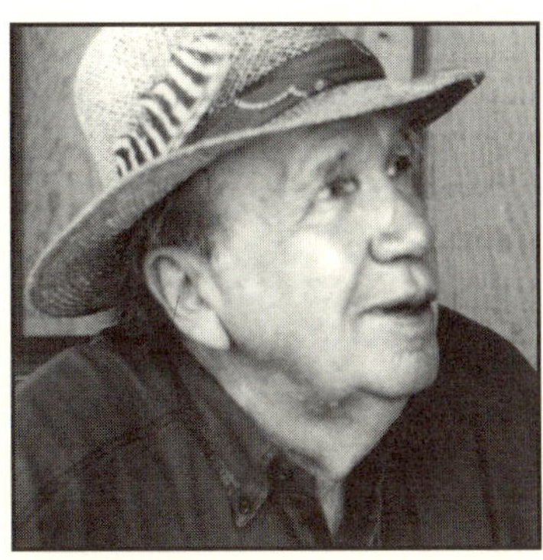

Will Campbell

Campbell attended Wake Forest, Tulane, and Yale after serving in World War II. He became a civil rights activist while he was director of religious life at Ole Miss and was later head of race relations for the National Council of Churches. He was the only white man to help organize the Southern Christian Leadership Conference. His iconoclastic vision and disillusionment with organized religion led to his becoming known as "a preacher without a church" and a "steeple dropout."

Among Campbell's writings are his award-winning autobiography *Brother to a Dragonfly* (1977), a novel, *The Glad River* (1982), *Forty Acres and a Goat* (1986), *The Convention* (1988), and *Providence* (1992). *And Also with You: Duncan Gray and the American Dilemma* (1997) was written as a tribute to Gray, the former Mississippi bishop of the Episcopal Church who, with Campbell, became embattled with conservative whites during the civil rights movement of the sixties at Ole Miss. Critics have noted that Campbell's writing can be searingly perceptive one minute and downright hilarious the next, but that it is always honest and grounded in the homespun wisdom he acquired while growing up in Amite County.

Despite bafflement over the views of their unorthodox native son, the community warmly received Campbell when he returned home as keynote speaker at a banquet given by the Pike County Arts Council in 1984. At the end of his talk he delivered to his audience the five words he had promised them at the beginning. "I love you very much," he said.

Campbell and his wife, Brenda, have three children and four grandchildren. They reside on a farm near Mt. Juliet, Tennessee. Friend to Waylon Jennings, Willie Nelson, Johnny Cash, and Tom T. Hall, Campbell spends time between writing books plucking his guitar.

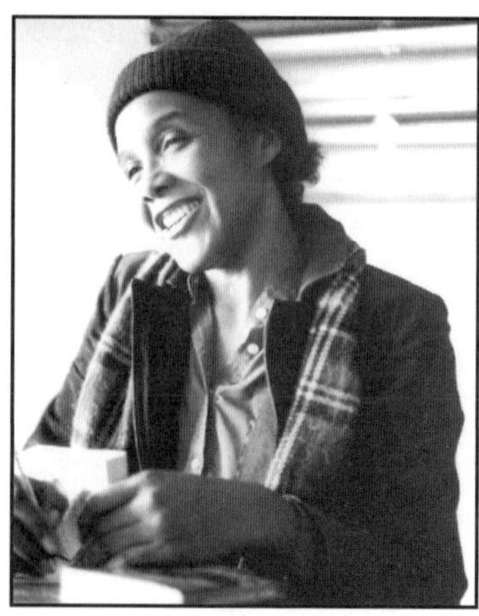
Anne Moody

Take Highway 48 west to Centreville. At Centreville, rejoin Highway 24 west. As you travel south, Mount Pleasant Baptist Church and cemetery are on your right.

Centreville

Mount Pleasant Baptist Church

Highway 24 West

This contemporary church set on a hill overlooks its century-old cemetery. The original church was founded for "people of color" in the early 1880s.

The daughter of black sharecroppers, Anne Moody (1940) was born in Centreville and lived intermittently in a section called Ash Quarters. She also lived for a time on the Clark property on Coon's Mill Road and Jackson Louisiana Road in Woodville. She attended Mount Pleasant School, which she describes in her autobiography *Coming of Age in Mississippi* (1968) as "a little raggly school building ready to collapse."

Despite poverty, by working part-time she was able to attend Natchez Junior College and Tougaloo College in Jackson. At Tougaloo, she became involved in the voter registration drives of the sixties. She gained national attention when she and others staged a sit-in at Woolworth's lunch counter in Jackson. She continued her involvement in civil rights as a fund raiser and public speaker for the Council on Racial Equality (CORE) and as a civil rights project coordinator at Yale.

In her autobiography, Moody gives a firsthand account of growing up in a segregated community and vividly describes the terrifying sit-in at Woolworth's where an angry white mob harassed, kicked, and beat the demonstrators while nearly ninety policemen watched through the windows and did nothing. "Before the sit-in," Moody wrote in her autobiography, "I had always hated the whites in Mississippi. Now I knew it was impossible for me to hate sickness."

Now in its eighteenth edition, *Coming of Age in Mississippi* is regarded as a significant documentation of civil rights struggles and is used as a text in high schools around the country. It has won many awards, including the Gold Medal Award from the National Council of Catholics and Jews. Moody has also written *Mr. Death* (1975), a collection of stories for children.

The I-55 tour ends here.

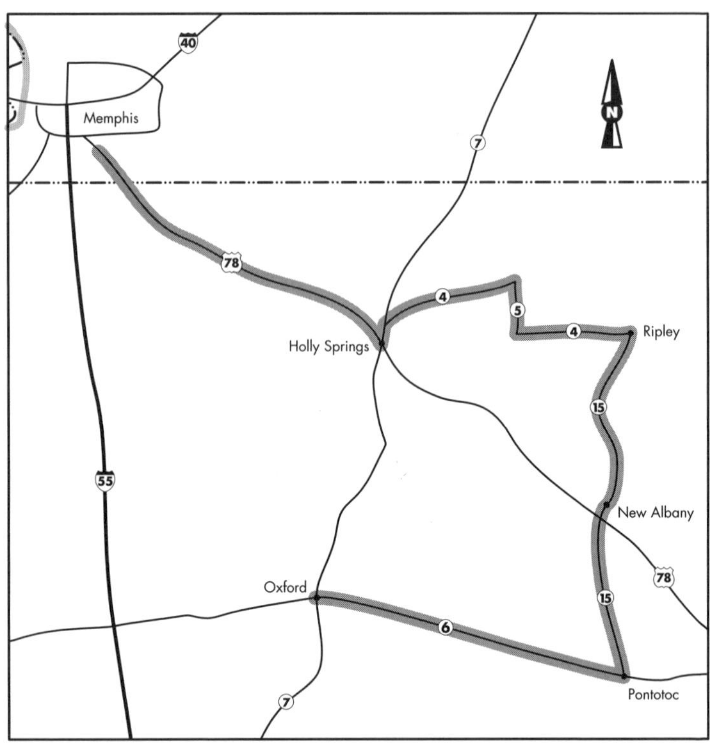

40
Memphis
7
N
78
4
5
4
Ripley
Holly Springs
15
55
New Albany
78
Oxford
15
6
Pontotoc
7

Yoknapatawpha Tour

Leaving Memphis, the tour follows Highway 78 south through the highlands of Mississippi to Holly Springs, then makes a loop through the area that William Faulkner made famous: Ripley, New Albany, Pontotoc, and Oxford.

This was once Chickasaw Indian land, but the Treaty of Pontotoc Creek in 1832 opened the area to white settlement and forced the Chickasaws on the Trail of Tears to Oklahoma. A mixture of rolling hills, rich river bottoms, and red-clay gullies, the region was settled quickly by immigrants from Tennessee, Alabama, Georgia, and the Carolinas.

Faulkner country includes the land that Nobelist William Faulkner (1897–1962) called his "little postage stamp of native soil" and which he explored fictionally in over two dozen novels, as well as the land associated with his brother John Faulkner and his great-grandfather, Colonel William C. Falkner, both well-known novelists. But these three men are by no means the only writers who ever lived and worked in Faulkner country. This tour will introduce you to poets, nineteenth- and twentieth-century authors whose books were national best sellers, other fiction writers, and memoirists with unforgettable tales.

Byhalia

William Faulkner died here in Wright's Sanitarium, a small private hospital. For over thirty years it was Faulkner's refuge where he went to dry out after drinking bouts. On July 6, 1962, he died of a thrombosis.

Holly Springs

Beautiful Holly Springs was once the most literary town in north Mississippi. After it was made the county seat of Marshall County in 1836, the town prospered. Rich cotton lands and a rail line linking it to New Orleans afforded Holly Springs the good life. Like the older Natchez to the south, Holly Springs had wealthy citizens, cotillions, music, drama, educational institutions, handsome houses, fine hotels, and a racetrack; it was also a summer resort known for its curative springs. A number of writers lived there in the nineteenth and twentieth centuries, including poets Robert Josselyn, Judge Lemuel Smith, and Charlemae Hill Rollins, novelists Sherwood Bonner and Joseph Holt Ingraham, and memoirists Anne Walter, Minnie Walter, and Sarah Jane Cohen.

Today two writers call Holly Springs home. Margaree King Mitchell, novelist and playwright, was born here. Poet Karen Mitchell was born in Columbus and grew up in Holly Springs. Her book of poetry, *Eating Hill*, was published in 1989.

William Faulkner was frequently in and out of Holly Springs to catch trains for various trips. It was at the Holly Springs depot that his proud family met him in 1918 as he stepped off the train from Toronto in his Royal Air Force uniform, complete with a Sam Browne belt, overseas cap, swagger stick, and trench coat. Faulkner's stepdaughter, Cho-Cho, attended the Mississippi Synodical College in Holly Springs. Later in life Faulkner chose the courthouse square as a place to rendezvous with writer Joan Williams. (See Arkabutla for more about Joan Williams.)

Each spring the Holly Springs Pilgrimage opens the doors of a number of antebellum houses for public visitation. Two of these houses were the childhood homes of literary figures.

Cedarhurst

708 Salem Avenue

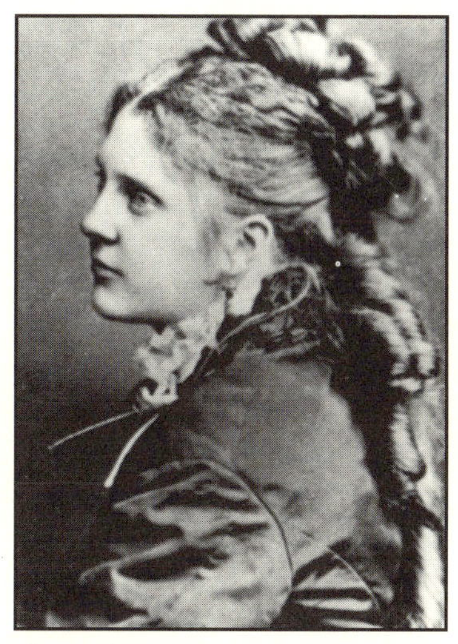
Sherwood Bonner

Holly Springs is much as Catherine Sherwood Bonner (1849–1883) would remember it. Many of the buildings that she knew still stand on the tree-lined streets. She was eight years old in 1857 when her father, Charles Bonner, a respected physician, built their home. Cedarhurst, one of Holly Springs's most identifiable landmarks, is a fanciful statement of the craze of mid-nineteenth-century America for romantic architecture.

The Bonners provided Sherwood all the ingredients of a beautiful childhood: material comfort, education, good books and conversation, laughter, and family concern. She could not foresee a Civil War that would turn her family out of their home, the turmoil and hardship of the war's aftermath, the 1878 yellow fever epidemic that would decimate her hometown and include her father and brother among the victims, and her own early death at the age of thirty-four.

Although the war deeply marred Bonner's adolescence, it was during that time that she became a published writer at the improbable age of thirteen. During the next several years, she endured the travail of Reconstruction conditions in Holly Springs, and at age twenty-one hastily married. Within two years she had had a child and made the decision to divorce her husband. She left her daughter with her sister and moved to Boston to pursue a writing career. She was introduced to the literary world there through the editor who had published the story she had written as a teenager. She became a close friend of William Dean Howells and Henry W. Longfellow and worked as Longfellow's assistant. There has been speculation that Bonner and Longfellow were lovers, but all that is really known is that he was helpful in her literary career, introducing her to editors and publishers and making suggestions concerning her fiction. When Harper Brothers Publishers accepted her novel, *Like unto Like*, set during the Civil War, she wrote to Longfellow, "How shall I thank you to whom I owe all."

Bonner's joy over the publication of her book must have turned to deep sorrow in 1878 when the yellow fever plague hit Holly Springs and she made the sad journey home to bury her father and brother. After she returned to Boston, her career blossomed. Her novel was out, and her stories began to appear regularly in *Harper's Monthly* and *Lippincott's*.

Three years later, in the spring of 1881, she discovered that she had life-threatening breast cancer. She worked tirelessly to prepare her stories for publication in book form. Drawing on her childhood in Holly Springs and on stories told her by the slave woman whom she loved and called "Gran'mammy," she produced two books which show her sense of the comic and her excellent portrayal of character. *Dialect Tales* was published in 1883, and *Sewanee River Tales* appeared in 1884, six months after her death.

Bonner had a fine ear for black dialect and a rich knowledge of black culture. Along with William Dean Howells, Stephen Crane, and Frank Norris, she helped to move American literature from nineteenth-century romance toward twentieth-century realism and naturalism.

Bonner returned to Holly Springs in the later days of her illness to be with her young daughter, then thirteen. She died here in the summer of 1883.

The Walter Place

339 W. Chulahoma Avenue

Nestled in a spacious lawn with dense magnolias, oaks, and evergreens around it, this house, with its handsome but curious architecture, suggests a compromise made by Mr. and Mrs. Harvey Washington Walter. They built a Greek Revival home flanked by two Gothic towers, incorporating both the classical and romantic architectures of the prewar era. The mood of the house turned dark, however, with the events of the times. Less than a decade after its construction, General Ulysses S. Grant selected it as his home where Mrs. Grant would join him after the capture of Holly Springs. The Walters reclaimed it after the Civil War, and in this spacious house brought up a large family. Like the Bonners, the Walter family suffered great devastation in the yellow fever epidemic of 1878. This house was turned into a hospital, the women and children of the house were sent out of town for safety, and Mr. Walter and three of his sons stayed to tend the sick. All four died.

Two of the Walter daughters became published writers. Minnie (1865–1939) married Henry C. Myers from Byhalia, a planter and later Mississippi's secretary of state. Using what she had learned during their summers in Biloxi and frequent visits to New Orleans, she wrote one of the early tourist guides to Mississippi, *Romance and Realism of the Southern Gulf Coast*, which was published in 1898. The couple moved to Memphis, where Minnie Myers edited the woman's page of the *Memphis Appeal* for years.

Her younger sister Anne became a doctor. Feeling that "the life of a social butterfly is only half a life," Anne earned her degree from the Women's Medical College of Pennsylvania, but her attempt to practice back in her hometown was thwarted. She wrote that she was forced to sit idly by while doctors far less skilled practiced bad obstetrics. She accepted a job to open a woman's hospital in Soochow, China. Her intention was to stay a year or so, but she remained in China for forty years, fighting superstition, disease, and fear. In her ten years at the Soochow hospital she added a children's ward and established the first coed medical school in China. In Soochow she met and married Dr. John Burrus Fearn, another Mississippian, in 1896. They moved to Shanghai in 1905 where she eventually opened her own hospital and practiced medicine for thirty-three years, witnessing the revolution of 1911, rebellions in 1913, and the White Russian invasion after World War I. She had a wide range of friends in China, including social leaders and diplomats as well as prostitutes and coolies. Her memoir, *My Days of Strength*, under the name Anne Walter Fearn, was published in 1939.

COTTAGE

Corner of East Salem and North Walthall Streets

The small cottage behind this house was the home of Sarah Jane Picken Cohen (1786–1862), a woman whose life was fraught with religious and social turmoil. She married Rabbi Alexander Cohen in Philadelphia when she was twenty, and had four daughters and two sons. The marriage foundered after twenty-five years when her gradual return to Christianity reached passionate proportions. She reverted to the Episcopal Church of her childhood after her separation from the rabbi. From 1841 until her death twenty-one years later, she lived around the country with first one daughter, then another, including daughter Henrietta Long in Holly Springs, who was married to a local druggist. While living here, Cohen published the autobiographical *Henry Luria: The Little Jewish Convert* (1860), a compilation of prose and poetry. Subtitled *Memoir of Mrs. S. J. Cohen*, the book was a wrenching account of one son's conversion to Christianity and his early death. It was dedicated "with the most enthusiastic feeling of admiration" to Joseph Holt Ingraham, rector of Christ Episcopal Church in Holly Springs and a writer himself. He was her writing mentor and religious counselor. Cohen died in this small cottage in 1862. The inscription on her monument in Hillcrest Cemetery is a passage from one of her poems.

Christ Episcopal Church

Randolph and Van Dorn Streets

Joseph Holt Ingraham (1809–1860) was a famous writer when he came to Holly Springs as rector of Christ Episcopal Church in 1858. (See Aberdeen and Natchez regarding his early career.) A Renaissance man, he wrote more than a hundred novels in his lifetime, was an advocate of free public schools, conducted a prison ministry in Tennessee, designed and built churches for Aberdeen and Okolona, and served as an Episcopal priest in several parishes in Mississippi, Alabama, and Tennessee.

After his ordination, he turned to writing religious novels. His story of the life of Christ, *The Prince of the House of David*, outsold Longfellow's *Hiawatha* and Whitman's *Leaves of Grass*, all three published in 1855.

While living in Holly Springs, he published the second and third books of his religious trilogy—*The Pillar of Fire* and *The Throne of David*. His last book, written in Holly Springs, was *The*

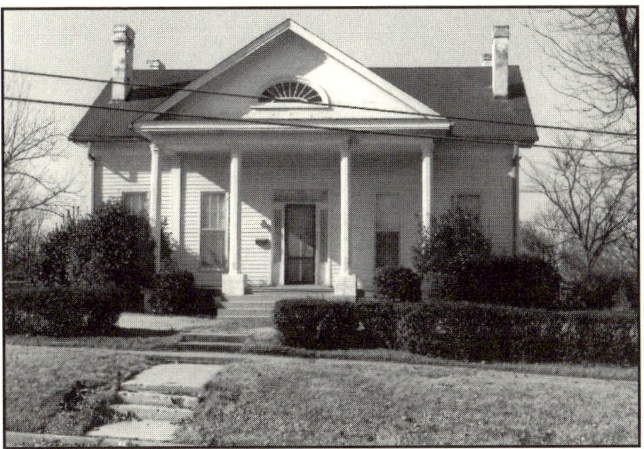

Ida B. Wells Art Gallery

Sunny South, or The Southerner at Home, an apologia and explanation of the South, published as the nation hurtled toward civil war. In December of 1860, three months after the book was published, Ingraham shot himself in this church. By some accounts it was accidental. His wife and teenage son survived him. The son, Prentiss, also became a famous and amazingly prolific novelist. (See Washington for his biography.)

Ida B. Wells–Barnett Family Art Gallery

220 N. Randolph Street

Originally called the Spires Bolling House, this antebellum house was built through the labor and talent of slaves, including James Wells, a skilled craftsman. His daughter, Ida B. Wells, one of the most important civil rights advocates of the nineteenth century, was born on the grounds just before the Emancipation Proclamation was signed. Her mother, Elizabeth, was a cook in this house. James Wells's owner in Tippah County, who was also his father, had apprenticed eighteen-year-old James to learn the building trades from Spires Bolling, a building contractor in Holly Springs. After Confederate Mississippi surrendered in 1865, James Wells was free to accept Bolling's offer to continue working for him as a skilled building craftsman assisting in much of Holly Springs's postwar construction. James and Elizabeth Wells

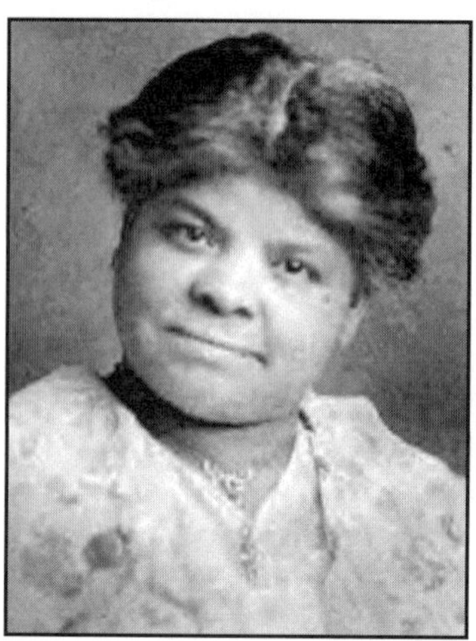
Ida B. Wells Barnett

eventually had four boys and four girls. (See below for Ida Wells's biography.)

Rust College

Randolph Street

Rust College was established in 1866 by the Methodist Church as Shaw University "for the education of Negroes." James Wells served on the board of trustees of the newly organized school. Ida Wells later wrote, "Our job was to go to school and learn all we could."

When Ida Wells was sixteen both of her parents and her infant brother died in the yellow fever epidemic of 1878, which killed over three hundred people in Holly Springs. Wells took on the task of rearing her five remaining brothers and sisters. With her family's savings, she attended Rust College. Although she was expelled two years later for insubordination, she continued to teach in local schools for three years. When her brothers were settled into apprenticeships, she took her sisters and moved to Memphis to live with her aunt. An important incident in her life when she was twenty-two presaged the different path her life would take.

While waiting to take the examination for teaching in the public schools of Memphis, she accepted a job in Woodstock, a rural community outside Memphis. Traveling from Memphis to Woodstock, she bought a ticket for the first-class ladies' car. Some eighty years before Rosa Parks refused to leave her seat on a Montgomery bus, Wells would not move out of a train seat for which she had paid. When she refused to obey the conductor's order to move to the smoker car, she was forcibly removed from the train. Backed by the Civil Rights Act of 1875, she filed and won a lawsuit against the Chesapeake and Ohio Railroad in 1887 and was awarded five hundred dollars in damages. The Tennessee Supreme Court shortly reversed the victory. Frustrated, she began writing political columns in church newspapers. Having secured a job in the Memphis public schools, she saved her money and became part owner of a small newspaper called *Free Speech and Headlight* in Memphis. In 1891 she was dismissed from the Memphis school system because of a strong article she had written about the board of education's unequal funding of the black schools. For the rest of her life she was an outspoken and courageous voice for civil rights, taking on the subjects of educational inequities, economic boycotts, lynchings, women's rights, and segregation, and helping found the NAACP. When her Memphis office was trashed because of her investigative work and hard-hitting reporting, she moved to New York and then to Chicago, where she married Ferdinand Lee Barnett in 1895 and continued her work. The couple had three children. Wells died in 1931. Though her published works during her lifetime were political in nature, she also wrote an autobiography, published nearly forty years after her death. *Crusade for Justice: The Autobiography of Ida B. Wells* (1970) was edited by her daughter, Alfreda M. Duster. The Ida B. Wells Commemorative Stamp was issued by the U.S. Post Office in 1990. She has been the subject of an award-winning documentary and of a biography, *To Keep the Waters Troubled* (1999).

Hillcrest Cemetery

South Center Drive

Old cedar trees and wrought-iron gates offer a peaceful entrance into the cemetery. All of the nineteenth-century writers of Holly Springs are buried here except the Walter sisters.

Joseph Holt Ingraham's grave is the most distinctive, with its tall monument topped by a cross and shaded by a giant yew tree. His friend Sarah Cohen is buried just south of Ingraham's grave, with her own poetry providing her epitaph. Sherwood Bonner, in accordance with her request, lies in an unmarked grave in the Bonner family plot.

In nearby Red Banks is the boyhood home of poet Neely Grant II, who lived in the house called Summer Trees for much of his childhood, from 1935 to 1945. After World War II his family moved abroad.

Grant now lives in Vienna with his wife, Eleonore Haupt-Stummer, an Austro-Hungarian baroness. He returns often to Mississippi, for many years visiting his grandparents in Tunica. His collection of poetry *Mississippi from a Picture Window* (1956) reveals deep family ties to the state. *Mississippi Knight* was published in 1994.

Leave Holly Springs on Highway 4. At Ashland, turn south on Highway 5, a scenic drive through hills covered with pine and hardwood trees. Go nine miles and turn off to Whippoorwill Valley, home of the literary Autry family.

Ewart Autry pastored the Pine Grove Baptist Church for more than thirty years. A sportsman and naturalist, Autry published numerous stories and sketches about Benton County, and his novel, *Ghost Hound of Thunder Valley*, won the Dodd, Mead Teacher and Librarian Award in 1964. Ewart's son James Autry is a respected poet now living in Des Moines and serving as president of the magazine group the Meredith Corporation. His published poems include *Life After Mississippi* (1989) and two other collections.

Retrace Highway 5 two miles and go east on Highway 4 to Ripley, fourteen miles. Follow Highway 4 to the town's courthouse square.

Ripley

Ripley is the birthplace of writer John Faulkner, the childhood home of Nobel Prize winner William Faulkner, and the place where their great-grandfather, novelist William C. Falkner, met a violent death. Ripley was incorporated in 1837, created out of the Indian lands. Colonel W. C. Falkner put it on the map in 1872 when he built the Ripley Railroad line, which ran from Ripley to Middleton, Tennessee, where it intersected with the Memphis-Charleston line. Ripley is still very much a railroad town. Modern-day tracks, which follow Colonel Falkner's original ones, run through a residential section, and the sound of train whistles and clacking wheels are reminders of the colonel's legacy.

Renfrow's Café

Main Street and West Spring Street
Courthouse Square

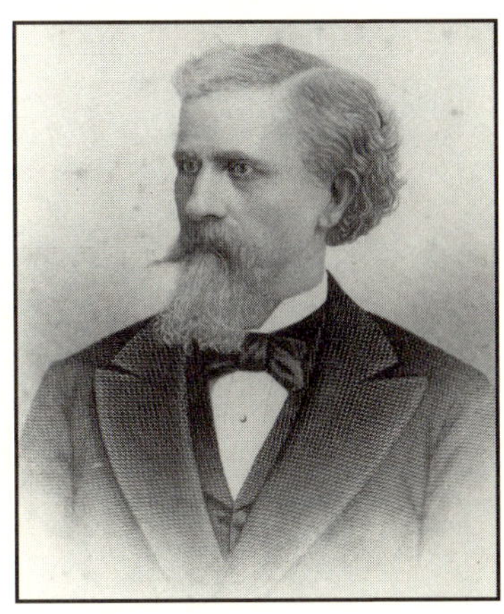
Colonel W. C. Falkner

After the Civil War, Colonel Falkner established the Ripley Railroad Company in partnership with R. J. Thurmond and subsequently bought out Thurmond's share. In 1889 Falkner was elected to the state legislature. On election night Falkner was gunned down on the courthouse square by Thurmond, his former partner. Falkner died the next day, and funeral services were held in the Ripley Presbyterian Church. Wealthy and prominent, Thurmond was acquitted for the crime committed in front of his Main Street office, which was on the site of Renfrow's Café.

Dixie-Net Building

301 North Main Street

This is the site of Colonel W. C. Falkner's home, called "the house of many gables." Facing Main Street, the house was centered on the entire block bordered by Cooper, Mulberry, and Union. Falkner bought the house from R. J. Thurmond shortly after the Civil War when it was a simple, one-story building. Late in 1884, Colonel Falkner had the house renovated and modeled on houses he had seen in Europe on a tour in 1883. The railroad ran behind the colonel's house along Union Street and is still operating there.

The house once dominated downtown Ripley but was gradually consigned to the wrecking crew. A portion of the lot was sold for the site of a new post office, no longer functioning but maintained by Dixie-Net as a historical structure. In 1937 the colonel's house was razed so that an apartment house (now owned by Dixie-Net) could be built next door. Many of the original architectural elements from the Falkner house are in

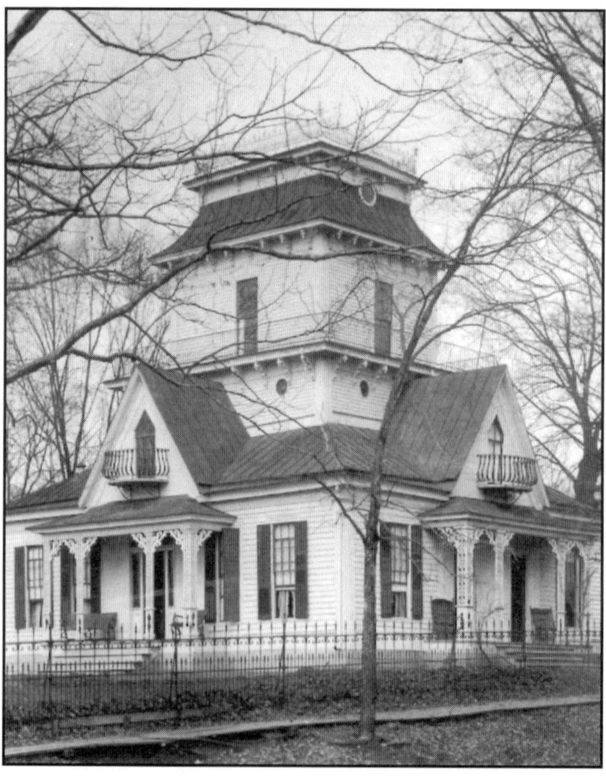

W. C. Falkner's house, Ripley

the building, including the stairway, wrought-iron balcony, and windows.

Dr. John Young Murry House

205 North Jackson Street

This was the home of William Faulkner's other great-grandfather, a physician who practiced medicine in Ripley for over sixty years. Dr. John Young Murry built the house in 1860. He served a term in the Mississippi legislature and was a state leader in the Masonic Order. His daughter Sallie married J. W. T. Falkner of Ripley, son of Colonel William C. Falkner. The J. W. T. Falkners and their three children moved to Oxford in 1885, and J. W. T. Falkner opened a law office there. Dr. Murry died in 1915.

Site of Murry Falkner Home

Jackson Street at Cooper

In a house on this corner, John Falkner was born in 1901 to Murry and Maud Falkner. With their infant son William, they had moved to Ripley from New Albany in 1898, nine years after the death of Colonel Falkner. At Colonel Falkner's death, his son J. W. T. Falkner inherited the railroad and named his son Murry treasurer of the company. Murry and Maud moved into a house on this site, a block from Murry's other grandfather, Dr. Murry. Their second and third sons were born here, Jack in 1899 and John in 1901. The family returned to Oxford in 1902 when J. W. T. Falkner sold the railroad. Murry and Maud's fourth son, Dean, was born in Oxford.

Ripley Public Library

398 N. Commerce Street

First editions of William C. Falkner's books, along with photographs and scrapbooks about the family, are housed here. Falkner has been called a novelist of impressive talent who avoided the nostalgia prevalent among the romantic writers of the New South. He wrote poetry and a travel book, as well as fiction. His most famous novel was *The White Rose of Memphis* (1881), which shocked his generation as much as his great-grandson's *Sanctuary* shocked a later generation.

Tippah County Historical Museum

106 Siddall Street

The most unusual Falkner item here is a stained-glass window rediscovered in a barn in the 1980s. Colonel Falkner's daughter Willie had donated the window to the First Baptist Church, which declined to use it, the story goes, because the colonel was not a Baptist. Whatever the story, Willie Falkner took it back from the church and installed it in her house, which was razed in the 1960s.

As you leave Ripley on Highway 15 south, follow the signs to the Ripley Cemetery.

Ripley Cemetery

Highway 15 South

The full-size marble statue of Colonel William C. Falkner (1826–1889) dominates the cemetery. The statue was imagined by Colonel Falkner himself and modeled by Chancey Rogers in Tennessee to convey Falkner's stature in the community. It was placed here in 1892.

In 1842, soon after north Mississippi was opened for settlement, William C. Falkner, a teenager, walked from his home in east Tennessee to north Mississippi to seek his fortune. He was a resident of Ripley by 1845, and it was here that his career began. He was prototypically the ambitious, self-made businessman in a frontier still marked by violence. He himself killed two men in self-defense, and he served in the Mexican War and the Civil War, where he earned the rank of colonel. He prospered as a planter, lawyer, railroad builder, and politician, while steadily writing books for over forty years. It is said that he financed his railroad, in part, from the sales of his novel *The White Rose of Memphis.* His great-grandson William Faulkner patterned the character of Colonel Sartoris in *The Unvanquished* and *Sartoris* after this colonel.

Buried in the family plot are the colonel's son, William Henry Falkner, shot by a jealous husband when he was a young man, and two of the colonel's infant children, Vance and Lizzie.

Continue on Highway 15 south to New Albany, twenty-one miles. This stretch of highway offers a microcosm of the area's economic history as it parallels the railroad founded by Colonel Falkner, and passes through cotton fields and factories. Near Cotton Plant, 7.5 miles north of New Albany, the highway and railroad pass the house once called Tippah Lodge, built by the flamboyant and wealthy Paul Rainey and alluded to in Faulkner's *The Reivers.* Take Highway 15 to Bankhead Street and turn right.

New Albany

Although New Albany's greatest claim to literary fame is as the birthplace of William Faulkner, the town is brought to life in the fiction of Borden Deal (1922–1985). The main business street,

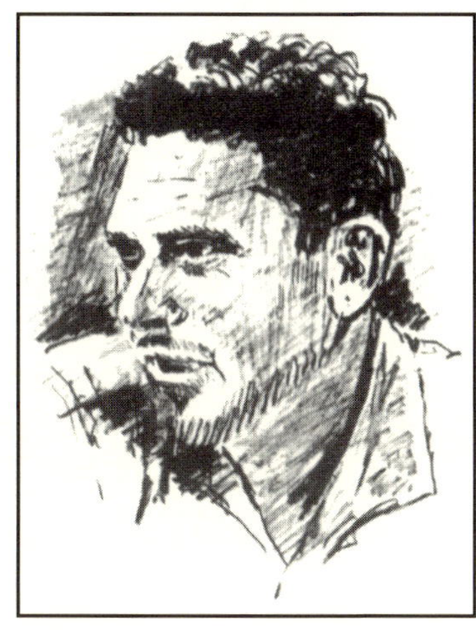
Borden Deal

Bankhead Street, with its handsome Union County Courthouse, is much as Deal saw it when he was a child. The settings of his autobiographical novels, *The Least One* and *The Other Room*, include the communities of Enterprise and Macedonia, where he grew up, but it was New Albany that excited his imagination. A Saturday treat was to come into town from his rural home. He loved movies at the Ritz Theatre, and he once walked twenty-eight miles roundtrip from Macedonia to see *Huckleberry Finn*. His favorite haunts were the county library, the Jockey Yard, and the offices of the *New Albany Gazette*. The Tallahatchie River bridge, which he crossed to get into town, is still here. It evoked for him his best memory of going to town on Saturday morning "with all the riches of New Albany just ahead," and walking home at sundown, "tired but with the richness of experience he had enjoyed."

Born in Pontotoc County and named Loyce Youth Deal, he grew up in the Union County communities of Ingomar, Enterprise, and Macedonia, and graduated from Macedonia Consolidated High School near Myrtle. After a series of colorful jobs ranging from fighting forest fires to working in a circus and on a showboat, he went to the University of Alabama to study creative writing with Hudson Strode. He began writing while holding a series of office jobs. His first publication, the short story "Exodus," was published in *Best American Short Stories of 1949*, and by 1955 he had become a full-time writer.

Aside from the numerous suspense thrillers and novels of erotica which he published under pseudonyms and in paperback, he became an important voice of the New South and achieved a level of success most writers dream about: stories published in prestigious collections, Hollywood adaptations of his novels, television dramas, translations into many languages, and a body of work considered by critics to be an important depiction of twentieth-century life in the American South.

In 1948 he legally changed his name to Borden, his father's name. Most of his work is under that name, although he also wrote under the pen names Lee Borden, Leigh Borden, and John Chickasaw, and, for the erotic novels written in the 1970s, he used Anonymous. He published over a hundred short stories and more than twenty novels. He was the recipient of Guggenheim and MacDowell Colony fellowships and awards by the American Library Association and the Alabama Library Association. Borden Deal died in Sarasota, Florida, where he lived the last five years of his life.

Ripley Railroad Tracks

The rest of Ripley is a Falkner story. The city was mostly torched during the Civil War, but by the late 1880s the railroad had come to town. In 1886, the Frisco Railroad beat Colonel Falkner's to town by nine months. Both tracks dominate the town and are still in operation as the Burlington Northern Santa Fe and Railnet. The tracks brought prosperity to New Albany, primarily through the furniture industry in the twentieth century.

Colonel William C. Falkner's Ripley Railroad was incorporated in 1871, building north from Ripley to Tennessee. The original path of the tracks built and operated by Colonel Falkner crosses the town east-west and goes over the Tallahatchie River, a major obstacle when the tracks were laid in 1887. By then the railroad extended south from Ripley to Pontotoc, passing through New Albany. It became the Gulf and Ship Island Railroad and was inherited by the colonel's son, John Wesley Thompson Falkner, who sold it in 1902. It later became the GM&O Railroad and is now called Railnet.

Union County Heritage Museum

112 Cleveland Street

The museum has a collection of Borden Deal and William Faulkner material, including a scale model of Faulkner's birthplace, first editions, family photographs, a portion of the colonel's fence from Ripley, and Ripley Railroad artifacts.

William Faulkner's Birthplace

204 Cleveland Street

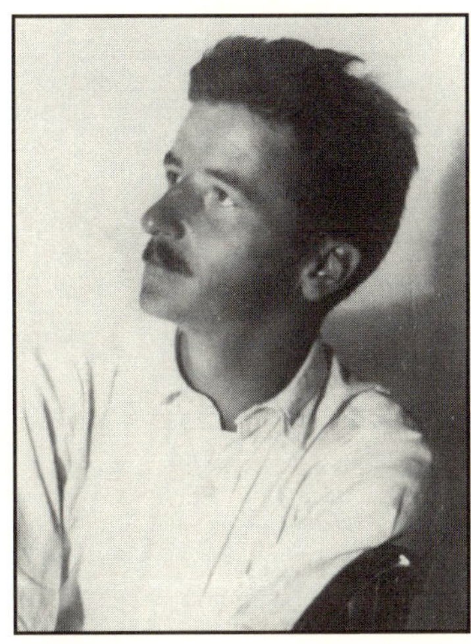

William Faulkner

A historical marker proclaims the site of a house now gone. On September 25, 1897, the first son of Maud Butler Falkner and Murry Cuthbert Falkner was born here. They named him William. The Falkners had been sent to New Albany in 1896 by Colonel William C. Falkner, Murry's father, who made Murry general passenger agent for the Ripley Railroad. The family lived in New Albany until William was eighteen months old and Murry moved to Ripley to accept a promotion with the railroad. The house was demolished in 1950.

Continue on Highway 15 south to Pontotoc, fifteen miles.

Pontotoc

Pontotoc was hacked out of the Chickasaw wilderness after the treaty of 1832 in order to establish a land office. It has many associations, mostly sad, with the Falkner family. William C. Falkner lived here briefly when he first arrived in Mississippi. Pontotoc later became the terminus of the railroad that he built to join the Gulf and Ship Island Railroad. Years later his grandson Murry was sent here to work for the railroad. When Murry got enmeshed in a quarrel between two women, he was shot twice by the brother of one of the women. Murry survived and was quickly transferred by his father back to Oxford. A generation later, the body of Murry's youngest son, Dean, victim of a small plane crash near Pontotoc, was laid out in the funeral parlor here.

A happier claim to literary fame for Pontotoc is the connection with poet James Gordon (see Lochinvar, below) and novelist Borden Deal, who was born in Pontotoc County, but grew up near New Albany (see New Albany).

Three miles south of Pontotoc a historical marker notes the existence of Lochinvar, a grand antebellum home off the highway up a sweeping gravel road.

Lochinvar

This estate was the birthplace and home of poet James Gordon. His father, who had acquired great wealth in land speculation after the removal of the Indians, built the house in 1840. Before the Civil War, Gordon wrote sporting sketches, some of which appeared in English journals, but he preferred writing poetry, and his collection *The Old Plantation and Other Poems* was published in 1909.

During the Civil War he raised and furnished his own company for action in the Battle of Corinth. In 1878 he was elected to the state legislature and was appointed United States senator in 1909 at the death of Senator McLaurin. He lost Lochinvar through financial setbacks in 1891 and moved to Okolona, where he died in 1912.

Turn west on Highway 6 toward Oxford. Ten miles down the road is Thaxton, where Dean Falkner's barnstorming plane crashed in a pasture. Five miles farther is Lafayette Springs, once a popular summer resort with a hotel and cottages. People of the surrounding area—including the Falkners—enjoyed its shady grounds, picturesque paths, and seven springs abounding in health-giving properties. Continue to downtown Oxford.

Oxford

The seat of Lafayette County, Oxford was the model for William Faulkner's fictional town of Jefferson, the county seat of the fictional Yoknapatawpha County. Perhaps because it is the town where Nobel laureate Faulkner lived and wrote, it has attracted a number of acclaimed writers, including John Grisham, Barry Hannah, Larry Brown, Willie Morris, Will Campbell, Stark Young, and John Faulkner. It has been the hometown of writers Jane Mullen, Cynthia Shearer, Jere Hoar, David Galef, John Crews, and Wylene Dunbar and of poet-artist Glennray Tutor. It is a graceful town, situated on a fertile plateau, forming a triangle with Ripley and New Albany of Faulknerian lore. It was named Oxford at its founding in the visionary hope that it would be the site of a fine university. The University of Mississippi was established here in 1844 after the town fought a hard battle to be chosen as the site. Today Oxford's shaded streets, bustling town square, and cultural opportunities have attracted a sizeable retirement community to commingle with the townspeople and university students. The Woman's Book Club, founded in 1895 and one of the oldest literary clubs in the state, is still active.

The Courthouse Square

The town square, the courthouse, the statue of the Confederate soldier, the old men who lounge on the courthouse benches, the hubbub on the streets, and the balconied storefronts are mostly as they were when Faulkner lived and wrote here. The Lafayette County courthouse was central to Faulkner's life and writings. It was built in 1840, destroyed by Union troops in 1864, rebuilt in 1872, enlarged in 1952, and renovated in 1981. As a child Billy Falkner played in and around the square, and, after dropping out of high school, hung around the square listening to the Civil War stories of the old men sitting in the shade of the courthouse. When his much-loved grandfather, J. W. T. Falkner, became old, Faulkner sometimes joined him as he spent most of his days sitting in the square, too deaf to have a conversation. William's grandmother, who ran the local United Daughters of the Confederacy, persuaded her husband to contribute the money for the Confederate statue, dedicated in 1907.

Faulkner helped prevent the demolition of the courthouse in 1947. Perhaps in gratitude, the city named an alley that runs off

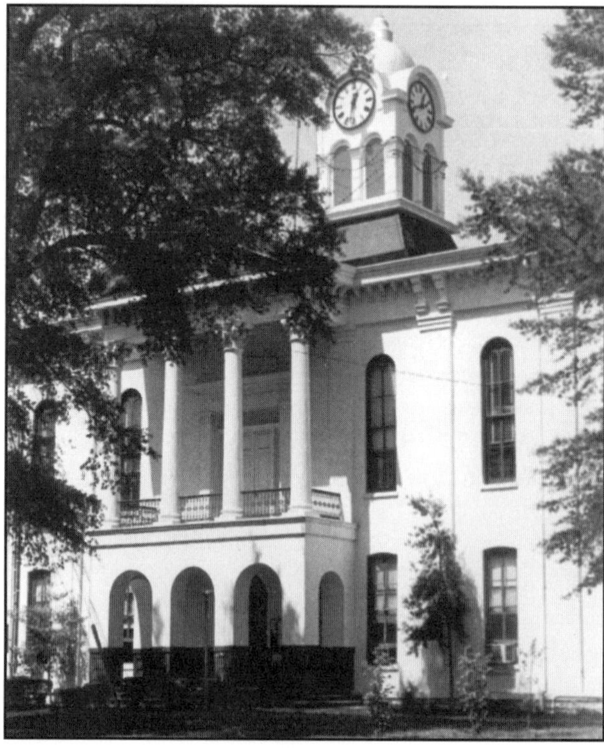

Lafayette County courthouse, Oxford

the square in his honor. But it is a dubious honor. According to Willie Morris, the alley is primarily the purview of winos. Seven feet wide, it runs between Shine Morgan's furniture store and the Gathright-Reed drugstore. The bronze statue of Faulkner on a courthouse bench in front of city hall is by sculptor William Beckwith, who completed it in 1997. It was commissioned by a group of Oxford citizens.

The square is one of the most ubiquitous landmarks in Mississippi fiction, appearing in the works of William Faulkner, Larry Brown, John Grisham, Barry Hannah, Willie Morris, and others.

Around the Square

The entire town square is designated as a National Historic Landmark. Faulkner was in and out of his father's businesses on the square, a livery stable and a hardware store, both gone. Beginning on the west side of the square and moving clockwise, one can find a number of literary sites.

• Jennie's Hallmark Shop

114 Courthouse Square

When *Intruder in the Dust* was filmed in 1949, the first office on the second floor of this building was used as the setting for Gavin Stevens's law office. It was also the real first office of Yoknapatawpha Press, established in 1975 by Howard Duvall, who sold the business to Lawrence and Dean Faulkner Wells in 1979.

• Duvall's

103 Courthouse Square

This is the site of the First National Bank Building, founded in 1910 by J. W. T. Falkner, who defied his father, Colonel W. C. Falkner, and moved to Oxford from Ripley in 1885. He became a successful lawyer and president of the First National Bank. He also grew close to his grandson, William Faulkner, who was briefly his bookkeeper. Faulkner used the bank as a model for the Sartoris Bank in *The Unvanquished* and *Sartoris.*

• Oxford Tourism Council

115 Courthouse Square

An exhibit on the life of William Faulkner featuring the photographs of Jack Cofield is on display here. Visitors can obtain pamphlets on Rowan Oak and a guide to the city.

• Square Books

160 Courthouse Square

One of the best bookstores in America occupies the site of Blaylock's Drug Store, a Victorian Italianate structure built around 1880. Owned by Richard and Lisa Howorth, Square Books was established in 1979 and moved to this building in 1986. With its emphasis on southern literature, Square Books is the literary hub of downtown Oxford. Upstairs in the bookstore is a place where readers and authors can drink coffee and discuss politics, best sellers, and football plays.

• Old Venice Pizza Company

1112 Van Buren Street

This is the site of the old Gathright-Reed Drug Store, a frequent destination for William Faulkner in his walks downtown. Proprietor Mac Reed was Faulkner's good friend whom he counted on to wrap and mail his manuscripts to his editors. Faulkner also borrowed heavily—mostly mysteries—from Mac Reed's paperback lending library.

• Off Square Books

1110 Van Buren Avenue

The literary hot spot in town is the annex to Square Books, five doors west of the bookstore, where owners Richard and Lisa Howorth frequently stage readings and book signings by authors and provide a place where readers and writers can meet. *Thacker Mountain*, a weekly literary radio program, is produced here. Emceed by Jim Dees, it features readings, interviews with writers, and a house band. (Thacker Mountain is a large hill on Old Taylor Road.)

• One Health Center

1006 Van Buren

This is clearly the site of the old Lyric Theatre, which premiered *Intruder in the Dust* in 1949. MGM brought Hollywood stars, beacon lights, and glamour to the square for the filming in Oxford and for the premier.

• Freeland and Freeland

1013 Jackson Avenue

This was the law office of Phil Stone, Faulkner's friend and mentor, who helped Faulkner get *The Marble Faun*, a book of poetry, published in 1924. He and Faulkner walked around the square selling copies of the book.

Phil Stone provided an important impetus to Faulkner in his writing. When they met, Stone was a twenty-one-year-old intellectual, with B.A. degrees from Ole Miss and Yale, where he concentrated in English and Greek literature. He took the teenage Faulkner under his tutorial wing, introducing him to important books, critiquing and editing Faulkner's writing, teaching him poetry. He also took Faulkner hunting and introduced him to the bordellos of Memphis and the French Quarter in New Orleans. Their friendship lasted for over forty years, and Stone's early influence was crucial to Faulkner's literary life.

West of the Square

• The Oxford American office

404 South 11th Street

Marc Smirnoff drifted into town from northern California in 1987 and stayed because of the bookstore. After working for several years at Square Books, in 1992 he founded *The Oxford American*, "The Southern Magazine of Good Writing." The first issue included a piece by John Grisham entitled "The Faulkner Thing." In 1994 Grisham boosted the struggling magazine by becoming co-owner and publisher. He not only supported it financially, but also gave *The Oxford American* first publishing rights to a new novel, *A Painted House*, which came out serially in 2000.

Expanding its original intention to publish southern fiction, the magazine focuses on other important aspects of southern culture and includes on its staff Roy Blount, Jr., John T. Edge, and Maude Schuyler Clay.

• The Belfry

1001 Jackson Avenue

This historic building was purchased by Grisham after his extraordinary literary success and served as his literary office for several years. It is the site of Oxford's first African American Methodist church. Grisham still owns the property.

• Isom Place

1003 Jefferson Avenue

This house is a candidate for the one described in Faulkner's "A Rose for Emily." Built in 1838–1843 and recently restored by architect Tom Howorth, it is now owned by the University of Mississippi and houses the Barksdale Reading Institute.

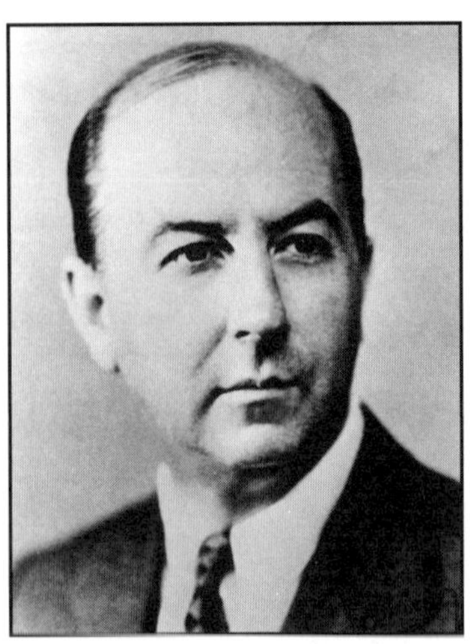
Stark Young

• **St. Peter's Episcopal Church**

113 S. Ninth Street

Faulkner's wife, Estelle, and daughter, Jill, attended St. Peter's, but William came along only on major holidays. Jill was married here, as was John Faulkner's son Jimmy. A stained glass window on the north side was installed in memory of John Faulkner. Funeral services for both William Faulkner and John Faulkner were held here.

• **Meek/Duvall/Doty House**

803 University Avenue

In Faulkner's youth, this was the home of Elma Meek. When Faulkner and Estelle Oldham married, they rented the east side and lived here after their honeymoon to Pascagoula in June 1929. The late Howard Duvall, Jr., founder of Yoknapatawpha Press in 1975, later owned the house.

• **Walton-Young House**

Fifth Street and University Avenue

Stark Young (1881–1963) is the most versatile literary talent ever produced in the state. He was born in Como, moved to Oxford when he was fourteen, graduated from Ole Miss in 1901, and, after getting his M.A. at Columbia University, taught at Ole Miss. In 1921 he moved to New York City and became one of America's greatest drama critics as well as a novelist, short story writer, poet, playwright, translator, essayist, and memoirist. Aside from his literary career, he was a painter and teacher. His best-selling novel, *So Red the Rose*, is about Mississippi during the Civil War.

Stark Young's widowed father, a physician, bought this house in 1895. Young returned here to visit every summer of his adult life, and he always retained a high regard and deep feelings for Oxford and Mississippi. Young died in New York in 1963 and was buried in Friendship Cemetery in Como.

The University of Mississippi bought the Stark Young House in 1974. It is used as a house museum. Young's personal papers are deposited in the J. D. Williams Library on campus.

• Memory House

406 University Avenue

This was the home of John Faulkner (1901–1963) and his wife, Lucille Ramey, called Dolly. John Falkner, William's younger brother, was born in Ripley and moved to Oxford with his family in 1902. He graduated from Ole Miss with a degree in civil engineering. He was an outdoorsman, an accomplished artist, and a writer. He added the "u" to his name when he began to write his satirical and comedic novels. His first published work, *Men Working* (1941), was followed by eight more novels and a memoir, *My Brother Bill: An Affectionate Reminiscence* (1963).

The house was built in 1838 and acquired by John Faulkner in 1944. To the rear is Bailey's Woods, which separates his property from that of his brother William by about two hundred yards. The University of Mississippi acquired Memory House from John Faulkner's sons in 1992 with funds donated by Louis K. Brandt. The house is now used as offices for the University Foundation.

• University of Mississippi

University Avenue

Through the years the university itself has attracted writers to its faculty, including contemporary writers Ellen Douglas, Willie Morris, Evans Harrington, Cynthia Shearer, Jere Hoar, David Galef, Jack Bass, John Crews, and Alice Cabaniss, as well as biographers Allen Cabaniss, John Pilkington, and James Webb. Writers who have attended Ole Miss are too numerous to mention.

After Faulkner dropped out of high school, he began hanging around the Ole Miss campus, attending dances (but not dancing), listening to W. C. Handy's band from Memphis, contributing drawings to the campus yearbook, wearing expensive clothes, and strolling aimlessly around. When he was twenty-two, his father gave him the choice of taking a job or going to Ole Miss. He entered as a non-degree student, rarely attended classes, decided

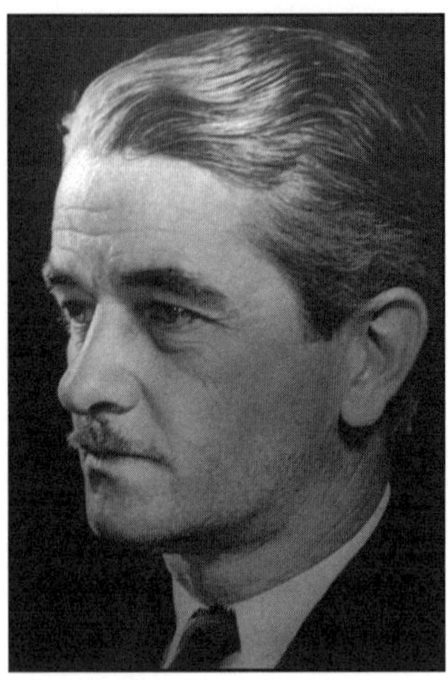
John Faulkner

he was a poet, and earned the nickname Count No 'Count. That first year Faulkner wrote poetry, criticism, and a short story, all of which appeared in the student newspaper. He met Ben Wasson from Greenville, a law student who shared his interest in poetry. In the fall of 1920 they helped form a campus dramatic club, the Marionettes. Faulkner was stage manager and property man, but by November he had dropped out of Ole Miss. He suffered through odd jobs that his father arranged. At the university he met Stark Young, who got him a job in a New York bookstore when he went to Manhattan in 1921 for several months.

Ventress Hall—Faulkner once helped paint Ventress Hall, tying himself to the steeple with ropes as he painted, a feat other painters considered too dangerous. This building closely resembles the house that Murry Falkner and his family lived in on campus, on the site where the Alumni House now stands.

Pharmacy Building—This was the site of the post office where Faulkner worked. In 1921 Faulkner returned from New York and got a job on campus as postmaster. He was a disaster in the position. George Healy, Jr., an Ole Miss student and later publisher of the *Times-Picayune* in New Orleans, recalled playing bridge with Faulkner in 1924 when the postal inspector arrived. Faulkner resigned from his job before he was fired. He left with the famous words, "Thank God I won't ever again have to be at the beck and call of every son of a bitch who's got two cents to buy a stamp."

Power Plant—In 1929 after his marriage, Faulkner worked here loading coal to the boiler. In the quiet hours of the night he would make a table out of a wheelbarrow and write. He began *As I Lay Dying* here and finished it in six weeks. He wrote parts of *Sanctuary* here. The furnaces no longer burn coal, and the big brick smokestack was demolished in the 1980s.

Alumni House—This is the site of the house that the university provided in 1920 to Murry Falkner. His son William occupied a small room in the tower. After dropping out of Ole Miss, Faulkner retired to his room, sometimes with a supply of corn liquor, and worked to write and illustrate an experimental play called *The Marionettes*, followed by a love poem about Estelle titled "Vision in Spring." In 1924 he finished *The Marble Faun* and, at Stone's urging, paid to have it published.

After living in New Orleans for two years with the literati of the French Quarter, including Sherwood Anderson, and spending June 1925 in Pascagoula and the rest of the summer and fall in Europe, Faulkner returned to Oxford. Financial problems forced Faulkner back home to live again with his parents. Here in his tower room he finally began writing about "that little patch up there in Mississippi," advice Sherwood Anderson had given him. He finished and revised *Flags in the Dust* five times and sent it off in January of 1928 to uninterested publishers. In April 1928 he began a novella here called *Twilight*, later named *The Sound and the Fury*, which was published in the fall. In January 1929, he began work on a potboiler, which he finished in May and later rewrote and published as *Sanctuary*. In the meantime, Ben Wasson edited the *Flags in the Dust* manuscript, and it was published as *Sartoris* in early 1929.

That spring, Faulkner wrote in the campus house for the last time. "A Rose for Emily" was bought by *Forum*, his first publication in a national magazine; other stories were sold to *Saturday Evening Post*, *The American Mercury*, and *Scribner's*.

Fulton Chapel—Faulkner delivered an address to his daughter's graduation class from University High School in this auditorium in 1951. In 1977 the Eudora Welty Symposium was held here. Later, in 1987, ceremonies were staged here to issue a postage stamp commemorating William Faulkner. Eudora Welty was present on the two latter occasions. Fulton Chapel was also the site of the second Oxford Conference for the Book (1994), featuring Barry Hannah, Stephen King, and John Grisham.

J. D. Williams Library—The Mississippi Collection, housed in this library, has books, papers, and clippings on hundreds of Mississippi writers and a fine Faulkner component, including photographs, papers, first editions, and oil paintings of William Faulkner and John Faulkner. The collection also includes William Faulkner's Nobel medal and citation.

Lyceum—Since it was built in 1846–1848, the Lyceum has always served as the location of the university's administrative offices, except when it was used as a hospital during the Civil War. It is the site of Augustus B. Longstreet's office when he was president of the university (1849–1856), and it was Murry Falkner's office when he was business manager.

Confederate Soldier Statue (Front of Lyceum)—The story goes that it was primarily Faulkner's grandmother who raised the money for this monument, intending it for the courthouse square. It arrived when she was out of town, and the other members of the local Daughters of the American Revolution had it placed here instead. The story of the switch was described in Faulkner's story "Shall Not Perish." J. W. T. Falkner had to donate additional funds for the statue on the courthouse square.

Barnard Observatory—The Center for the Study of Southern Culture is located in the old observatory building, built in 1857–1859 and restored in 1992. Founded in 1977, the center is the premiere research center for the Deep South, with collections of blues recordings, photographs, film, books, and papers concerning the culture of the South. William R. Ferris was named first director of the center in 1978, and Charles Regan Wilson assumed the position in 1998. The center is sponsor of the annual Faulkner and Yoknapatawpha Conference and the Oxford Conference for the Book.

Farley Hall—This building, formerly used as the law school, now houses the journalism department. John Grisham attended law school in this building and graduated in 1981.

Leave the campus by Sorority Row, turn left on Jackson Avenue and then right on College Hill Road (Highway 314). Continue on College Hill Road. In approximately three miles, turn right on Cedar Hill Drive (County Road 138).

• Cedar Hill Farm

114 Cedar Hill Drive

The Tara subdivision on the right sprawls over the land once part of Cedar Hill Farm, acquired by John Faulkner's son Jimmy in 1955. The 1850 house is the home of Jimmy Faulkner, author of *Across the Creek: Faulkner Family Stories* (1986). Stark Young is said to have written much of *So Red the Rose* while visiting here.

• College Hill Presbyterian Church

County Road 138

A few miles farther along the road is the College Hill Presbyterian Church, built as a chapel for a small college that was destroyed during the Civil War. It is the oldest church in the county. It appears as Seminary Hill in Faulkner's *The Town.* William Faulkner and Estelle Oldham were married here on July 20, 1929, with the Reverend Winn David Hedleston presiding. Estelle's minister at St. Peter's Episcopal Church had refused to marry a divorced person in his sanctuary. Five-tenths of a mile farther on College Hill Road is the antebellum house where Reverend Hedleston lived. There is still disagreement over whether the Faulkner-Oldham wedding took place on his lawn or in the church.

South of the Square

• Neilson House

712 South 11th Street

This house, now owned by Will and Patty Lewis, was built around 1857 by William S. Neilson. An incident that occurred in the yard during the Civil War was described in Stark Young's *So Red the*

Rose. A small boy, who had climbed into one of the magnolia trees to hide from Union raiders, was shot and instantly killed. The house is also a candidate for the house in Faulkner's "A Rose for Emily."

• Dean Faulkner Wells House

510 South Lamar Street

This site has long and complicated Faulkner associations. The original house on this site was "The Big Place," home of Faulkner's grandfather J. W. T. Falkner, who stirred Billy's heart and imagination with glorious stories about the old colonel, W. C. Falkner from Ripley. J. W. T., "the young colonel," gave Faulkner a powerful sense of family history and heritage. He died in 1922 when Faulkner was twenty-five. The house was moved in 1929 to the site of the Chevron Station, corner of University Avenue and South Lamar, and was finally demolished in 1980.

Murry and Maud Falkner, William Faulkner's parents, built their house around 1930 on the original site of "The Big Place." Maud lived here until her death in 1960.

It is now the home of Dean Faulkner Wells, William Faulkner's niece, and her husband, Lawrence Wells. Both writers, they own Yoknapatawpha Press. Dean Wells wrote *The Ghosts of Rowan Oak* (1980), *William Faulkner's Ghost Stories for Children* (1981), and *Belle-Ducks at the Peabody* (1984). Larry Wells's novels are *Rommel and the Rebel* (1986) and *Let the Band Play Dixie* (1987). As publishers they have produced books on subjects ranging from football to Faulkner. *The Great American Writers' Cookbook* got national attention in 1981.

The press, along with the university, sponsors the popular faux Faulkner writing contest, an annual event, and winners can be read in *Best of Bad Faulkner* (2000) published by the Yoknapatawpha Press and edited by Dean Faulkner Wells.

• BellSouth Company

701 South Lamar Street

This was the site of the Lem Oldham house. When Billy Falkner was a child, if he was not with his grandfather he was usually with a neighborhood girl named Estelle Oldham. As children, they decided to marry one day, but as teenagers their personalities took them in opposite directions. At twenty-one Estelle married a man she had met at Ole Miss. Eleven years later, after her divorce, Billy picked Estelle up at her house on this site. In his mother's Chevrolet, they drove to the courthouse for their marriage license.

• Betty Jane Gary House

910 Buchanan Avenue

Set on a lot that occupied a whole block, this was the home of Murry and Maud Falkner and their three sons from 1902 to 1905. William lived here from the age of five until he was eight and John from the age of one until he was four. Their maternal grandmother, Leila Butler, lived with them.

• Magnolia Grove

John Martin Place

923 South 13th Street

This was the model for the house that Faulkner described as the home of Benjy Compson in *The Sound and the Fury.*

• J. W. T. Falkner II House

706 S. Lamar Street

This was the home of Faulkner's uncle John, J. W. T. Falkner, attorney and brother of Murry Falkner.

• Stowers-Longest Home

1003 S. Lamar Street

This house was used as Gavin Stevens's home in the film *Intruder in the Dust.*

• Grisham House

908 Old Taylor Road

Across the street from Rowan Oak, this was once the home of writer Joan Williams and of Seymour Lawrence, noted director of the Atlantic Monthly Press (1955–1964) and then an independent publisher. John Grisham purchased the house from the Lawrence estate and donated it to the University of Mississippi to be used by participants in the John and Renée Grisham Visiting Writer Series, funded by the Grishams.

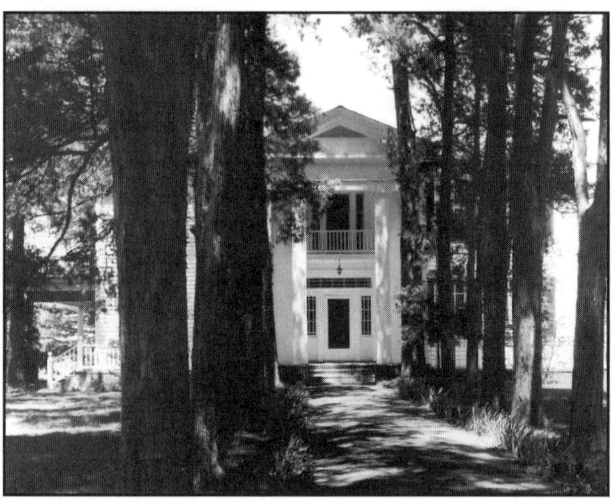

Rowan Oak

• Rowan Oak

Old Taylor Road

As the stock market crashed, Faulkner finally began to win his long financial struggle. In 1930 he was selling stories right and left and was able to buy a house. He had always liked the old Shegog place, a two-story, Greek Revival house built in 1844, with a smokehouse, a barn, and a wilderness tract of land adjoining it. Its portico with four columns and the curving, cedar-lined driveway gave it a patrician look, but his wife, Estelle, was dismayed. The house had no electricity or plumbing, and was sagging with rotted beams. By the end of the summer of 1930, doing much of the work himself, Faulkner had renovated the house. He called it Rowan Oak after the legend of the rowan tree, believed by the Celts to offer protection and safety. Faulkner designed and built the stable and later added a study to the house.

Alabama, his firstborn child, died here when she was only ten days old, devastating Faulkner and his wife. Two years later, his only other child, Jill, was born. She grew up at Rowan Oak, living here until her marriage in 1953. Faulkner's stepson, Malcolm Franklin (1923–1977), lived here and later wrote *Bitterweeds: Life with William Faulkner at Rowan Oak.*

From 1930 through 1951 Faulkner produced almost a book a year. Nearly all of his work was written here, although *Absalom,*

Absalom! was begun in Hollywood. It was here that he heard the devastating news of the death of his brother Dean in November 1935. His family stayed here while he bowed to the necessity of living in Hollywood as a scriptwriter, and it was here that Estelle heard the news of his death in 1962. Estelle lived at Rowan Oak until her death in 1972.

The house, acquired by the University of Mississippi in 1972, has been kept substantially as it was at Faulkner's death, including the outline of his novel *A Fable* (1954) handwritten on the wall of his study. The grounds of Rowan Oak are bordered by Old Taylor Road and University Woods. In 1993, it was named a National Literary Landmark by Friends of the Libraries, U.S.A.

North of the Square

• William R. Ferris House

1700 Jefferson Avenue

William Ferris (1942) was born in Vicksburg and raised on a farm in Warren County. He earned degrees from Davidson College and Northwestern University and a Ph.D. in folklore from the University of Pennsylvania. He was cofounder, with Judy Peiser, of the Center for Southern Folklore in Memphis and was the first director of the Center for the Study of Southern Culture at Ole Miss. He guided the center from 1977 to 1998, when he was appointed chair of the National Endowment for the Humanities in Washington, D.C.

He has published books, films, photographs, and countless articles on the folk culture of Mississippi. His books—all nonfiction—show a thoughtful and creative mind at work. They include the biography of Ray Lum, *You Live and Learn, Then You Die and Forget It All* (1993), *Blues from the Delta* (1978), and *Local Color* (1982),

• Longstreet House

634 North Lamar Street

Writer Augustus Baldwin Longstreet (1790–1870), who is credited with originating the genre called "southwestern humor," was the chancellor of the University of Mississippi from 1849 to 1856.

Born in Georgia and educated at Yale, Longstreet was an attorney, a judge, a Georgia representative, and a Methodist minister before serving as president of Emory College from 1839 to 1848 and then as chancellor at Ole Miss. He left here to become president of the University of South Carolina in 1858, but returned to Oxford at the outbreak of the Civil War. He lived here the rest of his life and is buried in St. Peter's Cemetery.

Longstreet published three books of fiction, but made his reputation with the book of humorous sketches entitled *Georgia Scenes* (1835). It marked the beginning of a school of southern writers interested in realism and Southern humor. Two other Mississippi writers, Joseph Beckham Cobb (see Columbus) and Joseph Glover Baldwin (DeKalb), were among those writing in a style that flourished in America from 1835 to 1861. Mark Twain would continue the tradition after the war.

• Barry Hannah House

211 Eagle Spring Road

Barry Hannah's startling prose—exuberant, fierce, funny, often outrageous—has made him a prestigious and popular writer-in-residence at the University of Mississippi. (See Clinton regarding his earlier life.) The career of this highly acclaimed writer is lit with awards: *Geronimo Rex* (1972) won the William Faulkner Prize for the best first novel of 1973 and was nominated for the National Book Award; *Airships* won the Arnold Gingrich Short Fiction Award in 1978 and the 1978 Award for Literature from the American Institute of Arts and Letters in 1979; *Ray* (1980) received a nomination for the American Book Awards in 1980; *Bats Out of Hell* (1993) won a 1994 Mississippi Institute of Arts and Letters award. His short story collection *High Lonesome* (1996) was nominated for the Pulitzer Prize, and in 1999 he received the Chubb Award for Fiction from the Fellowship of Southern Writers. *Boomerang* (1989) is considered his most autobiographical work. *Yonder Stands Your Orphan* was published in 2001.

Hannah has taught writing at Middlebury College, Clemson University, the University of Alabama, Memphis State University, the University of Iowa, and the University of Montana. In between these positions he moved to Hollywood in 1980 to write scripts for the director Robert Altman. On the faculty of Ole Miss since 1983, he has helped develop the talents of writers Cynthia Shearer, Donna Tartt, and Larry Brown. He lives here with his wife, Susan. Once asked what he liked about Oxford, he replied, "Benign neglect." As an example, he told the story of his barber, who asked him, "How much do you have to pay to get your books published?"

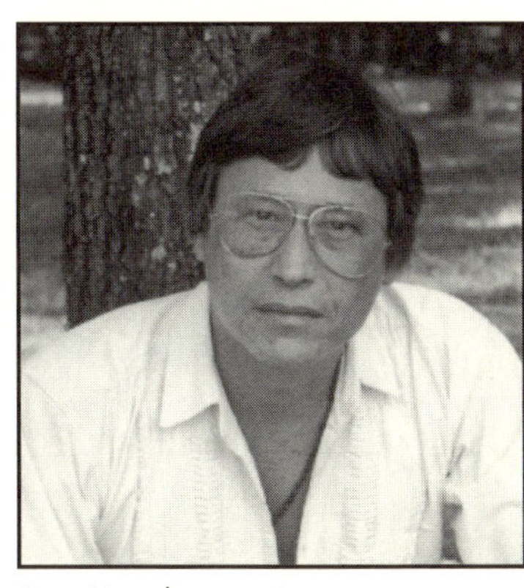
Barry Hannah

• St. Peter's Cemetery

Jefferson Avenue and North 16th Street

In the old section are the graves of Faulkner's paternal grandmother, Sallie Murry, who died in 1906, his maternal grandmother, "Damuddy," who died in June 1907, his grandfather, J. W. T. Falkner, his infant daughter, Alabama, his mother, Maud, his brothers, Dean, Jack, and John, and the family servant, Carolina Barr, known as "Mammy Callie." Augustus B. Longstreet is also buried in the old section. The graves of William Faulkner and wife, Estelle, are in the new section, in a lot to the northwest of the obelisk.

• Fire House No. 1

658 North Lamar Street

Writer Larry Brown has made this possibly the most famous firehouse in the South. He joined the Oxford Fire Department in 1973 and worked as a fireman for seventeen years. (See Yocona for his biography.)

There are several roads going out of Oxford, like wheel spokes. Almost every one of these leads to a literary site. Starting with the two o'clock position, take each spoke in order.

Spoke 1: Go seventeen miles northeast of Oxford on Highway 30 to Faulkner's farm, called Greenfield, or "The Farm."

Greenfield Farm

William Faulkner bought this farm on Puskus Creek in the northeast part of Lafayette County in the 1930s. On these 320 acres, called the old Joe Parks place, William, John, and their father, Murry, raised a few cattle and mules (one of William's favorite animals), as well as corn and hay for the livestock and for William's horses, which he kept at Rowan Oak. The Faulkner men hunted, fished, and had Fourth of July barbecues here. The gravel road going to town was called The Rock. Joan Williams writes about Puskus Creek in *The Wintering*.

Spoke 2: Go on Highway 6 east to Campground Road (County Road 217). Turn right and go 4/10 of a mile to County Road 238. Turn right to the campground.

Old Methodist Campground

Since 1870, this has been the site of weeklong revival meetings, usually held in August. The Falkners had a "tent" (cabin) here for many years, and Maud sometimes attended the revival. As a scoutmaster in Oxford, William once led his troop on an overnight hike and camped in the tabernacle.

Return to County Road 217. Turn left on Deer Run.

201 Deer Run

This was the house of Evans Harrington (1925–1997), a longtime and influential member of the Ole Miss English faculty. He was born in Birmingham and moved to Clinton before he was three. He served in the naval air corps from 1943 to 1945, then earned his B.A. at Mississippi College in 1948 and M.A. at the University of Mississippi in 1951. He joined the Ole Miss faculty in 1955, and remained there until his retirement. He was teacher and mentor to dozens of writers who studied at Ole Miss, and won the Henry Bellaman Foundation Award for Writing and Teaching Writing. A noted Faulkner scholar, he scripted the television documentary *William Faulkner, Land in Legend* and wrote short stories, essays, and novels, including *The Prisoner* (1956), *Willa* (1961), *Missy* (1961), and *Lily* (1964). The Evans Harrington Grant for a novel in progress is awarded annually by the Pirate's Alley Faulkner Society. The award is funded by one of Harrington's former students, mystery writer Julie Smith.

Spoke 3: From Highway 6 east take Highway 334; turn south to Yocona (eight miles). The road follows the route that Flem Snopes and wife, Eula Varner Snopes, took into Jefferson in *The Town*. From the first Yocona sign continue 1.3 miles.

Larry Brown House

945 Highway 334

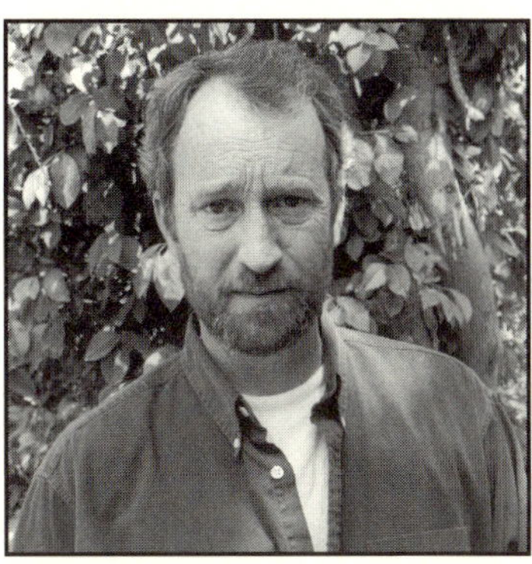

Larry Brown

After seventeen years with the Oxford Fire Department, Captain Larry Brown, burning with the desire to write, quit fighting fires in 1990 and turned full-time to the typewriter. From the publication of his first book, *Facing the Music* (1989), Brown has won critical acclaim for his hard-hitting, searing, funny, and direct style. He writes about the world of hard-loving, truck-driving, whiskey-drinking men, often out of luck and love. In 1992, his novel *Joe* won the Southern Book Critics Circle Award, and in 1997 he became the first two-time winner of that award with *Father and Son. Fay* (2000) has been called "his biggest, baddest and best" novel. He has written an adaptation of his novel *Dirty Work* (1989) for the stage and a movie script of *Joe*. The autobiographical *On Fire* (1994) recounts his years as a fireman. His second book of nonfiction, *Billy Ray's Farm* (2001) is a memoir about friends and family. He continues to write from this house, where he lives with his wife and children. His mother-in-law lives next door at 943. The Lafayette County and Oxford Public Library sponsor the Larry Brown Writers' Series, which offers readings and workshops.

Spoke 4. From Highway 6 turn south on Old Taylor Road and continue for about seven miles to Taylor.

Taylor Grocery

Once a stagecoach stop, Taylor is now a stop for serious artists. Over the years men and women pursuing various means of

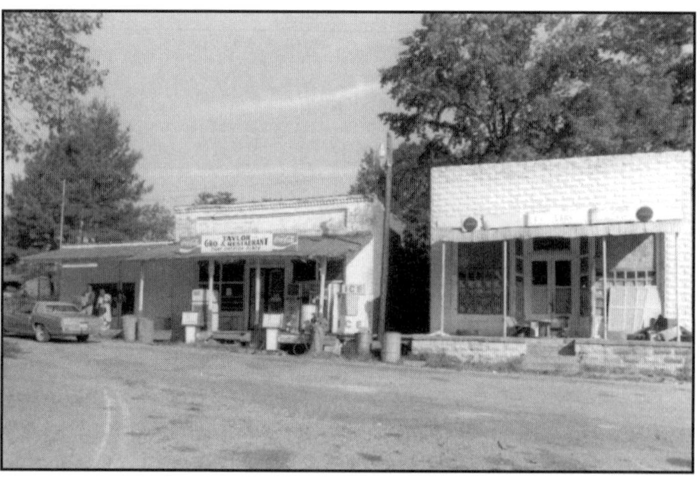

Taylor Grocery, Taylor

expression have settled down here for some serious work. Photographer Jane Rule Burdine presided over the town as mayor for several years. Taylor citizens include potters Keith Stewart and Obie Clark, sculptor Bill Beckwith, stone sculptor Jared Spears, and painters Alice Hammell and Jim Daigle. Furniture maker Marc Deloach and writer and photographer Christine Schultz are the mail carriers for the Taylor post office and operate the Taylor Arts gallery.

The Taylor Grocery has long been a gathering spot for the literati. The raw wood plank walls bear signatures and messages from local and visiting writers, who come here for fried catfish and music.

The road to Taylor was a favorite hiking and horse trail for Faulkner, who visited Taylor frequently. On the road about two miles south of Oxford was the old county poorhouse mentioned in *The Town* and *Sartoris.* Taylor is one of the few sites in his fictional Yoknapatawpha County for which Faulkner used the real name. In *Sanctuary* Temple Drake leaves a special train loaded with Ole Miss students at Taylor Depot to begin her woeful adventures.

Spoke 5: Take Highway 6 west, toward Batesville. Watch for a large yellow house on your left, delineated by a white fence tracing the contours of the rolling hills on which the estate sits.

John Grisham House

Highway 6 West

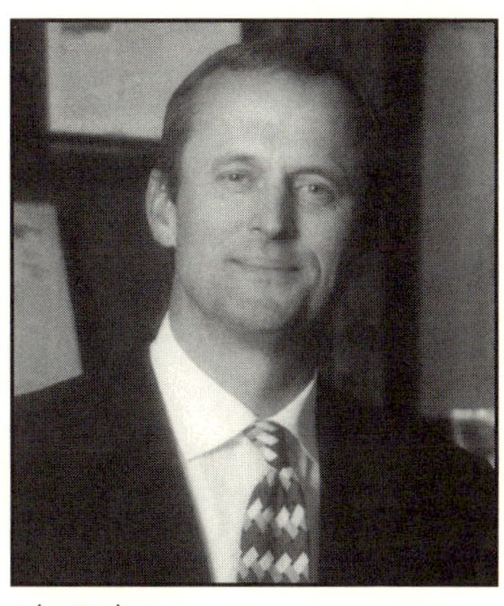
John Grisham

John Grisham (1955) is easily the most financially successful writer Mississippi has ever produced. Six of his nine legal mysteries have been made into Hollywood movies, and every book he writes makes the best-seller list. Grisham was born in Jonesboro, Arkansas, but grew up primarily in Southhaven, Mississippi. He first went to Oxford to attend law school. After he graduated, he and his wife, Renée, moved to Southhaven, where he practiced law from 1981 to 1991. He represented the northwestern area in the Mississippi legislature from 1984 to 1990. He and Renée returned to Oxford in 1991 and built their dream house on the hill with seventy acres surrounding it. The grounds include tennis courts, a baseball field, and a horse barn. Because zoning laws did not protect their homesite from encroaching commercialism, in 1994 the couple bought a home in Covesville, Virginia, where they and their children now spend most of their time. The Grishams have been generous to Oxford and Ole Miss, backing the *Oxford American* magazine and funding a writer-in-residence program at the university. Grisham's first book, *A Time to Kill* (1989), received scant attention, but *The Firm* (1990) was a major hit. Those two books and many that followed are based on actual cases or events in Mississippi.

Oxford is the end of the Yoknapatawpha tour.

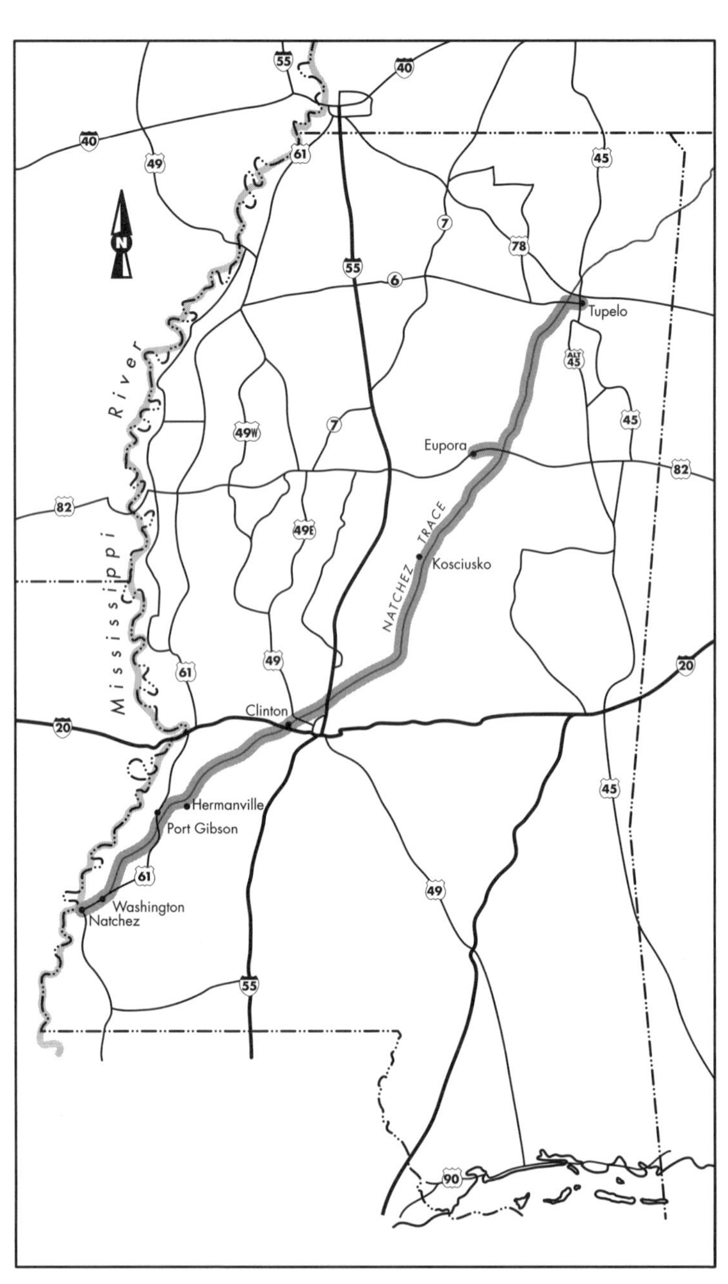

N
Mississippi River
NATCHEZ TRACE
Tupelo
Eupora
Kosciusko
Clinton
Hermanville
Port Gibson
Washington
Natchez
55
40
61
49
45
7
78
6
ALT 45
49W
82
49E
20
90

Natchez Trace Tour

The old Natchez Trace was a fabled road traveled by Indians, robbers, soldiers, settlers, boatmen, and such notables as Aaron Burr, Andrew Jackson, Meriwether Lewis, and John James Audubon. Now a national parkway, the Natchez Trace follows the old Indian trail that led from Natchez diagonally across the state to Nashville, Tennessee. In the 1730s, when the Mississippi River became a busy conduit for crops being brought downriver to Natchez and New Orleans, the Natchez Trace was the way home. Boatmen floated produce down the river, sold their flatboats, and walked back home. By 1810 the Trace was the most heavily traveled road in the Old Southwest, but, with the invention of the steamboat in 1812, it began gradually to revert to a forest pathway. In the late 1930s, the National Park Service began constructing a modern parkway that closely follows the course of the original Trace. More than 90 percent of the parkway is completed.

The sheer beauty of the Trace and its history and drama have inspired writers to use it as a setting for their fiction; these include Eliza Dupuy in the nineteenth century and Eudora Welty, James Street, Nevada Barr, and others in the twentieth century.

This tour starts where the original travelers started, in Natchez on the banks of the Mississippi River. It goes up the Trace through Washington,

Port Gibson, Hermanville, Clinton, Kosciusko, and Eupora, and ends in Tupelo. The traveler on the Trace today can still feel the sense of remoteness and isolation that Welty made palpable in her short stories "Livvie" and "A Still Moment."

Natchez

The Natchez country was considered a romantic and exotic land as soon as it was inhabited by the French. Pierre-François-Xavier de Charlevoix (1682–1761), a French-Canadian academic, traveled through the area in 1721–1722 and later wrote *Histoire et description générale de la Nouvelle France* (1744).

Over a half century later, without having ever visited the area, Frenchman François-Auguste-René de Chateaubriand (1768–1848) popularized it in France and the United States with his 1801 epic, *Atala, or the Love of Two Savages in the Desert*, a tale of the Natchez Indians. He based his descriptions of the land on Charlevoix's work.

Perched on a bluff overlooking the Mississippi River, Natchez flourished under the British and Spanish as cotton became king. Natchez was made an American city in 1798 and a Mississippi city in 1817, when Mississippi became the twentieth state in the union.

The houses and byways of Natchez have been used extensively in American fiction, biographies, and memoirs, as well as by Hollywood. Ellen Douglas (Josephine Haxton), whose family has been associated with Natchez for generations, set several of her stories here. (See Greenville and Jackson for her biography.) Natchez has starred in such movies as *Showboat*, *Raintree County*, *Huckleberry Finn*, *The Autobiography of Miss Jane Pittman*, and *Good Old Boy*, among others. Within some of its beautiful and impressive houses, men and women of letters were at work as early as 1799.

But literary works associated with Natchez have contained gritty realism as well as romanticism. Just after the turn of the twentieth century the impoverished area of Natchez was the birthplace of one of America's greatest black writers, Richard Wright (1908–1960), who chronicled the other side of life in Mississippi. (See Jackson for his biography.) Pennsylvania writer Nathaniel C.

Hale spent his boyhood in Natchez, and Barnard Shipp, a nineteenth-century poet, called it home. Twentieth-century writers include James Pipes, Margaret Samuels Ernst, Elizabeth Brandon Stanton, Verne Smith, Louis Lord, Morris Raphael, Isabella Brown, Larry Johnson, Jes Simmons, Julius Thompson, Robert Dalby, Greg Iles (see biography below), and Edgar Simmons, a native of Natchez whose poetry has been widely acclaimed and published in major periodicals. On the book jacket of Simmons's *Driving to Biloxi*, James Dickey wrote that "the poetry of Edgar Simmons is wild, various, and almost unbelievably inventive and energetic."

The strong literary heritage of Natchez is reflected in the annual Natchez Literary Celebration held each February. Organized in 1989 by Carolyn Vance Smith, it features readings and lectures by writers, tours to literary landmarks, book sales, book signings, and parties.

Out of the fabled high society of nineteenth-century Natchez, a trio of women emerged to become nationally known writers: Catherine Ware Warfield, Eliza Dupuy, and Sarah Ellis Dorsey. To imagine their milieu is to call up the exciting and elegant days in a booming and sophisticated river city before civil war changed everything. Their high-ceilinged drawing rooms were scenes of elegant parties, literary salons, and political gossip. During and after the Civil War, their experiences were harsh and difficult, and both eras fed their fiction. The lives of these three women were closely intertwined with the site now called Dunleith.

DUNLEITH

84 Homocitto Street

Before Dunleith was built, the house occupying this site was Routhland. Five nineteenth-century writers are associated with these two houses. Routhland burned in 1855 and was replaced by the current structure. Alfred Vidal Davis, who was the second owner of the house and renamed it Dunleith, was the great-grandfather of Ellen Douglas and great-great-grandfather of poet Brooks Haxton.

From the age of eight, Sarah Ann Ellis (1829–1879), daughter of Thomas George Percy Ellis, grew up in Routhland, which was

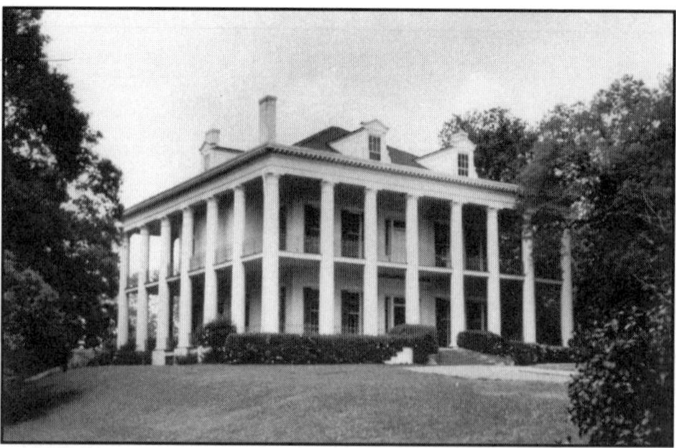

Dunleith, Natchez

the property of her mother, Mary Magdalene Routh. After one year there her father died, and two years later her mother married Charles Dahlgren. Their lives were filled with lavish social occasions, cultural opportunities, and travel. Dahlgren was a doting stepfather to the precocious Sarah Ann. He sent her to Philadelphia for her formal education. In 1853 her marriage to the much older Samuel Worthington Dorsey caused an estrangement between Sarah and her stepfather which lasted the rest of her life. Routhland burned to the ground two years after Sarah Ann had left home. She watched as her mother and stepfather built a second Routhland on the site. Now called Dunleith, it was a showplace even by Natchez standards. Her mother died two years after its completion.

Sarah Ann and her husband, Samuel Dorsey, lived at Elkridge, Dahlgren's plantation in Tensas Parish, Louisiana, across the river from Natchez, and maintained their social life in Natchez. Sarah Ellis Dorsey led a remarkable life. She tutored slaves when it was illegal to do so, teaching some sixty to seventy people to read and write. She adapted Anglican church services and arranged choral music for slaves. She was a strong advocate of female suffrage and women's rights, and even tried to establish an order of deaconesses in the Episcopal Church. During the Civil War, after their plantation house was burned, she served as a Confederate nurse in Texas. Though childless, she had a lifelong concern for children's well-being. Classically educated and a linguist, she had a strong interest in Greek, Roman, and Norse mythology which she used extensively in her writings.

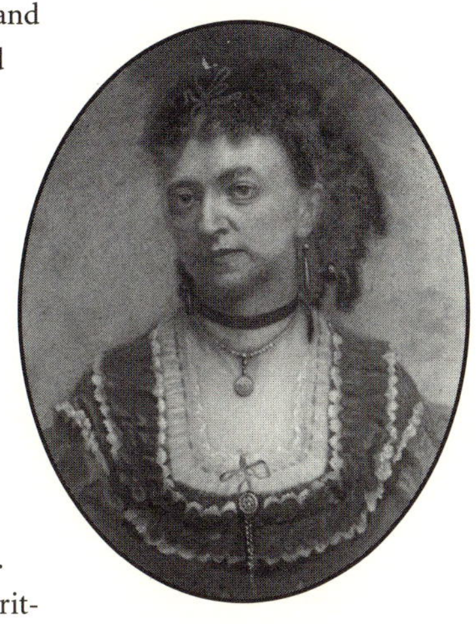

Sarah Ellis Dorsey

Between 1862 and 1877 she produced six fictional works, writing under the pen name "Filia." Her first novel, *Agnes Graham*, was autobiographical and was serialized in the *Southern Literary Messenger* in 1863–1864. *Lucia Dare* was her war novel, published in 1867. It was dedicated "to my aunt Mrs. Catharine A. Warfield, this book written at her request." In addition to books, she wrote several scientific and philosophic papers, including a daring one on Darwin.

At the end of the war she and her husband bought Beauvoir on the Mississippi Sound near Biloxi. Although her husband died before they could move from Natchez, Sarah spent the rest of her life at Beauvoir. She invited Jefferson Davis to live there and write his memoirs. When in 1878 doctors diagnosed her illness as cancer, she sold Beauvoir to Davis and bequeathed her remaining estate to Davis and his daughter. She died while under treatment in New Orleans and was buried in the Routh family cemetery on Homochitto Street across from the southwest corner of the grounds of Dunleith.

Eliza Dupuy (1814–1880) was Sarah's tutor as she was growing up at Routhland. A native of Virginia, Dupuy started writing in Kentucky to aid her family's precarious financial state. By 1840, her short stories were being published in the leading magazines of the era, *Godey's*, *The New World*, and *Knickerbocker's*. Perhaps through her literary reputation, she secured a job as governess at Routhland in Natchez, where literary activity abounded and was almost a social requirement. Dupuy's excitement about writing and love of books inspired young Sarah Ann.

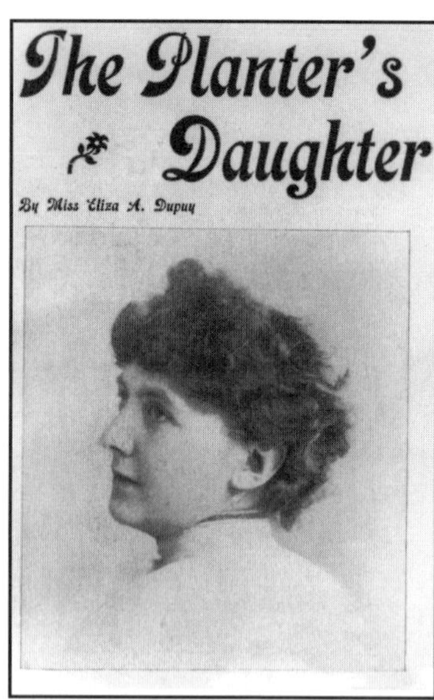

Eliza Dupuy, book jacket

While at Routhland, Dupuy wrote *The Conspirator* (1850), a fictional account of Aaron Burr's arrest and arraignment in Natchez. It was a huge success, selling more than twenty-five thousand copies and enabling Dupuy to give up the demanding job of governess. She moved to the country outside Natchez, where she wrote *The Country Neighborhood* (1855). That was the year Nathaniel Hawthorne took a swipe at the "damned mob of scribbling women." Dupuy would scribble and publish nine more books before she moved to New Orleans on the eve of the Civil War.

Many of Dupuy's novels ran in the *New York Ledger* during the years 1860 to 1868 under the pen name "Annie Young." She was the Jacqueline Susann of her day, known as a facile writer of melodrama and sensationalism. Her titles tell all: *The Discarded Wife, All for Love, The Cancelled Will, The Dethroned Heiress, The Gipsy's Warning,* and *The Mysterious Guest.* Her most famous novel, *The Planter's Daughter* (1858), was filled with murder, madness, and mayhem. Altogether, Dupuy published twenty-five novels between 1851 and 1872.

She returned to live in Kentucky during Reconstruction, but died in New Orleans on a visit in 1880. She was buried in Flemingsburg, Kentucky. Seven of her novels appear to have been written in Mississippi.

Sarah Ann Ellis had been born into one of the wealthiest and most influential families in the Mississippi Territory, a dynasty that would produce twentieth-century writers William Alexander Percy and Walker Percy. She was the granddaughter of Sarah Percy Ellis, whose daughters, Catherine Ann Ware (1816–1877) and Eleanor Ware (1820–1849), were writers. Both born in Natchez to Sarah Percy and her second husband, Nathaniel Ware, they became mentors to their niece, Sarah Ann Ellis.

After the birth of Eleanor, Sarah Percy was placed in a Philadelphia hospital for a mental disorder. Nathaniel Ware raised Catherine and Eleanor, with the help of a nurse and governess. The girls had every educational and material advantage available in America at the time. They traveled extensively, lived in Philadelphia and Cincinnati, and wintered in Natchez. They often visited their family at Routhland, where they met Eliza Dupuy, already an established writer. The three became good friends, pulled together by their close ages and interest in literature. They had literary gatherings at Routhland where they entertained their guests by reading from their works. Among the literati at these gatherings was novelist Joseph Holt Ingraham (see Washington, Holly Springs, and Aberdeen).

The Ware sisters began writing poetry and novels as teenagers. They collaborated on a manuscript entitled "Tales of the Weird and Wonderful." Eleanor married a cousin of Robert E. Lee and died of yellow fever before the age of thirty. Catherine married Robert Elisha Warfield, and lived in Galveston, Lexington, and Louisville, Kentucky, where she raised their six children.

Catherine did not write again for many years. Her niece from Natchez, Sarah Ellis Dorsey, finally persuaded her to write once more. Catherine Ware Warfield's first novel, *The Household of Bouverie* (1860, two volumes) was dedicated to Sarah. The novel was called by a contemporary critic "one of the most remarkable novels ever written by an American woman." Another cited her "unmistakable fire of genius." She was compared to Nathaniel Hawthorne and Edgar Allan Poe. She was snapped up by the nation's largest publisher, T. B. Peterson and Brothers, and wrote a spate of novels bearing romantic titles such as *Hester Howard's Temptation*, *The Cardinal's Daughter*, *Romance of the Green Seal*, and *Miriam's Memoirs*. Her novels had a seriousness of purpose and often showed the darker aspects of male and female relationships. She is considered one of the first important southern women novelists.

Eleanor Percy Ware (1820–1849) was four years younger than her sister, but they were inseparable, writing poetry and novels together. Ellen, as she was called, wrote a novel entitled *Agatha* when she was seventeen. It was never published, but in 1844 their intensely devoted father published a collection of their poetry, *The Wife of Leon and Other Poems.* Their second volume of poetry, *The Indian Chamber*, published in 1846, was dedicated to William Cullen Bryant in gratitude for his "indulgent opinions" of their first volume of poetry.

After Eleanor's marriage to Henry Lee, they lived on her estate in Hinds County and later on Deer Creek in Washington County. During a visit to Natchez in 1849 she died of yellow fever and is buried in Natchez. Her daughter Sarah Catherine Lee would become a novelist under the name Kate Ferguson (see Greenville).

Catherine and Eleanor Ware's father was also a writer. A native of South Carolina, Nathaniel A. Ware (1789–1854) moved in 1811 to the Mississippi Territory, where he served as the last secretary of the territory and as acting governor, and married the wealthy widow Sarah Percy Ellis. After her hospitalization in 1820, he moved his young girls to Philadelphia. They traveled extensively, but spent a great deal of time in Natchez. After both daughters married, he moved to Galveston where he later died of yellow fever. He published two books on political economics in his lifetime. His novel *Harvey Belden: Or, a True Narrative of Strange Adventures* was published in 1848.

The second owner of Routhland, Alfred Vidal Davis, took possession of the house around 1859 and renamed it Dunleith. He brought in from his plantation a teenage slave named John Roy Lynch, who worked at Dunleith as Davis's valet before Emancipation was proclaimed.

John Roy Lynch (1847–1939) went on to have a long and successful career as a politician, businessman, and author. He was the son of an Irishman and a slave woman who was widowed when Lynch was a young child. He grew up in Louisiana on Davis's plantation across the river from Natchez. Lynch was freed at age sixteen when Union forces occupied Natchez. With no formal education, he read constantly and became interested in the politics of Reconstruction. His remarkable career began four years after the Civil War when he was appointed a justice of the peace at age twenty-one, the first black man to hold public office in Mississippi. Later in that same year he was elected to the Mississippi House of Representatives where he served four years. At age twenty-six he became Mississippi's first black congressman. He attracted national attention through his impassioned work for the Civil Rights Bill of 1874.

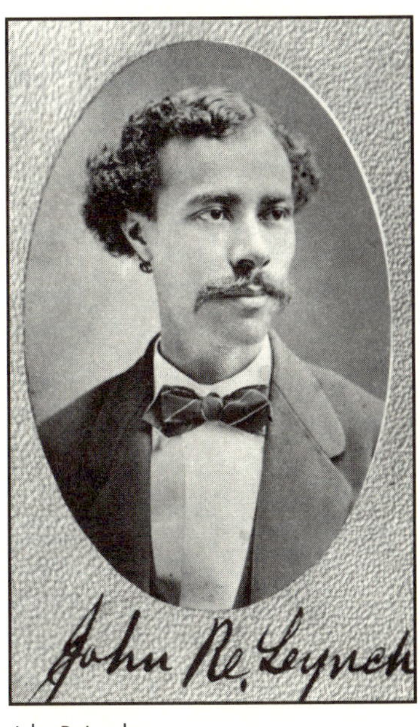

John R. Lynch

By 1876 Mississippi Democrats had overthrown Republican Reconstruction. Lynch lost his congressional seat, but he continued his struggle to improve life for the Negro. In 1912 he gave up on Mississippi and moved to Chicago, where he practiced law and was engaged in the real estate business. His memoirs were first published as *The Facts of Reconstruction* (1913), which he later revised. The book was published three decades after his death as *Reminiscences of an Active Life* (1970). He is buried in Chicago.

The Elms

Washington and Pine Streets

When the Elms was built in 1804 as his residence, John Henderson (1755–1841), a Natchez merchant and planter, was already Mississippi's first published author and its first poet. A native of Scotland, Henderson arrived in Natchez in 1775 during British rule and lived through Spanish rule, territorial days, and early statehood. Henderson was a leader in establishing the Presbyterian Church in the Mississippi Territory. As a response to Thomas Paine's *The Age of Reason*, published in 1794, Henderson wrote *Paine Detected, or The Unreasonableness of Paine's Age of Reason* as a witty rebuttal of Paine's "determined hatred to all revealed religion." The book, which also contains Henderson's poetry, was published by Mississippi's first printer, Andrew Marschalk, in 1799.

Pleasant Hill

310 South Pearl Street

Henderson's second home, Pleasant Hill, was built around 1840 at Pearl and Washington streets and was moved to its present location in 1858 by his son, Thomas Henderson. Henderson did not live to enjoy the house. Two of John Henderson's descendants are prominent writers today: Josephine Ayers Haxton, who writes under the name Ellen Douglas, and her son Brooks Haxton, a poet (see Greenville).

William Johnson House

210 State Street

One of the most remarkable memoirs in the South was written by William Johnson (1809–1851), an ex-slave who became a barber and landholder in Natchez. His two thousand hand-written pages cover the years 1835 to 1851 and record daily life when Natchez was at the peak of its prosperity. After a boundary dispute, a white man shot Johnson from ambush. Johnson died the next day. His murderer was not convicted, because black witnesses could not testify in court against a white defendant. His diary was published a century later as *William Johnson's Natchez: The Ante-Bellum Diary of a Free Negro* (1951).

Richmond

Government Fleet Street

Sarah Ann Ellis (1829–1879) was born in Richmond, the home of her parents, Thomas George Percy Ellis and Mary Routh Ellis, and of her grandmother, Sarah Percy Ellis Ware, during the last years of her life. The family divided their time between Richmond, their town home, and Woodlawn, their country home. When Sarah was eight, after the death of her grandmother, the family moved to Routhland (see Dunleith).

Use Ramada Inn's driveway on Highway 65/84 to reach the road to the Briars.

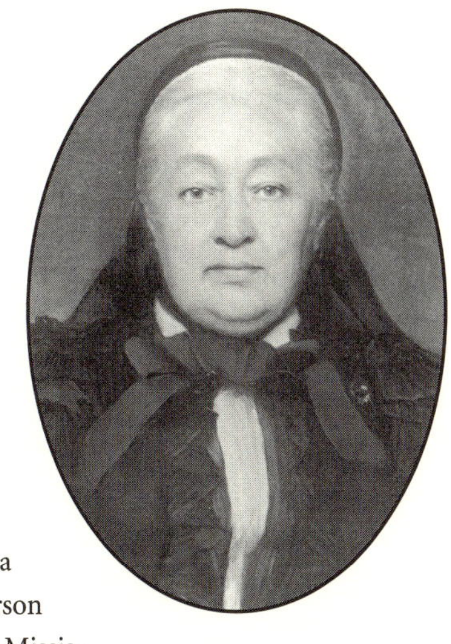
Varina Howell Davis

The Briars

31 Irving Lane

Varina Howell (1826–1906) was born into a wealthy Natchez family, and spent her childhood in this house rented by her family. She was privately tutored here and sent off to finishing school in Philadelphia for a year. She met the widowed Jefferson Davis shortly after she came back to Mississippi, and they were married in this house in 1845 when she was eighteen and he eighteen years her senior. The rest is history, literally. She was with him as he served in the U.S. Congress, returned from the Mexican War as a hero, became U.S. Secretary of War, was president of the Confederate States of America, was imprisoned for two years, lived in Europe, and finally resided in peace at Beauvoir, the surrounding land a gift from Sarah Ann Ellis Dorsey (see Dunleith). After Jefferson Davis's death at Beauvoir, Varina Davis began a memoir of his life. *Jefferson Davis, Ex-president of the Confederate States of America: A Memoir by His Wife* was published in 1890 (see Biloxi regarding her later life).

Bisland Road is on Highway 555 across from Pine Ridge Presbyterian Church.

Mount Repose

1 Bisland Road

Elizabeth Bisland (1861–1929) was the Nellie Bly of Natchez. She, in fact, raced Nellie Bly on a trip around the world in 1890 in a contest sponsored by rival newspapers. Working as an assistant editor of the New York *Cosmopolitan,* Bisland made the trip in seventy-two days, beating Phileas Fogg's record but losing to Nellie

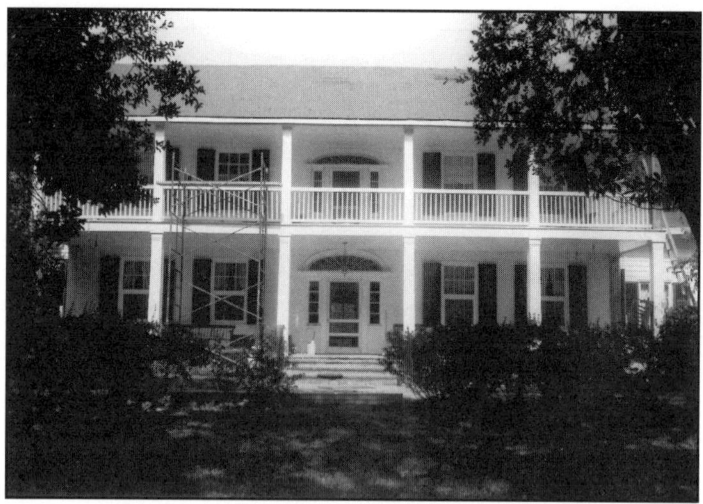

Mount Repose, Natchez

Bly by four days. Nevertheless her attempt and her book *A Flying Trip Around the World* (1891) brought her international fame.

Elizabeth Bisland lived here as a teenager. She moved to Mount Repose at fourteen when her parents inherited the house, built by kinsman William Bisland in 1824. Her family was able to give her the traditional education and cultural opportunities of the Natchez elite. After her marriage to an attorney, she lived and wrote in the elegant Oyster Bay area of Long Island. Her best-known novel was *A Candle of Understanding* (1903). She also wrote *The Life and Letters of Lafcadio Hearn* (1906) and *At the Sign of the Hobby Horse*, a collection of essays (1910).

Chattawa Cottage

710 North Union Street

Alice Walworth Graham (1905–1994) continued the tradition of successful women writers who were born and bred in the lush milieu of Natchez. Her intimate knowledge of the land, history, and culture of the town was handily used; she established a reputation as a writer of romances set in Natchez, including *Indigo Bend* (1954) and *The Natchez Woman* (1963). Although most of her novels were set in the historical context of Natchez, her later works took place in Edwardian England, and include *The Vows of the Peacock* (1955) and *Shield of Honor* (1957).

Graham's background was as romantic as her fictional characters. She was the great-grandniece of John James Audubon and a descendant of John P. Walworth, who built The Burn in 1836. She grew up in this house next door, daily visiting her grandfather and aunts at The Burn. With prestigious ancestors and a physician father, she fit into the social life of turn-of-the-century Natchez. She graduated from Natchez High School and St. Joseph's Convent. She attended Mississippi State College for Women and Louisiana State University before her marriage to Richard Norwood Graham. She published eight novels.

The Walworth family has been immortalized in the novel based on family history, *Pilgrimage: A Tale of Old Natchez* (1982) by Louise Wilbourn Collier.

Peter Isler House

508 Washington Street

Painting ornithological and quadruped specimens of North America earned John James Audubon (1765–1851) a special niche in American history. He came to the Natchez area to find new species of birds that he could paint, and made Natchez his home from 1822 to 1823. He supported himself by teaching at various locales in the city. It is known that he tutored the children of the Quegles family who lived in this house during those years.

In addition to being a fine painter of nature, Audubon was a writer of vivid prose. His detailed diaries have been published, as have his letters. He also wrote professionally, selling firsthand narratives of his adventures. A collection of these pieces was published as *Audubon's America: The Narratives and Experiences of John James Audubon,* edited by Donald Culross Peattie (1940). Three Mississippi pieces are included.

During Audubon's stay in Mississippi he explored the Delta swamp along the Yazoo River and wrote about his adventures. His account of early settlers, called squatters, a description of a cougar hunt, and a new arrival's view of Natchez give modern-day readers a glimpse of life in the raw wilderness of undeveloped Mississippi.

The Towers

801 Myrtle Avenue

Originally called The Gardenia, this house was described in Stark Young's *So Red the Rose* (1924), a novel about the Civil War. (See Oxford for Young's biography.)

Richard Wright House

20 Woodlawn Street

Mississippi's best-known African American writer, Richard Wright, lived in this house with his grandparents from the time he was three until he was six. (See Jackson for his biography.)

Dr. Jerry Iles House

205 Old Pond Road

This is the boyhood home of Greg Iles (1961). Iles began his writing career after his struggling rock band called it quits. To date he has published five novels that have been resounding successes, with one, *24 Hours*, turned into a Hollywood movie (Iles wrote the screenplay).

His first two World War II thrillers, *Spandau Phoenix* (1992) and *Black Cross* (1995), were both nationally praised. His third novel, *Mortal Fear* (1997), was set in the Mississippi Delta and his fourth, *The Quiet Game* (1999), in Natchez. His thriller *24 Hours* (2000) is set in Jackson and Biloxi. All of Iles's novels have been on the *New York Times* best-seller list. *Black Cross* received the Mississippi Author's Award for Fiction in 1995. *Deep Sleep* was published in 2001.

Iles was born in Stuttgart, Germany, where his father was head of the medical clinic at the U.S. embassy. The family moved to Natchez in 1963, and Iles was raised in this house. He graduated from the University of Mississippi in 1983, and now lives and writes in Natchez.

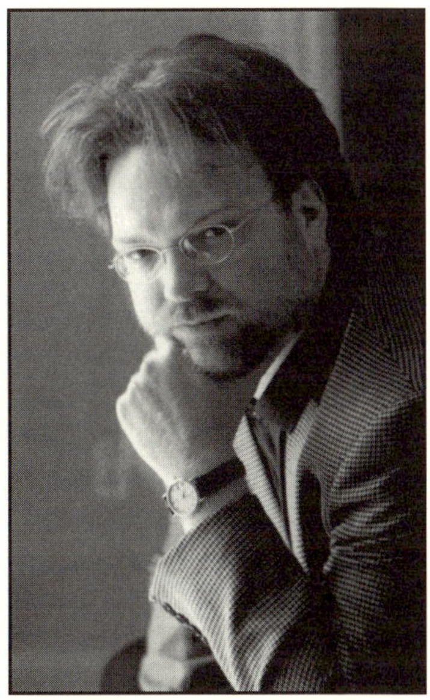
Greg Iles

George W. Healy, Jr. (1905–1980), longtime editor of the New Orleans *Times-Picayune*, was born and raised in Natchez, the grandson of Thomas Healy, portrait painter from Port Gibson. His charming autobiography, *A Lifetime on Deadline: Self-Portrait of a Southern Journalist* (1976), describes his childhood joy about being cast in some of the earliest films made in Natchez—*The Heart of Maryland*, filmed at D'Evereux, *Slippy Magee*, and *Uncle Tom's Cabin*. He started his newspaper career as a carrier for the *Natchez Democrat*. At Ole Miss he founded a humor magazine for which John Faulkner wrote and drew cartoons. Healy, focused on humor, declined work by William Faulkner. He worked for a Knoxville newspaper before joining the staff of the *Times-Picayune* in 1926. He moved through the ranks to become executive editor of both the *Times-Picayune* and the *States-Item*, the afternoon newspaper in New Orleans. He was also on the board of directors for the Associated Press from 1957 to 1966.

Dunbar Cemetery

Highway 61 South

A state historical marker designates the site of a cemetery and the columns of a long-gone house. The cemetery is the burial site for William Dunbar (c. 1751–1810), one of Natchez's most distinguished figures. Originally from Scotland, he moved to Natchez in 1784 and became a leading cultural force in the area. He was a scientist, naturalist, scholar, legislator, and writer. He was elected to the American Philosophical Society under the sponsorship of Thomas Jefferson. His letters and papers were compiled and published by the Mississippi Historical Society as *Life, Letters and Papers of William Dunbar . . .* (1930). His home, The Forest, no longer exists. The columns still standing are all that is left of his widow's home, also called The Forest. Dunbar's descendants include writers Ellen Douglas and Brooks Haxton.

Leaving Natchez, take Highway 61 twelve miles south to White Apple Village Road. Turn right and then left on Old Lower Woodville Road. A gate on the left leads to Laurel Hill Plantation.

Laurel Hill Plantation

The Gothic chapel built on the grounds in 1836 by plantation owner Dr. W. Newton Mercer is alone worth the trip to Laurel Hill Plantation. *The Unhurried Years: Memories of the Old Natchez Region* (1948) and *Laurel Hill & Later: The Record of a Teacher* (1954), both by Pierce Butler (1873–1955), will further introduce the site.

Butler was born in New Orleans, grew up on this Mississippi River plantation, and returned here after a distinguished academic career. He received his early education from his extended family and a tutor, then graduated from Tulane University. He studied at the Sorbonne in 1894 and earned his Ph.D. from Johns Hopkins University. He first taught at the University of Texas, where he met his wife, Cora Waldo, but the major part of his career was spent at Tulane University, where he was a professor of history and English and the dean of Newcomb College. After he retired to Laurel Hill in 1938, he wrote his two books of history and memoirs.

Return to Highway 61 north. Go three miles to the town of Washington.

Washington

Washington seems to be the outskirts of Natchez as the businesses along Highway 61 flow into Natchez, but it was once a discrete and important village. The capital of the Mississippi Territory in 1802 and the place where Mississippi's first constitution was written in 1817, it was a refined and cultured town on its own. It has two sites of literary interest.

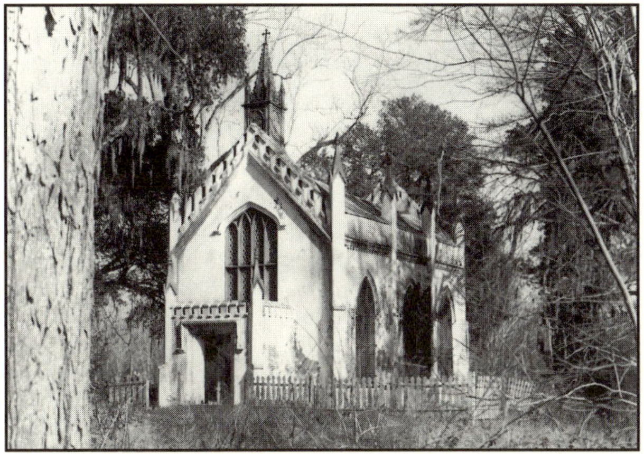

Chapel, Laurel Hill Plantation, Natchez

Meadvilla

One-half block off Highway 61

Benjamin Leonard Covington Wailes (1797–1862), a native of Georgia, moved to Washington when he was ten. He was educated at Jefferson College and worked as a surveyor and Indian agent before marrying into plantation society. He had wide intellectual interests and served as state geologist. He was on the board of trustees at Jefferson College and founded the Mississippi Historical Society. In addition to his 1854 report on the state's geology, he wrote a biography of Winthrop Sargent, unpublished, and *Memoir of Leonard Covington*, published in 1928.

Historic Jefferson College

Jefferson College, incorporated in 1802, was named in honor of President Thomas Jefferson. It was the first educational institution in the Mississippi Territory, an outpost of American civilization. It opened its doors in 1811 with fifteen students. By 1817, when Mississippi became a state, it was a full-fledged college and came to be a major influence on the intellectual and cultural development of the state. It has had many distinguished men associated with its history, including several writers.

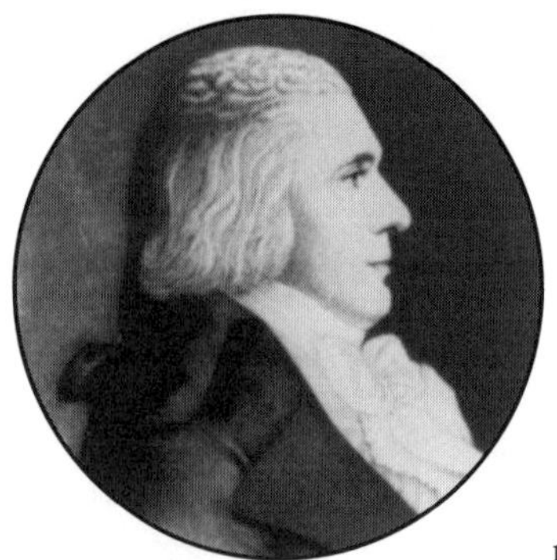

Joseph Holt Ingraham

The peripatetic writer Joseph Holt Ingraham (1809–1860) taught languages here. Born and raised in Maine and educated at Yale, he discovered and fell in love with Mississippi when he came south in 1830 to New Orleans and Natchez. He joined the faculty of Jefferson College that same year and married a young Natchez woman, Mary Elizabeth Odlin Brookes, in 1832. He has been called one of the most popular and prolific writers of his time and one of the most obscure in our time.

Ingraham began his amazing writing career with travel letters printed in the Natchez *Courier* beginning in 1833. These letters were collected and published as *The Southwest* by Harper and Brothers in 1835. They received acclaim and sold well. His first novel, *Lafitte: The Pirate of the Gulf* (1836), was a major commercial success. Ingraham wrote his best work during the next four years, publishing five books. In 1842 he began publishing paperback romances. He wrote over eighty of these popular novels. His output during the years 1842 to 1847 constituted nearly 10 percent of the novels printed in the United States in the 1840s. During the same five years he was also publishing stories, travel sketches, poems, and literary criticism in periodicals. No other novelist of the 1840s earned as much as he did, but he was always dogged with financial problems. He divided his time among Mississippi, Boston, New York, and Philadelphia to be near his publishers.

In 1847 he changed the direction of his life when he decided to go into the ministry. He moved to Nashville to study theology and taught there to support his family. Before he was ordained, his first official assignment was the missionary post of Aberdeen, a position that included charges in Okolona and Columbus as well. (See Aberdeen and Holly Springs regarding his later life.)

Joseph Holt Ingraham's son Prentiss Ingraham (1843–1904), an alumnus of Jefferson College, should be in the *Guinness Book of*

Records. He bested his father. In addition to his poems, short stories, and a dozen plays, Ingraham wrote six hundred novels and four hundred novelettes. The books were imitative, formulaic, and somewhat incoherent, but he was the preeminent writer of the popular "dime novels" of his day, the equivalent of contemporary television fare.

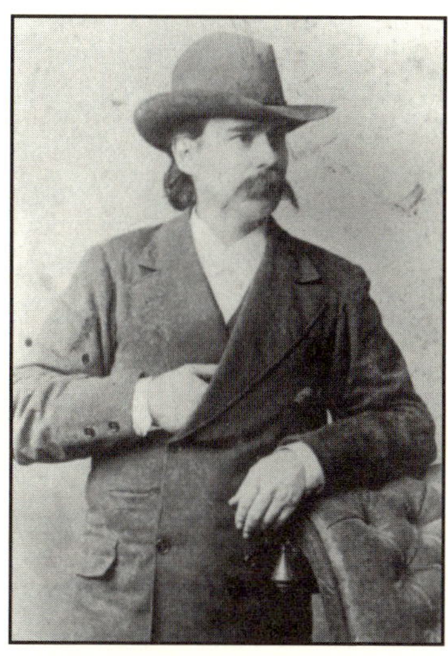
Prentiss Ingraham

Ingraham's work did, however, have one lasting effect on American consciousness. In over four hundred books about William "Buffalo Bill" Cody, he helped create the image of the American cowboy, influencing the way such men dressed, what arms they carried, and how they perceived themselves.

Prentiss Ingraham was born in Adams County at the home of his mother. After graduating from Jefferson College, he attended the Mobile Medical College, served as an officer in the Confederate army, and, after the war, became a soldier of fortune. He started his literary career in London in 1870 and wrote steadily for thirty-four years, living in New York City, Chicago, and Easton, Maryland. He died at Beauvoir, then a rest home for Confederate veterans. (See Biloxi for more on his career.)

Jeannette Ritchie Hadermann Walworth (1837–1918) grew up on the Jefferson College campus, where her father taught languages. She left home at age sixteen to be a governess in Louisiana, and after the Civil War moved to New Orleans to begin a career in journalism. Her first novels, *Forgiven at Last* (1870) and *Dead Men's Shoes* (1872), were published before she married Douglas Walworth of Natchez and moved with him to the Walworth plantation in Arkansas. The Walworths later lived in Memphis, where Walworth wrote for the *Commercial Appeal* as "Mother Goose," and then in New York where much of her work was serialized in magazines and newspapers. She wrote many of her novels in New

York, including *The Bar-Sinister* (1885), in which she intended to expose the evils of polygamy in Mormonism as *Uncle Tom's Cabin* had exposed the evils of slavery. In 1889, the Walworths moved back to Natchez, where Major Walworth became editor of the *Natchez Democrat.* Between then and 1914 when her husband died, Jeannette Walworth published seven novels while living in Natchez. They included *Uncle Scipio: A Story of Uncertain Days in the South* (1896) and *On the Winning Side* (1893), which was later reissued in the twentieth century as part of the Black Heritage Library Collection. She moved back to New Orleans, remarried, and kept writing. Over her fifty-year writing career, she published twenty-eight books.

Take Highway 61 north three miles to the Natchez Trace. Highway 552 West goes to the ghost town of Rodney, the setting for Eudora Welty's *The Robber Bridegroom.* Continue along the Trace and exit the Trace at Port Gibson.

Port Gibson

Since its beginning, Port Gibson has been a literary town. The first public library in Mississippi was chartered as the Mississippi Literary and Library Company of Gibson's Port in 1817. By the time of the Civil War, Port Gibson had taken its place as an important cultural center of the old Natchez territory. General Ulysses S. Grant reportedly spared the city, calling it "too beautiful to burn." It still has many of the stately churches and elegant homes that inspired his remark.

Irwin Russell House

411 Jackson Street

Irwin Russell (1853–1879), Mississippi's best-known poet in the nineteenth century, was born in this house, but not on this site. The house, now Leona's Beauty Shop, was moved here from the lot next to St. James Episcopal Church.

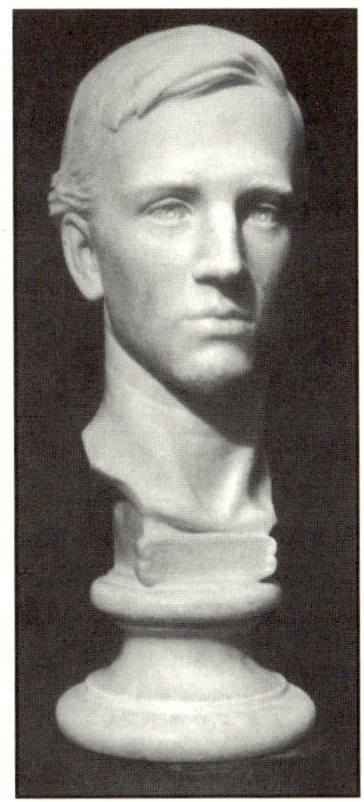

Irwin Russell

Russell was educated in the local schools and at the University of St. Louis in Missouri before returning home to read for the law. He practiced only a few years before he gave it up to be a professional writer. In Port Gibson he wrote a play, poetry, and an operetta in verse, *Christmas Night in the Quarters* (1878), before a yellow fever epidemic gave him reason to leave. He went to New York, where he briefly became a featured writer for *Scribner's Monthly.* He wrote chiefly Negro dialect poems, illustrated with his own line and silhouette drawings. Plagued by alcoholism, he soon left New York for New Orleans, where he worked for a few weeks at the *New Orleans Times.* He died of pneumonia at the age of twenty-six. A selection of his writings entitled *Poems* was published in 1888 with an introduction by Joel Chandler Harris. In 1917 an expanded version with his drawings was published as *Christmas Night in the Quarters and Other Poems.* His chief literary contribution was the treatment of the newly freed blacks as central characters in their own culture.

City Hall

1005 College Street

Constructed as the Port Gibson Female College, this building was once called the Irwin Russell Memorial. Irwin Russell's mother taught and was married in this building. Mementos of Russell's life and writings that were once housed here have been moved to the Grand Gulf Military Park museum. Another passing tribute by the city was a bridge across Bayou Pierre called the Irwin Russell Memorial Bridge.

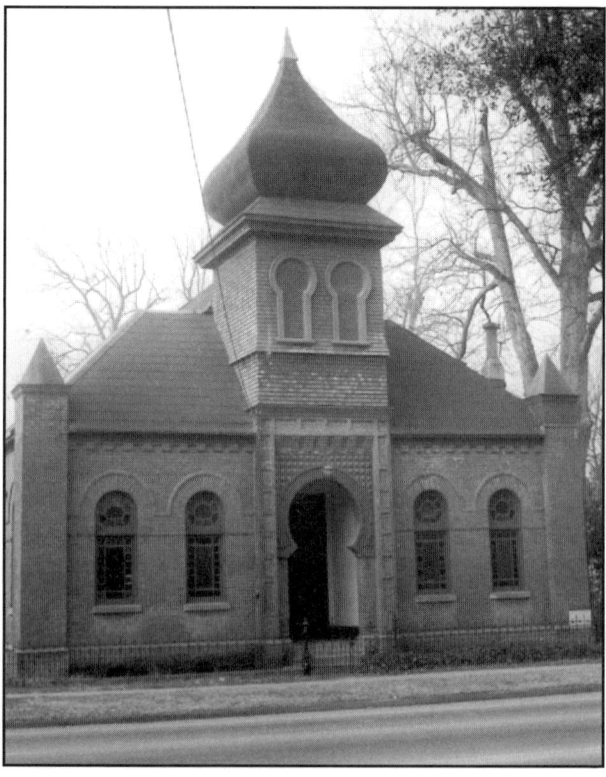

Temple Gemiluth Chassed, Port Gibson

Temple Gemiluth Chassed

704 Church Street

Port Gibson's Jewish families established a congregation in 1859 and held services in the Odd Fellows Hall until this synagogue was built in 1892. Among the twenty-two charter members were Samuel Ullman and his parents, who had arrived in Port Gibson in 1851. Samuel Ullman (1840–1922) was born in Bavaria and by age twenty-one was enlisted in the Confederate States Army. His poem "Youth," written during his service as a private in the Mississippi Infantry but not published until 1935, was made famous by General Douglas MacArthur and became widely read and admired in Japan.

Ullman moved to Birmingham in 1884 and had a distinguished career as a prominent merchant and civic leader. He was a member of Birmingham's board of education and had a high school named in his honor in 1901. At his retirement, he returned to writing poetry, and published *From a Summit of Years—Four Score* (1922).

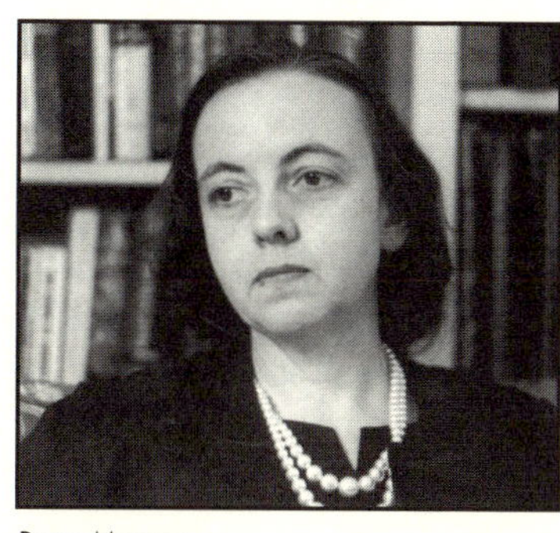
Berry Morgan

907 Church Street

Henry Hughes (1829–1862) was born and raised in this house and attended nearby Oakland College. Although not a writer of literature, he is notable as one of the first persons to use the term "sociology" in a title. His *Treatise on Sociology*, a proslavery argument, was published in 1854.

From U.S. 61 just south of town, go west on Old Colony Road for 1 1/2 miles to the Albena Plantation house on the right.

Albena Plantation House

3064 Old Colony Road

Berry Morgan (1919), a writer once called by Walker Percy "the most exciting novelist to come out of the South since Flannery O'Connor," did most of her adult writing in this house. She was born Betty Berry Taylor Brumfield at her grandparents' place, Hillcrest Plantation, near here. She worked as a secretary, realtor, and freelance editor before her first novel, *Pursuit*, was published in 1966. With it she won a Houghton Mifflin Literary Fellowship Award, which propelled her to write a second novel, *The Mystic Adventures of Roxie Stoner* (1974).

Morgan's evocation of Mississippi landscape and manner is flawless. Like Faulkner she creates a fictional world that closely resembles the real one. Port Gibson becomes King's Town. Morgan's short stories have appeared frequently in *The New Yorker*. She now lives in West Virginia and continues to write and publish stories.

Rosa Vertner Griffith (1828–1894) was raised by her aunt, Rosa Vertner, outside Port Gibson on Burlington Plantation, which no

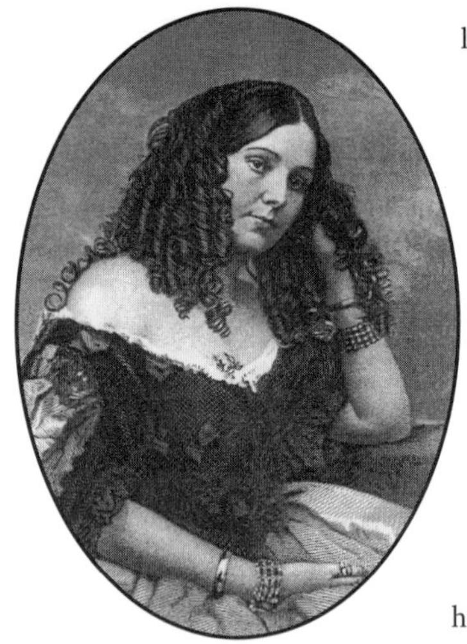
Rosa Vertner Johnson

longer exists. Born in Natchez, Rosa was adopted at the age of nine months by her aunt after Rosa's mother died. Rosa Griffith's poem "My Childhood Home" expressed her fondness for Burlington. When Rosa was ten the Vertners moved to Lexington, Kentucky, for her education, and Rosa spent most of the rest of her life there. She married first Claude M. Johnson of Lexington and had six children. After his death she married Alexander Jeffrey and had three more children. Under the names Rosa Vertner Jeffrey and Rosa Vertner Johnson, she published three volumes of poetry and two novels, *Marah* (1884) and *Woodburn* (1864).

From Port Gibson take Highway 18 seven miles east to Hermanville.

Hermanville

Hermanville is of interest as the subject of photographs by Eudora Welty and as the birthplace of one of the most intriguing writers to come out of Mississippi.

Maxwell Bodenheim (1892–1954) is remembered by some as the panhandler in Greenwich Village who, with his wife, was brutally murdered by a drifter in New York City. He was, however, at one time a luminary of American letters.

Bodenheim was born in Hermanville, which had been founded by his grandfather Herman whose daughter married Solomon Bodenheimer. Not successful as a merchant in Hermanville, Bodenheimer moved his family to Chicago when Maxwell was a child. Young Max was dismissed from high school, returned to the South, and worked in cotton fields. By the time he was twenty-two he was back in Chicago publishing his verse in prestigious publications under the shorter name of Bodenheim. During the next decade of his life, he was an active participant in Chicago's literary renaissance. He traveled the country and knew Edward Arlington Robinson, Eugene O'Neill, T. S. Eliot, and other leading writers of the post–World War I era. With Ben Hecht he founded and was associate editor of the *Literary Times*, an avant-garde newspaper in Chicago. The *New York Times* called Hecht and Bodenheim the Goths and Vandals of contemporary letters. After the demise of *Literary Times*, Bodenheim turned to creative writing as a way to make a living. He wrote stringent and respected critical reviews, poetry, and novels, but he seemed never to find financial stability. He was considered a Lothario with many women admirers, and his novel *Replenishing Jessica* (1925) garnered him a court appearance for pornography. Between 1918 and 1946 he published ten volumes of imagist poetry, highly respected, and a dozen novels. He died a pauper and a vagrant, unable to take care of himself or his third wife. At the time of his death his reputation as a serious writer was superceded by his reputation as a derelict who wrote poems to sell to Greenwich Village tourists and who begged for money with an "I am blind" sign.

Return to the Trace and continue north to Clinton. The Trace passes Rocky Springs, the site of Nevada Barr's mystery *Deep South*.

Clinton

Clinton is the birthplace of one of Mississippi's most distinguished poets, Sterling Plumpp, and of the novelist/story writer/poet Robert Canzoneri. It is the boyhood home of Barry Hannah, the one-time home of novelist Jack Butler and of romance writer Terri Herrington, and the current home of best-selling mystery writer Nevada Barr.

715 Oakwood Drive

Barry Hannah (1942) spent his boyhood in this house. Hannah was born in a Meridian hospital when his family lived in For-

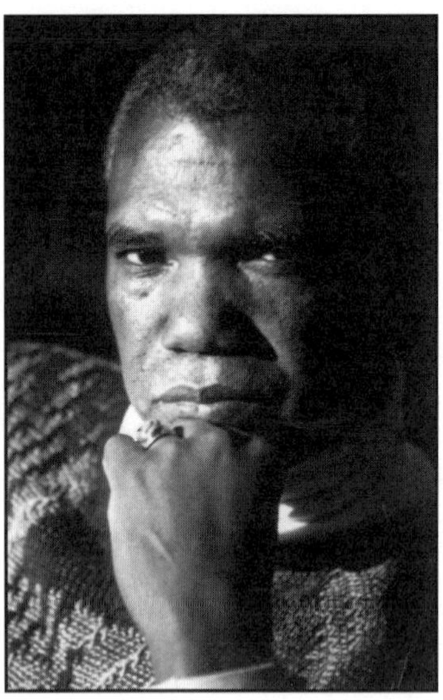
Sterling Plumpp

est; they moved to Pascagoula and then to Clinton, where he grew up and graduated from high school. He received his B.A. from Mississippi College and M.F.A. from the University of Arkansas. His first published novel, *Geronimo Rex* (1972), won the William Faulkner Prize and was nominated for the National Book Award. Since that time his work has been enthusiastically reviewed and marveled at by his peers. Cynthia Ozick wrote, "He takes fiction by surprise—scenes, shocks, sounds, and amazements: an explosive but meticulous originality." (See Oxford for additional biography.)

Holy Ghost Church

Convent Street and Cloister Street

Sterling Plumpp (1940) was born on a plantation out from Clinton and grew up in Jackson and Clinton. He finished high school at the Holy Ghost High School, which is now the community center here, and was baptized in the Holy Ghost Church in 1956. After he earned his B.A. from Roosevelt University, he was assistant professor in the black studies program at the University of Illinois. He is now a professor of creative writing at the University of Illinois. His books of poetry include *Portable Soul* (1969), *Half Black, Half Blacker* (1970), *Steps to Break the Circle* (1974), *Clinton* (1976), and *The Mojo Hands Call, I Must Go* (1982), which won the Carl Sandburg Literary Award for Poetry. His work is a strong evocation of the pain and joy of being black and southern.

Robert Canzoneri (1925) was born in Texas and grew up in Clinton, the son of a Sicilian Baptist minister and a Mississippi

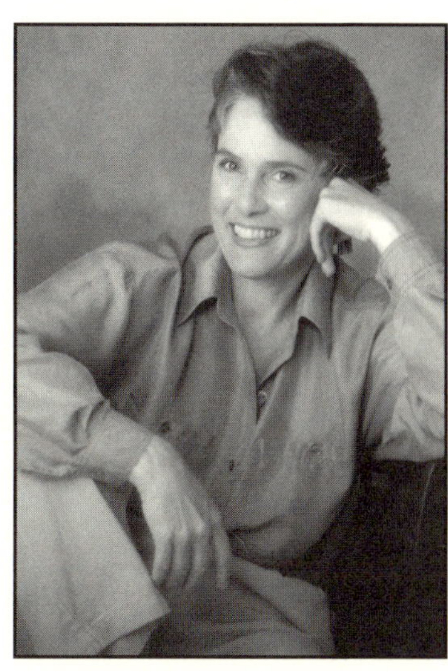
Nevada Barr

mother. After a stint in the navy during World War II, he returned home and earned a B.A. at Mississippi College and an M.A. at Ole Miss. He taught at several high schools and colleges before he returned to school and received his Ph.D. from Stanford University. In 1965 he settled in at Ohio State University, where he directed the creative writing program until his retirement. He received the Henry H. Bellamann Award in 1965.

Canzoneri drew heavily on his Mississippi background, and his published works include a civil rights memoir, *"I Do So Politely": A Voice from the South* (1965), a book of poetry, *Watch Us Pass* (1968), a comic novel, *Men with Little Hammers* (1969), a collection of short stories, *Barbed Wire and Other Stories* (1970), and his poignant autobiography, *A Highly Ramified Tree* (1976).

603 Merganser Trace

Nevada Barr (1952) arrived late on the scene in Clinton, a transplanted westerner, but she and the community have embraced one another warmly. Born in Nevada and raised in California, she is the successful writer of a series of mystery novels in which sleuth Anna Pigeon is on the case. Barr earned her graduate degree in acting at the University of California and began a successful career as an actress in New York. She published her first novel in 1984, but twisting circumstances took her in a new direction. She became a park ranger and began to write mystery novels with a common thread: each one is set in a national park. Her first mystery, *Track of the Cat* (1993), brought her the highest awards in mysterydom: the Agatha Award and the Anthony Award. Her settings are parks where Barr has worked or done extensive research. She moved to Mississippi and married a fellow ranger in the Natchez Trace National Park, where *Deep South* (2000) was set. Her book *Blood Lure* (2001) is set in Glacier National Park.

Mississippi College

200 West College Street

Mississippi College, the state's largest antebellum institution of higher education, was established in Clinton in 1826. It became a Baptist institution in 1850 and is still sponsored by the Baptist Church. Among the literary alumni are Barry Hannah, Robert Canzoneri, and Louis Dollarhide, who for many years was a book and arts critic for the *Jackson Daily News*.

Nearby Raymond is the birthplace of Muna Lee (1895–1965). Muna Lee's early interest in poetry shaped her life. She wrote most of her poems from 1912 to 1930, publishing a collection called *Sea-Change* in 1923. In 1919 she married Luis Muñoz Marin, poet, journalist, and future governor of Puerto Rico. She began translating Spanish poetry for the American magazine *Poetry*, and during her lifetime translated over twenty Spanish poets into English. In an abrupt turn in the 1930s, she coauthored with Maurice Guiness five murder mysteries under the pen name Newton Gayle. Her life and writing took a final turn when she entered politics, working for women's equal rights. She was one of the first women to address the Pan-American Conference and helped establish the Inter-American Commission of Women. In 1941 she moved to Washington as a cultural affairs specialist. She continued her translations of Spanish poems, wrote a children's book, and did all of the research for *The American Story*, radio programs presented by Archibald MacLeish, who was Librarian of Congress. She later became a foreign affairs officer, a job which she held until two months before her death.

To continue the Natchez Trace tour, bypass Jackson to Natchez Trace north. Leave Clinton on I-20 east to I-220. Take I-220 north to I-55 north. Immediately after turning onto I-55, look for the Natchez Trace exit and resume travel north on the Trace. At Kosciusko, take the exit at the Kosciusko Museum and Information Center.

Kosciusko

Kosciusko is best known as the birthplace of two national figures, Oprah Winfrey and James Meredith. It can also claim poets Jack Fenwick and Joyce Hollingsworth-Barkley, biographer Preston Hughes, and an important literary educator, Blanche Colton Williams.

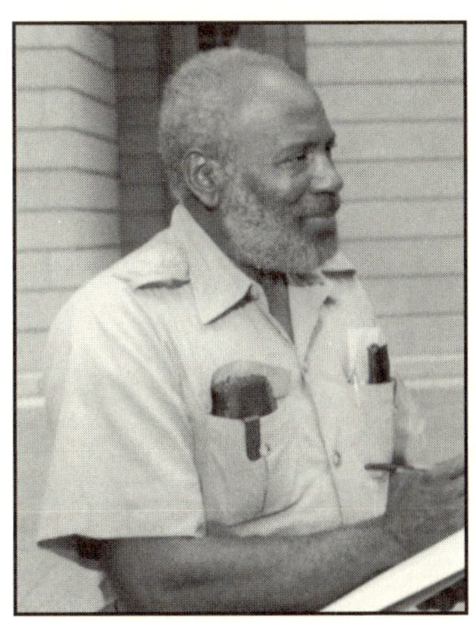
James Meredith

Beale Street

James Meredith (1933) played a major and courageous role in bringing about the demise of legal segregation in Mississippi. His attempt to enter the University of Mississippi, which was all white at the time, precipitated a riot on the campus, but he persevered, enrolling and earning his B.A degree in 1963. Continuing his commitment to the civil rights movement, he staged a walk from Memphis to Jackson in 1966. On the second day he was shot on Highway 51. His account of the Ole Miss period is the subject of his autobiographical *Three Years in Mississippi* (1966). Meredith graduated from Columbia Law School in 1968 and returned to Mississippi in 1971. He has made extensive trips to Africa to promote trade and teach conservation and tree farming to Africans. He now lives in Jackson.

In *Three Years in Mississippi*, Meredith describes Kosciusko and the house where he was born four miles from town on the eighty-four-acre farm of his father, Moses Meredith, the first member of his family ever to own a piece of land. He wrote, "The greatest intangible that the house had to offer was pride. The second was order. If these are taken away, only poverty is left." Meredith bought the farmhouse from his father in 1960 so that his father could build a house in town.

Take Highway 12 east toward the Trace. Turn left on Oprah Winfrey Road, formerly Buffalo Road.

Oprah Winfrey Road

The road renamed to honor Oprah Winfrey passes Buffalo Community Center, which was her first church, then passes her family cemetery and the site of her birthplace.

Oprah Gail Winfrey was born here in 1954. She was named for a biblical character, Orpah, but the name was misspelled and turned into "Oprah." Having endured a childhood filled with sorrow and difficulty, she has become one of the most influential woman in contemporary culture. She produces and hosts the syndicated television program *The Oprah Winfrey Show*, publishes and edits the magazine *O*, and is active in such areas as education, social awareness, and health. She is an acclaimed actress, producer, and writer, and she is a lover of books. Oprah's Book Club, an on-air reading club which she started in 1996, is a national phenomenon, creating overnight best sellers. "I want to get the whole country excited about reading," she said.

Her rise to fame started when she competed in 1971 in the Miss Black America pageant. In 1973 she became the first black and first woman hired to anchor television news in Nashville. From there she moved to Baltimore to cohost *People Are Talking*, and in 1986 she began *The Oprah Winfrey Show*. That same year she was nominated for an Oscar for her performance in *The Color Purple*. In 1998, she produced and starred in the film version of Toni Morrison's *Beloved*.

Winfrey is the subject of a number of biographies, and her own words have been published in *Oprah Winfrey Speaks: Insights from the World's Most Influential Voice* (1997) and *The Uncommon Wisdom of Oprah Winfrey: A Portrait in Her Own Words* (1999).

Winfrey's philanthropy and interests have continued to expand, and today she is one of the most admired and recognized figures in America. Since 1988, January 29 has been Oprah Winfrey Day in Kosciusko.

Fame came to Blanche Colton Williams (1879–1944) from teaching other people how to write stories rather than from writing them herself. After attending Kosciusko High School and Mississippi University for Women, she went to Columbia University for her M.A. and Ph.D. degrees and remained there to teach. In 1926 she became chair of the English department of Hunter College, a division of Columbia, and taught there until her retirement in 1939. She wrote the first practical guide to creative writing, *Handbook on Story Writing* (1917) and over the years published many more books on the techniques of writing and understanding literature. She served as chair of the O. Henry Memorial Award Committee from 1919 to 1932 and worked with the annual publication of the *O. Henry Memorial Prize Short Stories*, which were edited in the 1940s by another Mississippian, Herschel Brickell (see Yazoo City).

Follow Highway 12 east to rejoin the Trace. Continue up the Trace for about thirty miles and take Highway 9 to Eupora.

Eupora

James Robert Peery House

207 Gold Street

James Robert Peery (1900–1954) had two best-selling novels just before World War II, *Stark Summer* and *God Rides a Gale.* Both novels were set in Mississippi in the thirties.

He grew up in this house, and lived in Eupora until after the war, when he moved to Jackson to be news editor of WJDX and Jackson bureau chief of United Press.

To rejoin the Trace take Highway 82 east out of Eupora and continue to Tupelo.

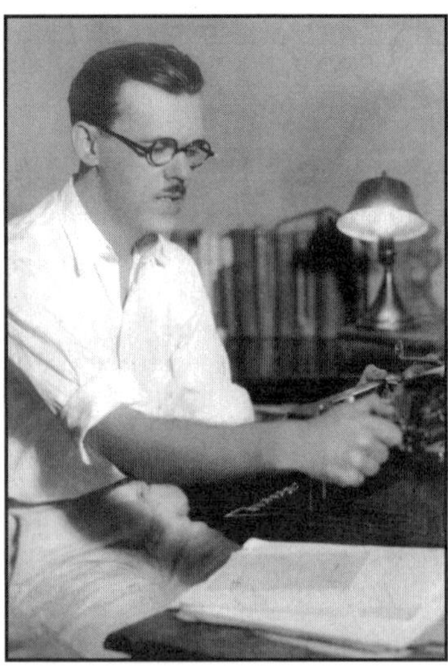
James Robert Peery

Tupelo

Tupelo, a vibrant and prosperous city, is nestled in the wooded hills and valleys where Chickasaw Indians once lived. Positioned on the Natchez Trace, it was familiar to settlers long before its incorporation in 1870. Its colorful history early and late is chronicled by Phyllis Harper in her *Tupelo Daily Journal* column. Writers have thrived here. It is the hometown of fiction writer Kenneth Holditch, mystery writer John Armistead, prolific romance novelist Peggy Webb, and poets Samuel Prestridge and Sue C. Spigner. Novelist Dorothy Shawhan was born in nearby Verona and grew up here. (See Cleveland for her biography.)

Clayton Home

425 North Church Street

This site is associated with two writers, a memoirist and a poet, father and granddaughter. The house was the childhood home of Erin Clayton Pitner, whose book of poetry *Stones and Roses* was published in 1993. A sense of place in the natural world of north Mississippi is evoked in her verse. Her grandfather, Washington Lafayette Clayton (1836–1921), was a journalist and local historian. He lived in the original house on this site. His memoir, *Olden Times Revisited: W. L. Clayton's Pen Pictures*, was published in 1982 by his great-granddaughter.

Pegues Funeral Home Parking Lot

543 Jefferson Street

This site has been unlucky for houses. The first one here was destroyed by fire and the second by tornado; the third was razed to make a parking lot. But it was the family homeplace for three generations of writers. The matriarch of the family, Mrs. C. P. Long, was a prolific though unpublished writer of novels; her daughter Olivia Long Napoli wrote *Grit, Greed and Guts* (1980), a memoir about Tupelo. It was a member of the third generation, however, who achieved success, as a writer of crime fiction. Genevieve Long Pou (1919), granddaughter of Mrs. C. P. Long and niece of Olivia Napoli, wrote six books in the Doubleday Crime Club series (1953–1961) under the name Genevieve Holden. Pou graduated from Tupelo High School, attended the University of Mississippi, and graduated from the University of Georgia School of Journalism in 1941. Her first novel was *Killer Loose* (1953).

Elvis Presley Birthplace

While not the home of a writer, this house figures in countless biographies of Elvis Presley. Presley is also the subject of numerous plays, films, songs, and poems.

Tupelo marks the end of the Natchez Trace tour. From here the Trace cuts across a corner of Alabama and continues to Nashville, Tennessee.

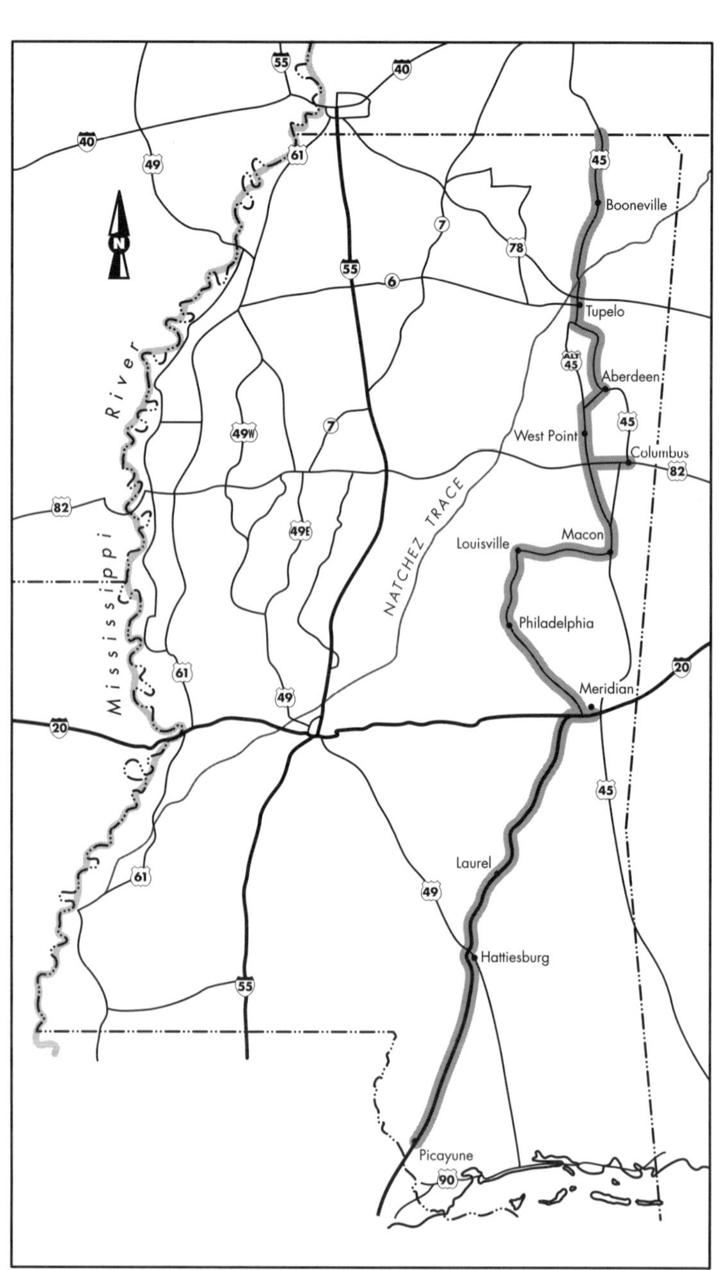

55
40
40
61
49
45
Booneville
7
78
55
6
Tupelo
ALT 45
Aberdeen
49W
7
West Point
45
Columbus
82
82
49E
NATCHEZ TRACE
Louisville
Macon
Mississippi River
Philadelphia
61
20
Meridian
49
20
45
Laurel
61
49
Hattiesburg
55
Picayune
90

East and South Mississippi Tour

This tour begins in Corinth, in the foothills of Appalachia, passes through the Black Prairie, one of the state's richest agricultural areas, to the Piney Woods, once a place of great virgin forests and still heavily wooded with second growth, and then goes southwest to Picayune, home of the Crosby Arboretum, a regional nature center. The tour generally follows Highway 45 south to Booneville, Tupelo, Aberdeen, West Point, Columbus, Macon (with a side trip to Louisville and Philadelphia), then to Meridian and Laurel on Highway 59. From there the tour cuts down Highway 59, a diagonal, to Hattiesburg, and ends in Picayune.

Corinth

Corinth, with its beautiful Grecian name, was once proudly called Cross City because it marked the junction of two railroads, the new technology that would assure its future. It prospered and was renamed in 1855 for the great crossroads city of Greece.

The same railroad tracks that brought prosperity became a liability less than a decade later when opposing armies focused on

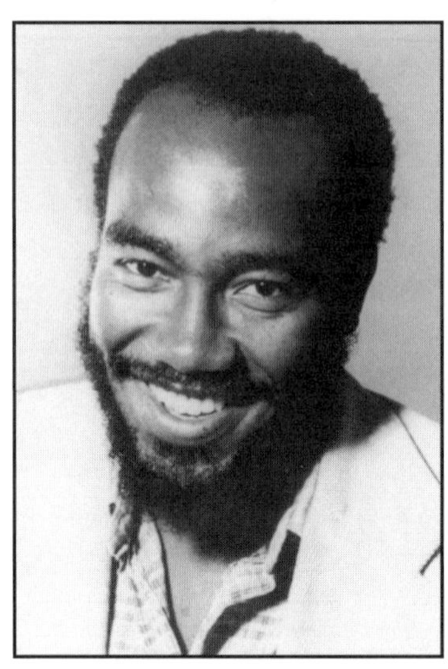
Etheridge Knight

them. The Civil War's Battle of Shiloh, Siege of Corinth, and Battle of Corinth were all fought to control the transportation lines that ran through the town.

Today Corinth is a city of poets. Henry Dalton, Jonathan Brooks, and Etheridge Knight are the bearers of this claim. It is also the childhood home of novelist Frances Gaither and the virtual hometown of Thomas Hal Phillips, who is from nearby Kossuth.

Poet Etheridge Knight (1931–1991) was born in Corinth and grew up in Mississippi and Paducah, Kentucky. Knight dropped out of school in the eighth grade and eventually joined the army. His first book was published while he was incarcerated in the Indiana state prison for robbery to support a drug habit. In an interview, he explained why he wrote poetry: "I died in Korea from a shrapnel wound and narcotics resurrected me. I died in 1960 from a prison sentence and poetry brought me back to life."

His hard-hitting, idiosyncratic verse is an urban voice, but such poems as "The Idea of Ancestry" and "The Bones of My Father" strongly reflect his Mississippi background. His poetry has been published in four books, *Poems from Prison* (1968), *Belly Song and Other Poems* (1973), *Born of a Woman: New and Selected Poems* (1980), and *The Essential Etheridge Knight* (1986). Knight was awarded fellowships by the Guggenheim Foundation and the National Endowment for the Arts and in 1985 was recognized by the Poetry Society of America for distinguished achievement in poetry. He was also a novelist, a short story writer, and a popular lecturer on the college circuit.

615 Second Street

Frances Jones Gaither (1889–1955) moved with her family to Corinth from Tennessee when she was a small child and was raised here. After she graduated from Mississippi University for Women in 1909, she married Rice Gaither, a newspaperman. They moved to New York, where he worked for the *New York Times* for many years.

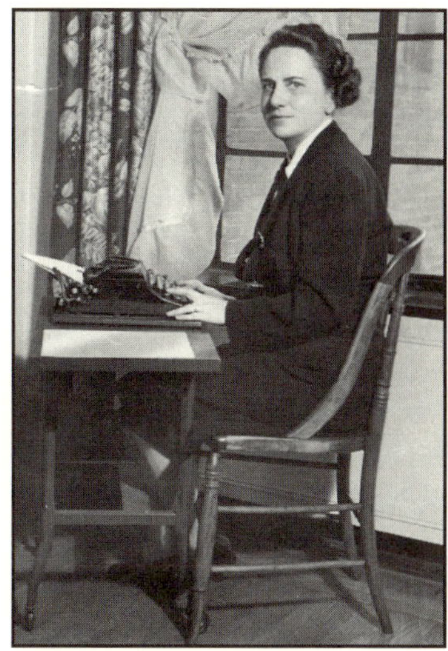
Frances Jones Gaither

Frances Gaither maintained interest in southern history and explored in three novels the institution of slavery: *Double Muscadine* (1949), *The Red Cock Crows* (1944), and *Follow the Drinking Gourd* (1940). She also produced three children's novels, all dealing with various aspects of southern history. In addition she wrote short stories, pageants, and a biography of La Salle. Gaither received national attention when *Double Muscadine* was selected for the Book-of-the-Month Club in 1949.

2001 Maple Road

This was the home of poet and musician Henry Dalton (1909–1999) and his wife from 1950 until his death. Dalton was born in Rienzi and graduated from Union University in Jackson, Tennessee, in 1930. He did graduate work at the University of Alabama and the University of Virginia after serving in World War II. He taught high school English and math for several years before he joined the U. S. Postal Department in Corinth, where he worked until 1969.

Dalton was a mentor to novelist Thomas Hal Phillips and to poet Jonathan Brooks. His books of poetry, *Hill Born* (1954) and *Process of Becoming* (1977), strongly evoke the hills and the country people of northeast Mississippi.

1520 East 5th Street

Poet Jonathan Brooks (1905–1945) wrote his gentle poetry in this house. He was born in Holmes County, the son of share-

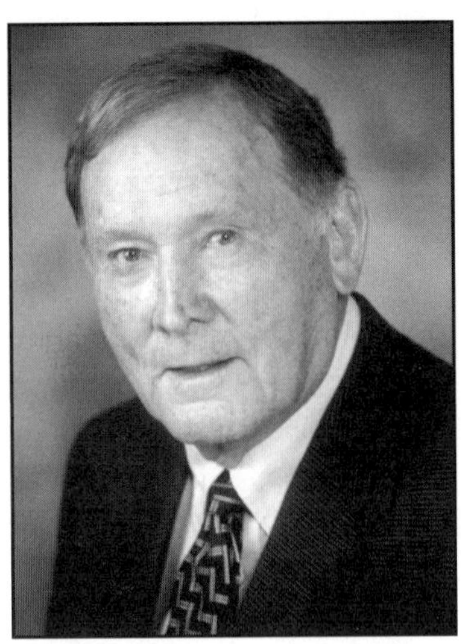

Thomas Hal Phillips

croppers. His mother arranged for him to attend high school in Missouri. He graduated from Tougaloo College and immediately took a job there as assistant to the president. After his marriage in 1933, he moved to Corinth and built this house in 1938. His wife taught school while he, an ordained Baptist minister, served as assistant pastor at St. Marks Missionary Baptist Church.

Brooks's poems, which are distinguished by poignant imagery and mysticism, appeared in several journals of the period. He mused on race relations, nature, and faith. Langston Hughes said, "Jonathan Brooks wrote the most beautiful poem I know to have come out of World War II in the English language—the poem 'She Said.' Had he lived, I think he would have been one of our major poets."

Brooks died of a heart attack at the age of forty. *Resurrection and Other Poems* was published three years after his death.

Novelist Thomas Hal Phillips (1922) was born on a farm about five miles west of Corinth, near Kossuth, and now lives in Corinth. He went to public schools in Kossuth and attended Hinds Junior College. After he received his B.S. degree from Mississippi State University, he joined the United States Navy. When World War II was over he enrolled in creative writing courses at the University of Alabama and earned a master's degree. His first novel, *The Bitterweed Path* (1950), was his master's thesis. Phillips taught at Southern Methodist University, spent a year in France on a Fulbright Fellowship, and returned home to be a full-time writer. When movie rights were purchased for his fifth novel, *The Loved and the Unloved* (1955), he moved to Hollywood and became a successful screenwriter. He divided his time between California and Corinth, where he lived for over a quarter of a century at the Phillips Brothers Truck Stop on Highway 72, which he and his brother had opened in 1960. In Hollywood he worked with director Robert Altman, writing scripts for *Nashville, California Split, Buffalo Bill and the Indians,* and *Thieves Like Us.* His other work in film included scripts for *Ode to Billie Joe, Roll of Thunder, Hear My Cry, Huckleberry Finn* and several Tarzan movies.

Phillips has received many awards, including the O. Henry Prize Award, a Julius Rosenwald Fellowship, two Guggenheim Fellowships, and a Saxton Memorial Award. He succeeded his brother as the northern representative on the Mississippi Public Service Commission in 1960 and served until 1963 when he resigned to manage his brother's unsuccessful gubernatorial bid.

Phillips's novel *Kangaroo Hollow* was first published in 1954 and reprinted by the University Press of Mississippi in 2000. Like his other acclaimed novels, it is set in northeast Mississippi, his neck of the woods, his Yoknapatawpha County. His novel *Red Midnight* was published in 2002, also by University Press of Mississippi.

From Corinth take Highway 45 south toward Booneville.

Booneville

This is the hometown of the poet and Faulkner scholar Robert W. Hamblin (1938) and of the famous wit George E. Allen.

George E. Allen Library

Highway 145

George E. Allen (1896–1973) wrote his memoir *Presidents Who Have Known Me* (1950) about his longtime involvement in Washington politics. Allen was born and raised in Booneville. After earning his law degree from Cumberland University, he practiced law briefly in Okolona, then moved to Chicago where he became a hotel executive, a partner in some twenty hotels, and a millionaire at the age of twenty-nine. At his death he was on the board of directors of more than thirty major corporations.

Mississippi's senator Pat Harrison, a friend, introduced Allen to Franklin Delano Roosevelt, who appointed him commissioner of Washington, D.C., in 1933. He subsequently served in

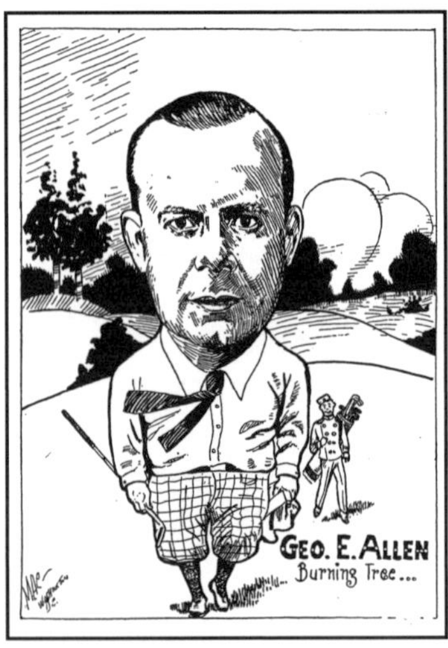

George E. Allen

high-ranking posts under Harry S. Truman and Dwight D. Eisenhower, whose friendship during World War II caused Allen to jump from the Democratic Party to the Republican Party. Allen requested that he be buried in Booneville, and he left the city a bequest for a new library, which was named in his honor and dedicated in 1976.

Continue south on Highway 45 toward Tupelo.

Baldwyn

Although he was born in Shannon, below Tupelo, Louis Cochran (1899–1974) grew up in Baldwyn. The community provided a quiet childhood, in strong contrast to Cochran's later multifaceted career as teacher, school superintendent, journalist, attorney, and FBI agent.

Louis Cochran began his writing career with a fanciful children's book, *The Lowly Gnome and Other Stories*, and quickly moved to novels based on his intimate knowledge of the people, events, and characteristics of Mississippi, including *Black Earth* (1937), *Boss Man* (1939), and *Row's End* (1954). Both *Flood Tides* (1931) and *Hallelujah, Mississippi* (1955) had autobiographical elements. He published seven novels between 1931 and 1963, but his most popular book was his autobiography, *FBI Man: A Personal History* (1964), reissued in London in 1965. He died in Nashville, Tennessee, where he had spent the final ten years of his life.

Baldwyn is also the birthplace and hometown of Claude Gentry, history and nature writer, novelist, and biographer. Gentry's occupations would fill a small notebook. A man for all seasons, he called himself "a tenth-grade dropout," but the range of his interests was extraordinary. An insurance businessman, he established and wrote for the *Baldwyn News* from 1939 to 1947, was on the staff of *Deep South*, a Mississippi magazine, and published monographs on religion and Civil War history in addition to his books and articles. He was considered an authority on the Civil War. He established the Brice's Cross Roads Museum and worked on the film *Shiloh: A Portrait of a Battle.* In the tradition of the dime novels of the nineteenth century, he published a series called the Freedom Hills novelettes. His twenty-seven books were all self-published under the name Magnolia Publishers. His last book, *Four Score and More in Dixie*, was an autobiography.

Baldwyn is also the home of memoirist Aileen Richs Hoover. Nearby Itawamba County is the home turf of poet Elmo Howell, a graduate of Ole Miss and the University of Florida and a member of the faculty of Memphis State University from 1957 to 1983. He has written three historic travel guides to Mississippi and six books of poetry including *Winter Verses* (1989) and *Mt. Pleasant* (2001).

Tupelo

For Tupelo's literary sites, see the Natchez Trace Tour.

From Tupelo take Highway 45 south. At Shannon, take Highway 45 toward Aberdeen.

Okolona

This small town was the birthplace of William Raspberry (1935), syndicated newspaper columnist and author of *Looking Back at Us* (1991), the home of James Gordon (1833–1912), politician, planter, and writer (see Pontotoc), and the one-time home of Charles Wilson, mystery writer.

At Okolona rejoin Highway 45 to Aberdeen. Highway 45, which becomes Commerce Street inside the city limits of Aberdeen, passes handsome houses with spacious lawns leading to a Magnolia-lined boulevard and a prosperous downtown.

Aberdeen

Aberdeen literally owes its being to the Tombigbee River. Its founder, Robert Gordon, admired the terrain on a trip down the river, and, when he was given his choice of Chickasaw land after the Treaty of Pontotoc, he picked this spot and set up a trading post. He founded the town in 1832 and named it for his home in Scotland. The river made Aberdeen a busy shipping port and brought prosperity. Called the "Queen City of the Tombigbee," it was the second-largest city in Mississippi during the decade before the Civil War. Aberdeen has excellent examples of almost every period and style of southern architecture. It has historically been a seat of culture in the area, home to nineteenth-century writers Mary Louise Sims, Edward Goodwin, Mary Halbert Davis, and Reuben Davis and twentieth-century writers William A. Evans, Augustus Frey Hamilton, Charles Granville Hamilton, Frank Trippett, and poet Patsy Clark Pace.

Sunset Hill

803 West Commerce Avenue

A Mississippi Historical Society marker calls attention to a large 1847 Greek Revival house as you enter town. Reuben Davis (1813–1890) came to Aberdeen from Alabama in 1832 to practice law. He had an honored career in Mississippi: he was a colonel in the war with Mexico, a state legislator, a United States Congressman, a brigadier general in the Confederate army, and a Mississippi representative to the Confederate Congress in Richmond. His first wife, Mary Halbert, wrote poetry under the name "Hinda." She died at the outbreak of the Civil War. After the war Davis remarried and moved into this 1847 Greek Revival house and with his second wife raised his family here.

Davis wrote *Recollections of Mississippi and Mississippians* in his old age, a reminiscence composed with gusto and insight. It was published in 1889, a year before his death. His grand-nephew, Reuben G. Davis, was a novelist in the Mississippi Delta.

St. John's Episcopal Church

Commerce Avenue

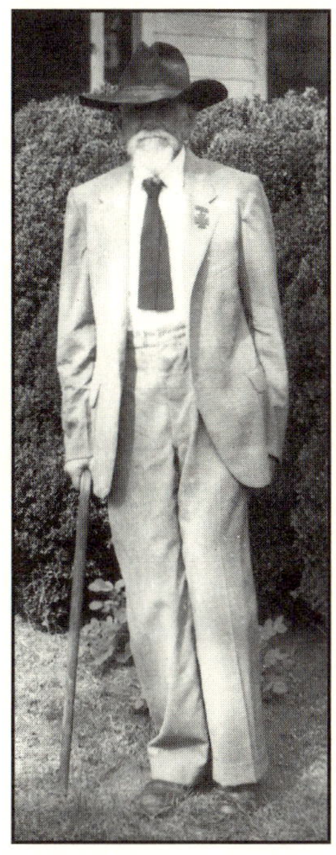

Reuben Davis

This church was built by writer/clergyman Joseph Holt Ingraham (1809–1860). He came to Aberdeen in 1851 to take charge of St. John's Mission, his first assignment leading to his ordination to the priesthood. While in Aberdeen, he also had charges in Okolona and Columbus and organized a new parish in Pontotoc. In his two years in Aberdeen he began a campaign to build a church, which he designed and constructed "with the aid of two young men and nine slaves." After his ordination Ingraham was sent to Mobile in 1853. (See Natchez for information about his early life and Holly Springs regarding his later life.) A subsequent rector at St. John's, Charles G. Hamilton, was also a writer (see below).

Gregg-Hamilton House

410 South Meridian Street

This was the home of Charles Granville Hamilton (1905–1984), who came to Aberdeen as rector of St. John's Episcopal Church in 1931 and served there until 1942. He married Mary Elizabeth Casey in 1939, and they bought this antebellum house in 1971. A fine example of a planter's cottage, it is designated a Mississippi Landmark and is on the National Register of Historic Places.

In his rich life Hamilton was a minister, teacher, writer, poet, historian, state legislator, and political activist. Although he was

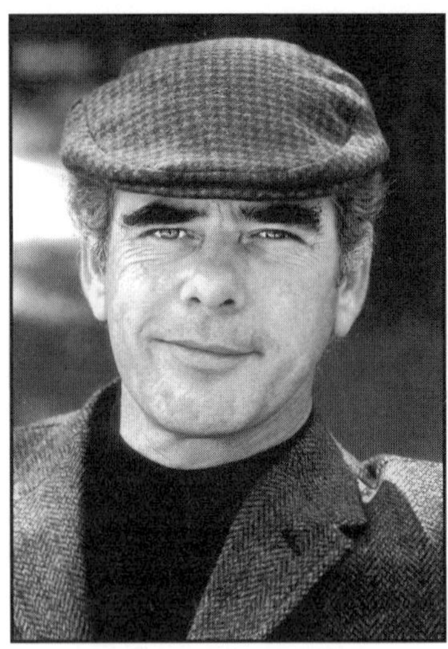
Frank Trippett

a native of Pennsylvania and grew up in Kentucky, Hamilton's poetry sings of Mississippi. He captures fine details in lines such as "a family so honest they never were put on the jury" and "farming around slot machines and cocacolas, minds consecrated to the status quo." His poem "The Flag Was Flame" is a Civil War epic which he worked on for over two decades. He wrote a poem for the centennial of Aberdeen, "where the Bible is honored and the *Commercial Appeal* is read." He also published historical and religious writings, and in 1939 compiled *Lyric Monroe*, an anthology of poems about Monroe County.

Leftwich House

503 S. Franklin Street

Born in Columbus, Frank Trippett (1926–1998) was raised in the flamboyant 1883 house of his grandmother, Mrs. George Leftwich, on a street still referred to as Silk Stocking Row. Called "Trip," he graduated in 1944 from Aberdeen High School, where he first exhibited a wide range of interests in music, boxing, and writing. He served in the navy air corps in World War II.

His broad interests were reflected in his college career; he attended Mississippi College, Duke University, the University of Mississippi, Vandercook College of Music, and the State University of New York. He chose journalism as his field and excelled as a reporter and essayist. His first job was with the Meridian *Star*. He later became an associate editor of *Newsweek*, senior editor of *Look*, and senior writer and essayist for *Time* from 1977 until his death. He won many awards for political, legal, scientific, and general reporting. Bill Emerson, editor of *The Saturday Evening Post*, said of Trippett, "He was one of the really mind-blowing talents of his generation as a journalist, essayist, poet, story teller and as a man rambling about town."

Trippett and his wife lived in Larchmont, New York, where they raised their four children. His books include *The States, United They Fell* (1966), an analysis of state legislatures, and *The First Horsemen* (1974), a narrative history of the Scythian culture. In his first novel, *Child Ellen* (1975), Trippett established the fictional world of Nemisisipiana. Written as the first of seven projected novels dealing with the characters and history of the state of Nemisisipiana, *Child Ellen* covered the period of World War II through the *Brown vs. Board of Education* ruling. His last book, *Hymning and Hawing About America* (2001) was published posthumously.

SURISTAN

Highway 25

Nothing remains but the cypresses of Suristan to mark the mansion built by Reuben Davis and his first wife, the poet "Hinda." The name she gave her house, Suristan, and her nom de plume indicate her fascination with the Orient.

The Davises built the house in the 1840s on the highest point in Aberdeen overlooking the Tombigbee River. On the grounds she constructed a large mound of concentric circles supported by brick walls. The mound was surrounded by a moat fed by three artesian wells and flanked by cypress trees. According to a local historian, Hinda sat atop the mound writing her poetry and gazing at swans swimming in the moat. She made Suristan a gathering place for local writers. Hinda lived and wrote at Suristan for some twenty years, traveling to Cuba and other places from which she sent back dispatches to Aberdeen's *Sunny South*. The house burned in the decade before the Civil War, and in 1861 Mary Halbert Davis died. The eight cypresses that she had planted around the pool were saved by the citizens of Aberdeen when the four-lane bypass was built in 1975.

Leave Aberdeen on Highway 25 south for ten miles to Alternate Highway 45 and turn south again to West Point, eight miles.

West Point

West Point has produced a variety of writers, from poets James Hull and James Lynch to biographer Louis Harlan and prominent publisher and writer Iris Vinton.

Pulitzer Prize winner Louis R. Harlan (1922) was born in West Point, where his father grew alfalfa in the fields nearby after World War I. The family moved to Tennessee when Harlan was three and on to Atlanta where he graduated from Emory University. He served in the U. S. Navy during World War II, then got his M.A. from Vanderbilt and his Ph.D. from Johns Hopkins, and taught at the University of Maryland. He was awarded the Pulitzer Prize in 1984 for *Booker T. Washington: The Wizard of Tuskegee, 1901–1905*. He had published an earlier biography entitled *Booker T. Washington: The Making of a Black Leader, 1856–1901* (1972), as well as several academic works.

Born in West Point, Iris Vinton (1905) was prominent in the New York publishing world of children's and young people's books. She was head of publications for the Boys Clubs of America, served on the editorial board of Scholastic Books and Magazines, and was with the Initial Teaching Alphabet Foundation. She was herself a prolific writer, publishing sixteen books, mostly biographies for young people.

542 Calhoun Street

James Daniel Lynch (1836–1903) gained national fame as a poet when his poem "Columbia Saluting the Nations" was chosen as the official salutation of the Chicago world's fair in 1893. Born in Virginia, he came to Columbus to be a teacher of Greek and Latin at Franklin Academy in 1860. He soon married a woman from West Point, and they made this house their home. He joined the Confederate army, practiced law, farmed, became a judge, and even ran a matrimonial bureau out of New Orleans. He was well known locally for his political writing—a study of Reconstruction in Kemper County and *The Bench and Bar of Mississippi*—but achieved national recognition with his poetry. His poem "The Siege of the Alamo" hung on the wall of the Alamo mission during his lifetime. He and his wife lived in this house until 1893, when they moved to Texas; he died there a decade later.

Leaving West Point, take Highway 50 east twelve miles back to Highway 45 and turn south to Columbus, four miles.

Columbus

Settled in 1817, Columbus is the seat of Lowndes County. It is a beautiful city that would not have fit its original name, Possum Town. Like Natchez, settled one hundred years earlier, Columbus was a wealthy social-commercial center for plantation aristocracy. Their land lay in the prairies west of Columbus; their river was the Tombigbee; their port was Mobile. The area's wealth produced a sophisticated cultural and aesthetic life expressed through handsome buildings, many of which are still standing. It is the home of Mississippi University for Women, one of the state's most beautiful campuses.

The literary claims of Columbus are extensive, beginning in the nineteenth century with writers Joseph B. Cobb, Samuel Berryhill, and Alexander B. Meek. In the twentieth century, Columbus had a wide range of writers in addition to those associated with sites: Luke Wallin, who wrote for young adults, autobiographer Julian Sherrod and novelist Phillip Thompson, poet J. Dudley Bearden and poet/playwright Sarah Frances Jacob. It is the birthplace of contemporary poets Karen Mitchell, who grew up in Holly Springs, and Samuel Prestridge, who grew up in Tupelo. The Columbus Reading Circle, organized in 1892, is believed to be the oldest literary club in Mississippi.

Mississippi Welcome Center

Tennessee Williams House

300 Main Street

This house was the first home of Tennessee Williams, America's master of poetic drama. Once the rectory of St. Paul's Episcopal Church, this 1878 Victorian house was moved from College Street to its present location to be used by the city as a welcome center.

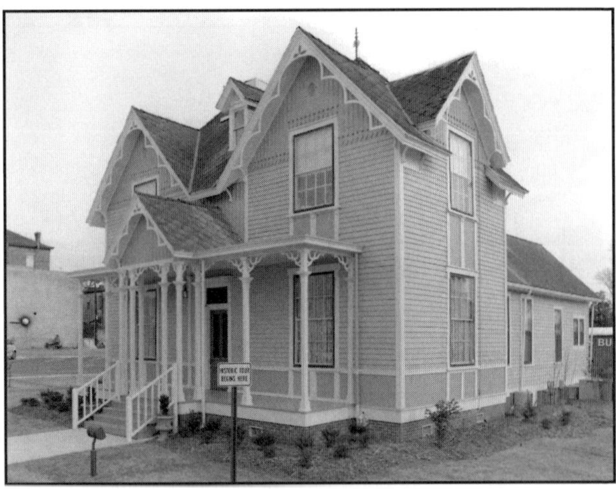

Tennessee Williams's birthplace, Columbus

Thomas Lanier Williams (1911–1983), later to be known as Tennessee Williams, was born to Edwina Dakin Williams in a Columbus clinic on March 26, 1911, and brought home to the rectory. Then twenty-seven, Edwina had stayed with her parents for most of her marriage to Cornelius C. Williams. During her first pregnancy she had come home to live, and after her daughter, Rose, was born, Edwina remained at the rectory for the next several years. The new baby was called Tom, and by the time he was born, his father, Cornelius, was selling shoes and clothing up and down the Delta and often visiting his family in Columbus. Edwina had resumed an active social life in Columbus.

At that time Columbus was a town of some four thousand, with a highly developed sense of the genteel life—stability, manners, the art of hospitality, an unhurried and pleasant existence for the families with the financial means to enjoy it. Like the rest of the South, Columbus was a racially segregated society shored up by a belief in a fixed, divinely ordained social order. Tom Williams and his sister, Rose, were cared for by a young black woman named Ozzie who would move with them as Reverend Dakin accepted calls from other churches. By the end of 1913, the family and Ozzie had moved to a pastorate in Nashville, but they soon returned to Mississippi. (See Clarksdale for additional information on Tennessee Williams in Mississippi.)

St. Paul's Episcopal Church

318 College Street

In 1905, Reverend Walter Edwin Dakin became pastor of St. Paul's Episcopal Church after serving in Port Gibson, Natchez, and Vicksburg. In Columbus he charmed the town with his elegant manner and social ease. His serious and hardworking wife, Rose, and his twenty-one-year-old daughter, Edwina, accompanied him, and all three fit immediately into the parish and community life. Edwina, a beautiful, archetypal "southern belle," was the object of much attention by the young men of the town. While she was appearing in a local production of *The Mikado* in early 1906, she met a promising young man named Cornelius Williams, who traveled for a telephone company. They married in this church on June 2, 1907, and left at once for Gulfport. Their daughter, Rose, and son Tom (later called Tennessee) were baptized in this church as infants, and played on its lawn as toddlers.

Site of the Original Gilmer Hotel

321 Main Street

Charles Henri Ford (1908), a legend in America's avant-garde movement, is one of the most influential poets and artists of this century. He is known as America's first surrealist poet and as an artist, filmmaker, and publisher of the work of international surrealists.

Born in Hazlehurst at the Ford Hotel, which was owned by his grandfather, he lived in Brookhaven and then in Memphis and other Tennessee towns before moving with his family to Columbus. His sister, Ruth, went on to become a renowned actress, collaborating with William Faulkner on the stage adaptation of *Requiem for a Nun.*

In Columbus the family lived in the Gilmer Hotel, where his father managed the coffee shop. In 1929, Ford published a small magazine in Columbus entitled *Blues: A Magazine of New Rhythms.* Although it only lasted for nine issues, it was an astonishing feat, showcasing the new schools of modern art and literature, publishing works by William Carlos Williams, Gertrude

Stein, Ezra Pound, E. E. Cummings, Erskine Caldwell, and other literary luminaries. He moved to New York, then on to France. During his first few years abroad, at the age of twenty-five, Ford coauthored one of the nation's first homoerotic novels, *The Young and the Evil* (1933), written with Parker Tyler and banned in England and America.

From 1940 to 1947, Ford was editor and publisher of the magazine *View.* Published in New York, *View* featured avant-garde artists and writers, including Joseph Cornell, Allen Ginsberg, and Randall Jarrell. Ford is credited with putting America into the international mainstream of literary surrealism. He published the American contingent of surrealist novels, including those of Paul Bowles, Parker Tyler, and Edouard Roditti.

Ford's fifteen books of poetry include *A Pamphlet of Sonnets* (1936), *The Garden of Disorder and Other Poems* (1938), *ABCs* (1940), *The Overturned Lake* (1941), *A Night with Jupiter and Other Fantastic Stories* (1949), *Spare Parts* (1966), *Om Krishna* (1978), *Secret Haiku* (1982) and *Out of the Labyrinth* (1991). Many famous artists have illustrated his books, including Noguchi, Cornell, Matta, Tanguy, and Tchelitchew.

In 2001, at the age of ninety-three, he published *Water from a Bucket,* which Edmund White called Ford's masterpiece. A memoir, it covers the years 1948 to 1957 and his friendships with Jean Cocteau, George Balanchine, Salvador Dali, Jean Genet, Ned Rorem, Gertrude Stein, Paul Bowles, Djuna Barnes, Tennessee Williams, and Truman Capote, as well as the Russian painter Pavel Tchelitchew, who was his companion for two decades.

Ford is also a graphic artist, filmmaker, and photographer. His work has been exhibited in London, Paris, and New York. His motion pictures include *Poem Posters* (1966) and *Johnny Minotaur* (1972). He now lives primarily in New York City with residences in Paris and on the island of Crete.

Lehmquen

613 South Second Street

Robert Ivy, Jr., is an architect and the author of the lavishly illustrated book *Fay Jones* (1992) about the life and work of the esteemed architect from Arkansas. He is also editor of the magazine *Architectural Record*, the nation's oldest architectural journal. Ivy and his wife divide their time between this house in Columbus and New York.

922 N. Fourth Avenue

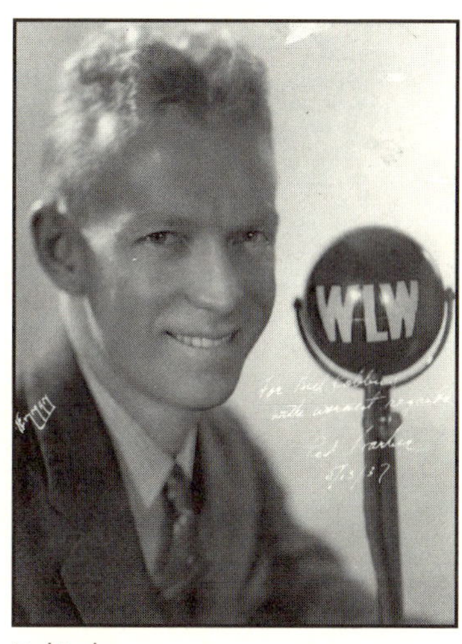

Red Barber

Red Barber was born Walter Lanier Barber (1908–1992) in Columbus, his mother's hometown. His father was a railroad conductor and his mother a schoolteacher. When he was ten his family left Columbus and moved to Florida, where he later studied at the University of Florida, then went into sports broadcasting. As a broadcaster from 1939 to 1953 he was known as the voice of the Brooklyn Dodgers, and from 1954 to 1966 the voice of the New York Yankees. He won the Frick Award for broadcasting excellence. His southern drawl and down-home stories helped baseball become the nation's favorite sport. He moved back to Florida in 1966 and switched to writing a sports column and working in television.

Red Barber's nonfiction books include *The Rhubarb Patch: The Story of the Modern Brooklyn Dodgers* (1954), *The Broadcasters* (1970), *Show Me the Way to Go Home* (1971), and *When All Hell Broke Loose in Baseball* (1982). His autobiography, *Rhubarb in the Catbird Seat,* was published in 1968.

Hickory Sticks

1206 7th Street North

This was the home of Frances and Robert Ivy, authors of the charming *A Boy's Will: A Mississippi Memoir* (1991). The memoir was written about Robert Ivy's life in this house. They are the parents of Robert Ivy, Jr. (see Lehmquen, above); Frances Ivy now lives at 324 S. Third Street.

Mississippi University for Women

Entrance on College Street

Now called "the W," the Industrial Institute and College was the first state-supported institution for women in the United States. It opened in 1884 and today is considered one of the leading universities of its size in the South.

The university can count numerous writers among its alumnae, in fields as diverse as biology, sociology, history and art history. Regarding fiction, the W has the distinction of being able to claim one of America's foremost writers, Eudora Welty. She describes her student days there in *One Writer's Beginnings.* She was active as a cartoonist and poet and as a writer for the school paper and of comic skits for the student body. The administration building has been named Eudora Welty Hall. The inscription in marble comes from *One Writer's Beginnings*: "All serious daring starts from within."

Magnolia Hill

1106 12th Street North

Because of a happenstance created by the Civil War, fabled author, traveler, and lawyer Lee Meriwether (1862–1966) was born in this raised cottage built in 1832. In 1862 General William T. Sherman began to banish wives of Confederate officers from Memphis. Eliza Meriwether, then pregnant, had to leave her home and take her two sons to Holly Springs, where her husband was camped with General Nathan Bedford Forrest. The Confederate army moved south, and Mrs. Meriwether and her two sons moved with them. When they reached Columbus, she had to stop for the birth of her baby. He was born on Christmas night in the home of widow Rebecca Winston, who had lived in this house since 1843. The newborn boy was named for General Robert E. Lee, and the Meriwether family returned eventually to Memphis.

Lee Meriwether started his career as a newspaper reporter, became an attorney, and practiced law in St. Louis for seventy years. During World War I he was assigned to an embassy in Paris. He wrote his first travel book in 1886 and over his lifetime published more than two dozen books, mostly about travel. He lived to be 103 and, like Forrest Gump, met many great figures of his time. He sat on the knees of Jefferson Davis, at age twelve visited in the home of Mark Twain, knew Leon Trotsky in Paris, and was present at the opening of King Tut's tomb. He wrote two autobiographical works, *Postscripts on My Life* and *My First 98 Years, 1862–1960* (1960).

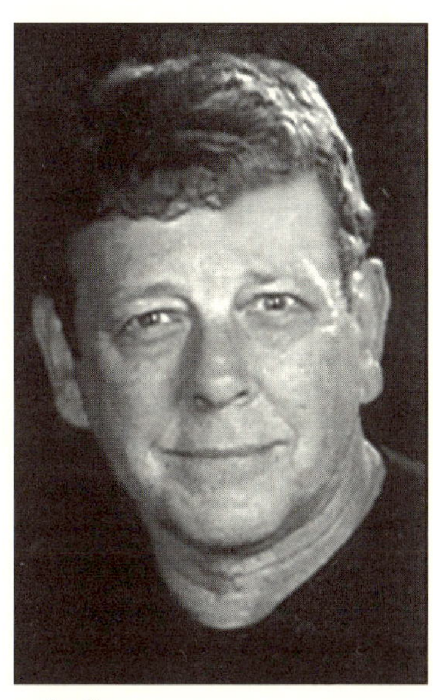
Paul Ruffin

124 Sand Road

Paul Ruffin (1941) has made a mark both as an academician and as a versatile and accomplished writer. Born in Alabama, he moved to Columbus when he was seven and went to public schools there. After a brief tour of duty with the army, he earned his B.A. and M.A. degrees from Mississippi State University and later obtained his Ph.D. at the University of Southern Mississippi. He has published four collections of poetry, one of which, *Circling*, won a Mississippi Institute of Arts and Letters award in 1997. His short stories and essays have been published in numerous journals and magazines. A collection of his short stories, *The Man Who Would Be God*, was published in 1993. He teaches and directs the creative writing program at Sam Houston State University in Texas. He is the founder and director of the *Texas Review* Press. Works in progress include three novels, a memoir, and a book of poetry.

Friendship Cemetery

Fourth Street South and 13th Avenue

The cemetery contains the only sites left that can be associated with two nineteenth-century writers who lived and worked in Columbus. Joseph Beckham Cobb (1819–1858), a native of Georgia, came to Mississippi as a young man, bought land, and created a cotton plantation which he called Longwood. He was elected to the state legislature in 1841 and ran unsuccessfully for Congress in 1853. He valued his large library and spent his life writing.

In 1850, he published a novel, *The Creole* (1850), set in Louisiana during the War of 1812. His other books, *Mississippi Scenes* (1851) and *Leisure Labors* (1858), are both collections of essays ranging from literary criticism to social and political observations. Several of his essays give a vivid picture of the town of Columbus. The Cobb family grave plot, with monuments for his two infant sons, does not have a monument for Cobb himself.

Alexander B. Meek was speaker of the house of the Alabama legislature and became Alabama's best-known poet with the publication of *Red Eagle* (1855) and *Songs and Poems of the South* (1857). After his wife's death in 1863 he moved to Columbus to be with his brother and soon married Eliza Jane Cannon, his brother's mother-in-law. Before he was able to publish more poetry, Meek died in 1865 at the age of fifty-one. His marble grave marker refers to him as a poet, orator, historian, statesman, and founder of Alabama's public school system. His poem "The Mocking Bird" still appears in some anthologies.

Leave Columbus on Highway 82 west for four miles, then turn south on Highway 45 to Macon, twenty-seven miles.

Macon

Carved out of Indian lands and made beautiful by antebellum Greek Revival houses, Macon was the home of nineteenth-century poet William Ward and Civil War reporter Louis Dupré. It is the birthplace of the prolific novelist Ben Ames Williams, novelist/historian Marie Bankhead Owen, and contemporary writers Loyle Hairston, Jewel Miller, Jack Holman, and Gordon Hansen.

A poet of more recent times is T. R. Hummer (1950). A native of Macon, he earned his B.A. and M.A. degrees at the University of Southern Mississippi and his Ph.D. at the University of Utah. His first collection was *Translation of Light* (1976), and he has published five other volumes of poetry, including *The 18,000-*

Ton Olympic Dream (1990). He has received a Guggenheim Fellowship, a National Endowment for the Arts Fellowship, and the 1999 Hanes Poetry Prize from the Fellowship of Southern Writers. Hummer has served as editor in chief of *The New England Review* and *The Kenyon Review.* In 2001 he was named editor in chief of *The Georgia Review.*

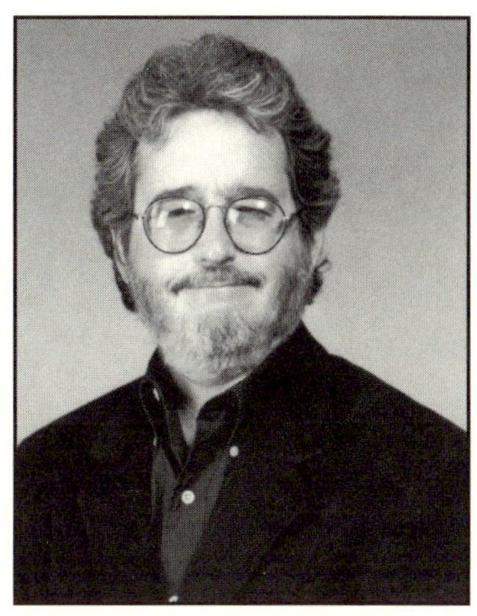

T. R. Hummer

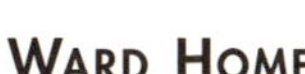

Ward Home

310 North Street

This was the home of poet William Ward (1823–1888). Born in Connecticut, Ward came south in 1839 to join his brother in Columbus and learn the jewelry trade. In the 1850s he moved to Macon to set up his own shop. He built this house in 1858 after his marriage to a local schoolteacher who was from England. Ward became editor of the *Macon Beacon,* where most of his poems were published. He was best known for one poem, "Katie Did," a standard piece in Mississippi schoolbooks in the first half of the twentieth century.

McGehee-Ames House

1234 Magnolia Drive

Ben Ames Williams (1889–1953) is remembered primarily as the author of *Leave Her to Heaven* (1944), popularized by Hollywood. His literary legacy, however, is huge, including some three dozen novels, 432 short stories, and several nonfiction books.

He was born in Macon at the home of his grandmother, Sarah J. Longstreet Ames, and lived with his parents on the Ecford Place. Both houses are now gone.

When he was an infant, his parents, Dan and Sarah Ames Williams, moved the family to his father's home state of Ohio, where he became a newspaper editor. The family later lived in

Wales, his father having been appointed to the American consulate there. During all of those years the young Williams often visited Macon, sometimes staying in this house.

Williams graduated from Dartmouth College in 1910 and began to work as a journalist by day and a fiction writer by night. In 1916 he quit his job on the Boston *American* to become a full-time writer. He and his wife and children lived in Chestnut Hill, a suburb of Boston, and he remained there for the rest of his life.

By the mid-twenties Ben Ames Williams had become a household name through his stories in the *Saturday Evening Post* and *Colliers.* By the 1930s he was an established writer; his fiction ranged from serious novels to those that were serialized in magazines, from historical to mystery novels and adventure stories. His short stories are collected in three books.

Williams believed in "the potency of place." In an autobiographical sketch, he wrote, "Born in Mississippi, I spent some months of each year for eleven years in Macon, and the South persists in me." The only works that deal with the South are his mammoth (1,514 pages) *House Divided* (1947) about the effect of the Civil War on five major characters and *The Unconquered* (1953), about the dark and angry Reconstruction era.

The Williams family had a farm in Searsmont, Maine, where he died of a heart attack while playing a game of curling, a sport that he loved and in which he excelled as an international competitor. As a measure of his fame, *Time, Newsweek,* and *Publisher's Weekly* all carried his obituary. His literary and personal papers are in the Dartmouth College archives.

Site of the Bankhead House

State Road 14

Eight miles east of Macon

It should be said that Marie Bankhead Owen (1869–1958) was an Alabamian by any measure. Only by a quirk of timing can Mississippi claim her; she was born near Macon on her uncle's plantation where her parents were living during and just after the Civil War. She was raised in Montgomery, the daughter of a United States congressman and senator. She herself raised her niece, Tallulah Bankhead. Her novel, *Yvonne of Braithwaite* (1927), was set on a Missisisippi Delta plantation. Many other historical novels she wrote remain unpublished. Her major career was as archivist and historian for the state of Alabama.

From Macon take Highway 14 west to Louisville.

Louisville

One of the nation's great historians, Thomas D. Clark (1903) was born and raised on a farm near Louisville. After dropping out of school to work in a sawmill, he graduated from Choctaw County Agricultural High School and then from the University of Mississippi in 1929. He received a scholarship and earned his M.A. from the University of Kentucky. After getting his Ph.D. from Duke University, he returned to the University of Kentucky and became head of the history department in 1942.

He had a distinguished career as scholar, teacher, and writer, publishing over two dozen books ranging from a history of the country store to *The Southern Country Editor* (1948). He also published a biography, *Simon Kenton, Kentucky Scout* (1943).

Clark taught at Indiana University for seven years and then returned to Louisville. He was a founder of the Organization of American Historians, and was named Kentucky's Historian Laureate for life.

Leave Louisville on Highway 15 south to Philadelphia. The highway goes through Noxapater, home of writer Winston Caperton.

Philadelphia

Philadelphia is built on the site of a large Choctaw town called Lune Bu Osh, which translates to Burnt Frog. Chartered in 1841, it prospered when the railroad came in 1905.

Turner Catledge (1901–1983), editor of the most powerful newspaper in the nation, was born in New Prospect near Ackerman and

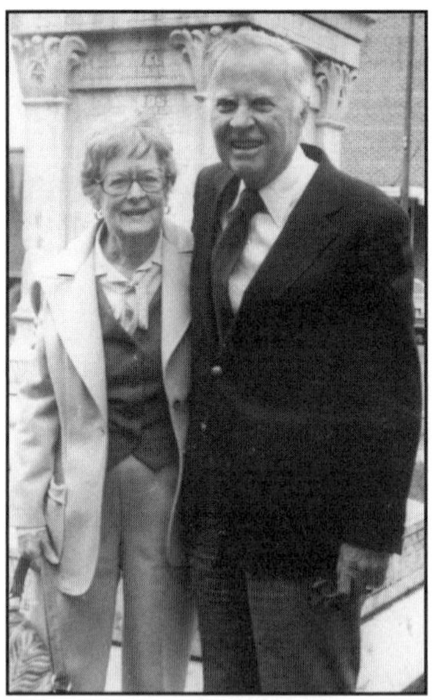
Florence Mars and Turner Catledge

moved to Philadelphia when he was three. He attended Mississippi State University from 1919 to 1922 when it was still called Mississippi A & M. After graduation he went into newspaper work and launched a career that followed a steady upward trajectory. He was hired by the *Tunica Times* in 1922, worked briefly as managing editor of the *Tupelo Journal*, and then moved to the Memphis *Commercial Appeal*, the *Baltimore Sun*, and, in 1929, to the *New York Times*, an association that lasted more than forty years.

Catledge worked at the *New York Times* as a city reporter, a national correspondent, and a political reporter in the Washington bureau; in 1951 he landed the prestigious job of managing editor, a position he held until 1964 when he was made executive editor. He was president of the *New York Times* from 1968 to 1970. When he retired in 1970 Catledge and his wife moved to New Orleans, where he wrote his autobiography, *My Life and The Times*. In an interview in 1978, he said, "I had a wonderful time as a reporter. Why should it be otherwise? It was a lot easier than plowing a field in Mississippi."

Mars House

518 Poplar Avenue

This house, built in 1902, is the home of Florence Mars (1923), a feisty cattle farmer and freelance photographer. She had the courage to buck her community's apathy toward local Ku Klux Klan activities during the civil rights movement. She later wrote *Witness in Philadelphia* (1977) describing the turmoil that gripped the state from 1954 to 1968, climaxed by the savage killing of three civil rights workers in Philadelphia by local men. *Witness in Philadelphia* was made into the Hollywood film *Mississippi Burning*.

Leave Philadelphia on Highway 19 south to Meridian.

Meridian

It could be said that Meridian had a shaky literary start. The men who named it thought the word *meridian* meant junction. They intended for railroads to cross here, and, after the town was settled in 1836, the railroads indeed came, bringing prosperity. Meridian has suffered two great disasters: the Civil War, which precipitated three battles here, and a yellow fever epidemic.

Meridian can clearly claim the garden writer Ben Arthur Davis and the great country lyricist Jimmie Rodgers. Several other noted writers lived at some time in Meridian: Wyatt Cooper of Quitman, the Oklahoma novelist John Hewett Culp, the Alabama novelist Mark Childress, Pulitzer Prize–winning cartoonist Doug Marlette (now at work on a novel), and James Street, who often visited his parents after his father moved here as a state judge. Meridian is the birthplace and boyhood home of Florida writer Edwin Granberry and the current home of Dennis J. Mitchell, biographer of Frank E. Smith. It also claims Carl Milner Holloway, J. Gregory Keyes, poets Randolph Bates, Pauline Simmons Busbee, Stephen Owen, and David Moore, and techno-thriller writer Bill Buchanan. Nearby Collinsville is the home of a poet laureate of Mississippi, Winifred Hamrick Farrar. But the major literary claims to be made by Meridian are Edward Kimbrough and Howard Bahr.

Kimbrough House

2719 24th Street

But for his early death at forty-seven, William Edward Kimbrough (1918–1965) might have been one of Mississippi's most powerful voices, a worthy successor to Faulkner. His three novels and many short stories draw heavily on Mississippi's social, cultural, and political milieu.

He was born in Meridian and spent his preschool years and teenage years here, graduating from Meridian High School. In between those times his family lived in Tampa and New Orleans. Kimbrough spent his teenage years in this house and maintained

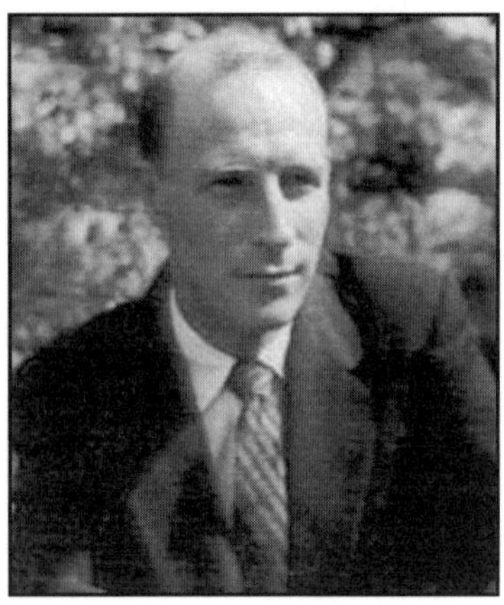

Ed Kimbrough

it until his death. He is buried in Meridian's Rose Hill cemetery.

He attended George Washington University and studied creative writing with Hudson Strode at the University of Alabama, where he received his B.A. and M.A. degrees. He taught creative writing with Strode from 1941 to 1950, was a Fulbright Fellow at the universities of Paris and Strasbourg, and taught at the University of Michigan, Colorado State University, and Loyola University in New Orleans.

Kimbrough wrote his first novel when he was nineteen. *From Hell to Breakfast* (1941), not published until he was twenty-three, is held together by the machinations of a Mississippi political campaign. The *Meridian Star* observed that the novel "set Meridian on its ear." Kimbrough was awarded the Julius Rosenwald Fellowship for fiction. His second novel, *Night Fire* (1946), dealt with racial prejudice and labor troubles in the South. His last novel, *The Secret Pilgrim* (1949), is a psychological drama set in Meridian and built around events there. A number of his short stories were published in national magazines. At the time of his death he was writing a philosophical novel, tentatively entitled *The Wild Pollen*, set in the old St. Louis Street cemetery in New Orleans, where he lived. He was the public relations director for the Port of New Orleans and a reporter for the *New Orleans Item.*

2711 7th Street

Howard Bahr (1946) was born in Meridian, christened at St. Patrick's Catholic Church, and attended Stevenson Primary School. He lived in this house with his mother and grandfather, who was the band director at Meridian High School. The house has been many things since then: a beauty parlor, a radio station, a children's shop. "The house still stands, stronger than ever, planted firmly in the earth right where we left it," he wrote in 1991.

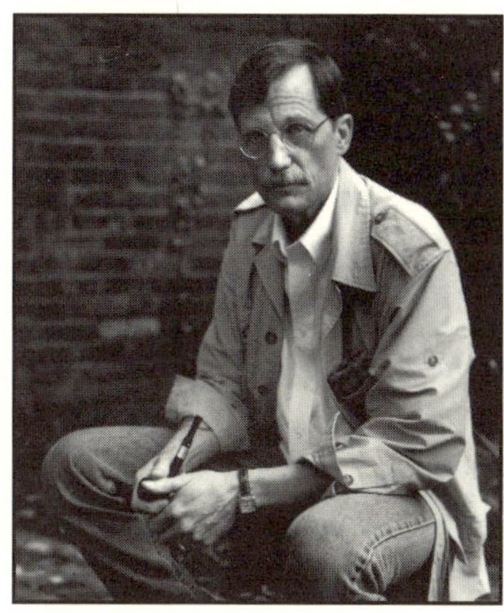
Howard Bahr

Bahr moved away from Meridian when he was ten. He graduated from high school in Illinois and returned to Mississippi to attend Ole Miss, where he earned his B.A. and M.A. degrees. He was an assistant professor at the University of Mississippi and served as curator of Rowan Oak, William Faulkner's house in Oxford, from 1984 to 1993. In 1987 he published a children's book set during the Civil War, *Home for Christmas.* It would presage his two novels, *The Black Flower* (1998) and *And the Year of Jubilo* (2000), both set during and just after the Civil War. In a recent interview Bahr said, "The Civil War period has interested me a great deal. I know that time better and feel comfortable in it." He won the Mississippi Library Association fiction award in 1998 for *The Black Flower* and a Mississippi Institute of Arts and Letters award in 2001 for *And the Year of Jubilo.* He now teaches at Motlow State Community College in Fayetteville, Tennessee.

Jimmie Rodgers Museum

Highland Park

41st Avenue and 19th Street

This museum pays tribute to the life of Jimmie Rodgers, considered by music scholars to be one of the most influential country singers of the twentieth century. Rodgers was the first person elected to the Country Music Hall of Fame and is called the "father of country music." After his death, his widow, Carrie Williamson Rodgers, wrote a biography of the great singer entitled *My Husband, Jimmie Rodgers* (1935).

Born in Pine Springs, Mississippi, in 1897 Rodgers began working on railroad crews when he was fourteen. He played the guitar and banjo and picked up music from railroad men and black musicians in Meridian. In 1920, while still working for the railroad, he married Carrie Williamson of Meridian. By 1923 Rodgers was unemployed and in bad health. Carrie helped support their family by holding odd jobs, working as a waitress, stenographer, and newstand clerk. At twenty-seven, Jimmie Rodgers, desperate for work, formed a string band and began making stage appearances and occasionally singing on radio station WWNC in Asheville, North Carolina. When Carrie Rodgers heard that an RCA Victor talent scout was auditioning musicians, she urged him to go to Bristol, Tennessee, to be heard. In 1927 he recorded his first song, "Sleep Baby Sleep," a hit record that sold over a million copies. During the next six years he became one of the most popular singers in America. His sixty records sold twenty million copies and made him a millionaire. He and Carrie moved into a Texas mansion near a sanitorium so that his tuberculosis could be treated. In 1933 he sailed from Galveston to New York City for a recording session. He managed to record twelve songs before he collapsed. He died in a suite at the Taft Hotel, and Carrie brought his body by train back to Meridian for burial at the Oak Grove Cemetery in Bonita.

After Jimmie's death, Carrie Rodgers wrote his biography and began working with other young country-western artists Johnny Cash and Ernest Tubb. When she died in Texas in 1961, Johnny Cash sent a thousand matched red roses in the shape of a musical note to her gravesite in Oak Grove Cemetery.

Leave Meridian on Highway 59 to Laurel. En route, Highway 18 swings over to Quitman.

Quitman

Quitman is the hometown of Wyatt Cooper (1927–1978), a country boy born and raised on a farm, who startled his hometown in 1966 when he married Gloria Vanderbilt. Life with Vanderbilt, an artist, member of a famous family, and former wife of Leopold Stokowski, spun his life in a new direction. His book about his marriage, *Families: A Memoir and a Celebration*, was published in 1975.

When he was fifteen, his mother moved to New Orleans with her children. Cooper returned to Mississippi to attend Meridian

Junior College and to work as a radio announcer before he went to the University of California at Berkeley to study theater. He later became an actor and a writer of plays, screenplays, television scripts, and magazine pieces. He was technical adviser for the film version of Faulkner's *Sanctuary*. He wrote the screenplay for *The Chapman Report* and collaborated with friend Truman Capote on the television script of *The Glass House*. Capote called Cooper "one of the most civilized men in the world." For years he was on international best-dressed lists and lectured around the nation. Cooper died at the age of fifty-one.

Laurel

Laurel was once known as a city of millionaires. It is located in the heart of the Piney Woods, an area that attracted the northern timber industry, which led to the town's wealth. After the cutting of the big forests, Laurel sustained its growth with success in the pulpwood industry. Masonite was invented here. Laurel is the home of the first art museum in the state, the Lauren Rogers Museum, which opened in 1924, and the hometown of Leontyne Price of Metropolitan Opera fame. It is also the hometown of poets Douglas Gray and Joan Johnson, novelist Eric Harry, memoirist Charles Marsh, and novelist James Street.

James Street House

725 Sixth Avenue

Almost every one of James Street's novels was a national best seller, and two were made into movies. Although his success came many years after he had moved far away from Laurel, he wrote about Mississippi in most of his work.

Born in Lumberton, James Howell Street (1903–1954) moved to this house when he was seven. At fourteen he began working for the *Laurel Daily Leader*, which launched him on the journalistic career that took him to New York City. There he wrote his first book, *Look Away!* (1936), sketches of Mississippi life. By 1937 he had turned to full-time story writing. His first five novels were set in Mississippi, beginning with *Oh, Promised Land* (1940). The

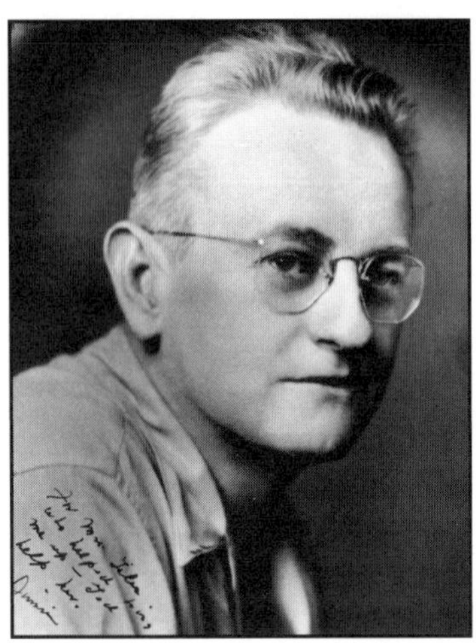
James Street

most popular of these Mississippi novels, *Tap Roots* (1942), was made into a movie starring Susan Hayward. The movie had its southern premier in Laurel in 1948 at the Ritz Theatre. The film was boycotted in nearby Meridian after Street remarked that "the Dixiecrat movement stinks." Street cared passionately about the state and the direction it began to take after World War II.

During 1940–1941 Street lived in Natchez in order to write *In My Father's House*, set in Jones County. His dog books, *The Biscuit Eater* (1941) and *Good-bye, My Lady* (1954), were also set in Mississippi. He returned to New York for four more years, and in 1945 he moved to Chapel Hill, North Carolina, where he died almost a decade later. While living in the East he was called a "Vermont Yankee" in a Jackson newspaper. He responded, "I'm a Mississippian living in Connecticut and doing business in New York. That's bad enough, don't tack the Vermont tag on me."

8 Highland Woods

Charles Marsh (1958) was born in Mobile and moved to Laurel as a teenager in 1967 when his father accepted pastorage of the First Baptist Church here. *The Last Days: A Son's Story of Sin and Segregation at the Dawn of a New South* (2001) is a memoir of the South's titanic civil rights struggle played out in microcosm. In this small southern town lived the Imperial Wizard of the White Knights of the Mississippi Ku Klux Klan, who intimidated and silenced the largely Christian community, their good will overwhelmed by racist beliefs and a fierce clinging to the status quo. Marsh traces his father's reluctant but finally triumphant leadership in attempting to challenge the orthodoxy of a segregated society.

Marsh earned his B.A. at Gordon College, his master's of theological studies at Harvard Divinity School, and his M.A. and Ph.D. in philosophical theology at the University of Virginia. He taught at Loyola College in Maryland from 1990 to 1999. He now lives with his family in Charlottesville, Virginia, where he is a professor of religion at the University of Virginia and director of the Project on Lived Theology.

The nearby community of Soso on Highway 28 is the hometown of Rebecca Hill (1944). Born in Memphis, Hill grew up in Mississippi and set her first novel, *Blue Rise* (1983), in the state. She graduated from Grinnell College in Iowa and received her M.A. from Harvard. Her novels *Among Birches* (1986) and *Killing Time in St. Cloud* (with Judith Guest, 1988) are both set in Minnesota. Hill donated her original manuscripts to the Mississippi Department of Archives and History in 1993.

Leave Laurel by Highway 59 south and head to Hattiesburg.

Hattiesburg

Hattiesburg was once a small logging community; as the railroads arrived, it grew to become a city of locomotives and commerce. Today it is a center of education with two institutions of higher learning, the University of Southern Mississippi and William Carey College, and a military center, nearby Camp Shelby.

Hattiesburg is the birthplace of poet and fiction writer William Mills and of Linda Peavey, who writes fiction, poetry, and essays. It has been the home of several writers including Elliott Chaze, Elizabeth Bowne-Minn, Julie Fleming, Mary Ann Wells, poets Sybil Pittman Estess and Sandra Napier-Dyess, and romance writer Carolyn Thornton. The town's latest literary star is Lee Durkee, who was born in Hawaii and raised in Hattiesburg, where his father taught at the University of Southern Mississippi. Durkee's first novel, *Rides of the Midway* (2001), has drawn high praise, and he has been placed in "the great tradition of Mississippi literature."

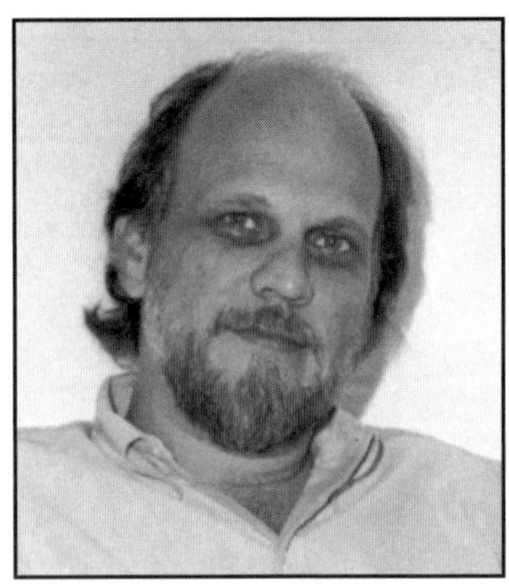
Frederick Barthelme

Nearby Petal was once the home of P. D. East, editor/writer, and native Melinda Haynes, author of the extraordinary novels *Mother of Pearl* (1999) and *Chalktown* (2001). Her first novel was Oprah Winfrey's twenty-fourth book club pick in 1999.

University of Southern Mississippi

Enter on Hardy Street at 29th Avenue

For several years the university, with its Center for Writers at USM, has been a hotbed of faculty writers, including poets Angela Ball, Jean Davidson, Philip Kolin, and Rosewell Graves Lowrey, memoirists Noel Polk and Thomas D. Young, biographer James G. Hollandsworth, Jr., and fiction writers Gordon Weaver and the Barthelme brothers.

Frederick Barthelme (1943), a native of Houston, Texas, has been the head of the Center for Writers at the University of Southern Mississippi since 1978 and an acclaimed writer since 1983 when *Moon Deluxe*, his first major collection of short stories, was published. Since then he has continued to write dazzling fiction that exhibits a tense balance between comedy and darkness. His short stories and novels, always dealing with contemporary life, are often set in Hattiesburg or on the Gulf Coast. He has published eleven books, including the autobiographical *Double Down: Reflections on Gambling and Loss* (1999), cowritten with his brother. He has written two screenplays and has edited the *Mississippi Review* since 1977. His book of short stories *The Law of Averages* was published in 2001.

Steve Barthelme, Frederick's brother, is also a professor of writing at the university and writes fiction, nonfiction, and poetry. He broke onto the scene with the publication of a collection of short stories entitled *And He Tells the Little Horse the Whole Story* (1987). He coauthored *Double Down: Reflections on Gambling and Loss* (1999).

The university's library houses the Lena de Grummond Children's Literature Collection, a nationally known research collection featuring manuscripts and illustrations of children's books. It was begun in 1966 by Dr. Grummond, a professor of library science from 1965 to 1970. Among its fifty thousand items are an unpublished Kate Greenaway manuscript, original illustrations for *Curious George*, and an edition of Aesop's *Fables* published in 1530.

411 Sixth Avenue

Elliott Chaze (1915–1990) arrived in Hattiesburg when he was thirty-six as a reporter for the *Hattiesburg American*. In 1970 he was made city editor, a post he held until his retirement in 1980. Chaze was born in Mamou, Louisiana, and graduated from high school in Alexandria, Louisiana. He attended Washington and Lee, Tulane, and Oklahoma University, from which he graduated in 1937. He arrived in Mississippi after working with the Associated Press in New Orleans, serving in the army in World War II, and writing for a newspaper in Denver. He lived in this house from 1969 until his death.

During his life in Hattiesburg, he wrote nine novels, a collection of humorous essays, and many short stories that were published in *Life* and *Look*. He made use of wide-ranging subject matter and settings, from occupied Japan to Colorado. His novels *Tiger in the Honeysuckle* (1965) and *Wettermark* (1969) are both set in Mississippi; Hattiesburg is called Catherine. His first novel, *The Stainless Steel Kimono* (1947), was said to be a favorite of Ernest Hemingway.

Continue south on Highway 59, passing Lumberton, birthplace of James Street and his hometown until he was seven years old. (See Laurel for Street's biography.)

Picayune

The town of Picayune, on the banks of the Hobolochitto River, began life with the timber industry, and was once a leading mill town. When the railroad was built to accommodate the timber,

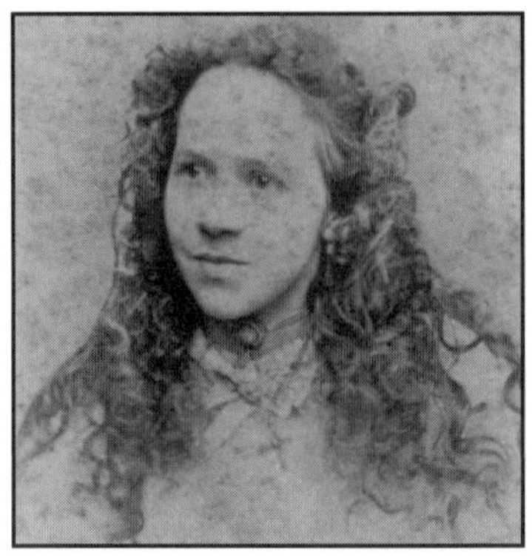

Eliza Jane Poitevant Nicholson

Eliza Poitevant Nicholson (see below) had the opportunity to name two towns on the line. She named Nicholson for her husband and changed Hobolochitto to Picayune, after her New Orleans newspaper, still extant as the *Times-Picayune.* Today Picayune is best known for the Crosby Arboretum, established by the L. O. Crosby family, and its magnificent Pinecote Pavilion designed by Fay Jones.

The life and times of Picayune were chronicled for many years by Samuel Grady Thigpen (1890–1981), who published a series of memoirs and stories about the town, including *A Boy in Rural Mississippi and Other Stories* (1966) and *Work and Play in Grandpa's Day* (1969). Picayune is also the home of writers Georgia Mitchell, Pat Harrison Spiers, Nat Lovell, Gladys Lynge, and Tommy Frierson.

THE HERMITAGE

1 River Road off 3rd Street

Now abandoned, this was the childhood home of the first woman in the nation to run a daily newspaper. At age twenty-seven, Eliza Jane Poitevant (1849–1896) became the owner-publisher of the New Orleans *Picayune* (forerunner of the *Times-Picayune).* Hers was one of the first newspapers in the nation to recognize the changes that the Civil War had made in women's place in society. She remade the face of newspapers, introducing columns especially for women—articles on health and beauty and a column of personal advice. Other innovations were articles on consumer problems, a generous use of illustrations, a cartoon weather report, and society notes, an idea borrowed from the eastern press. A popular feature of her Sunday edition was "Woman's World and Work."

Despite her extraordinary work in the publishing world, she was at heart a poet. Born near Pearlington on the Pearl River, she began to write poetry as a teenager under the name "Pearl Rivers."

She graduated from Amite Female Academy in 1867 and, to the consternation of her family, left home to pursue a career amid the strife and danger of postwar New Orleans. Her poetry, first published in the *New York Home Journal* in 1860, provided an introduction in New Orleans to the owner and editor of the *Picayune*, A. M. Holbrook, whom she married in 1872. After his death she married George Nicholson, the *Picayune*'s business manager, and together they forged a successful newspaper and raised two sons. Nicholson's book of poetry, *Lyrics by "Pearl Rivers,"* was published in 1873. It evokes the woods and fauna of south Mississippi, which she loved.

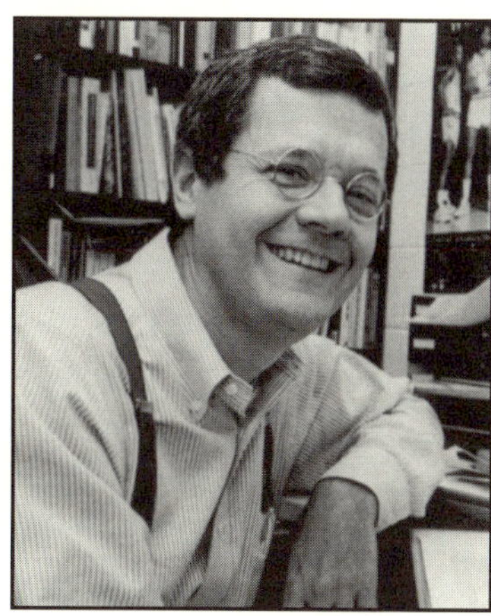

Noel Polk

815 Williams Avenue

Noel Polk (1943), a native of Picayune, was raised in this house and attended Picayune public schools. He earned his B.A. and M.A. degrees from Mississippi College and his Ph.D. from the University of South Carolina. He taught there and at the University of Texas in Arlington before he joined the faculty of the University of Southern Mississippi in 1977. A noted Welty and Faulkner scholar, he wrote an insightful and charming memoir of his life in Picayune, *Outside the Southern Myth* (1997).

Picayune is the end of the tour, but Highway 59 will take you to the Gulf Coast, where another tour begins.

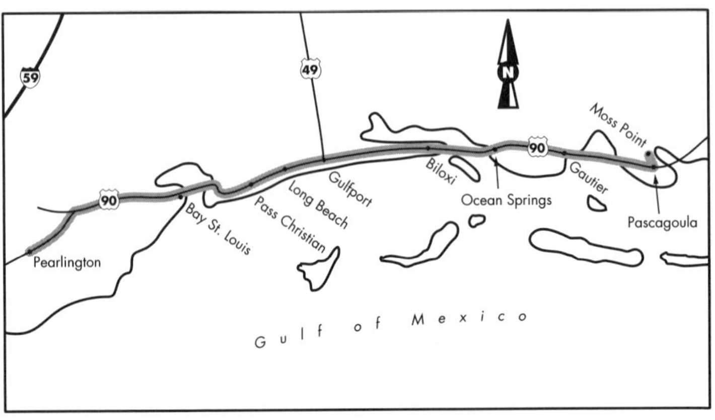
59
49
N
Moss Point
90
Biloxi
Gautier
Gulfport
Long Beach
Ocean Springs
Pascagoula
Pass Christian
Bay St. Louis
90
Pearlington
Gulf of Mexico

Gulf Coast Tour

The Gulf Coast tour begins in Pearlington on scenic Highway 90 on the Gulf of Mexico and continues to Bay St. Louis, Pass Christian, Long Beach, Gulfport, Biloxi, Ocean Springs, Gautier, Pascagoula, and Moss Point.

Pearlington

Born in Natchez, John Francis Hamtramck Claiborne (1807–1884) had a home here called Laurel Wood, a Louisiana-style plantation house located off Highway 90, south of Pearlington, facing Mulatto Bayou. The house was demolished some time after World War II by a pulpwood company. In the early 1850s, when talk of secession arose, Claiborne, a "states' rights Unionist," removed himself from politics and retreated to Laurel Wood.

A nephew of W. C. C. Claiborne, the first governor of the Mississippi Territory, Claiborne's father was commander of the Mississippi Volunteers in the War of 1812. Claiborne himself became involved in public life when he served a term in the U.S. Congress. He had a rich and varied career as a journalist, politician, planter, and author.

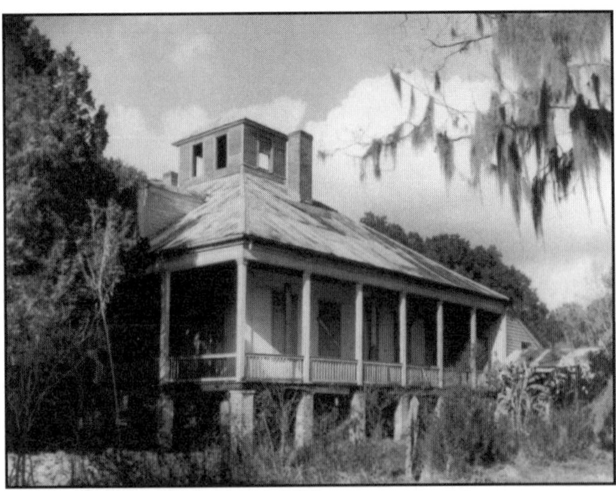

Laurel Wood, Pearlington

Called "the father of Mississippi history," he published two biographies in 1860, *The Life and Times of General Sam Dale* and *Correspondence of John A. Quitman*, but he is best known for *Mississippi as a Province, Territory and State, with Biographical Notices of Eminent Citizens*, published in 1880. Papers and data for the book are collected in part in the Claiborne Collection at the Mississippi Department of Archives and History in Jackson. It was originally a two-volume work; the second volume was destroyed by fire while Claiborne was living at Dumbarton, his wife's family home near Natchez. Grief stricken over his loss, Claiborne died two months later.

In the essays on his travels through the piney woods of Mississippi and Louisiana, Claiborne made detailed observations in an elegant style, and critics have praised his writing for over twelve decades. In contemporary times historian John K. Bettersworth compared him to Herodotus, and poet James Whitehead called him "Faulknerian" and "Carlylian."

Bay St. Louis

Only a little over fifty miles from New Orleans, Bay St. Louis has always been a favorite vacation spot for New Orleans aristocrats and wealthy Natchez planters. Native Sara Dodge Kimbrough wrote a memoir of her father, an artist. She also wrote *Drawn from Life* (1976) about four American artists who were friends in Paris during the 1880s.

Turn off Highway 90 onto North Beach Boulevard. Go south to South Beach Boulevard.

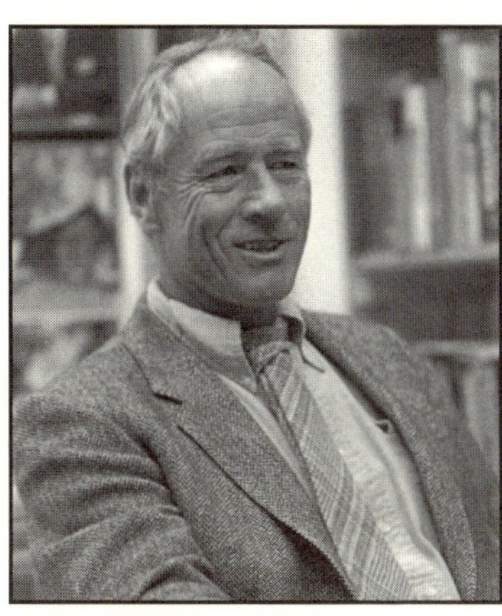
Stephen Ambrose

Ambrose House
977 South Beach Boulevard

Stephen Ambrose (1936) lives part of every year in this contemporary grey-blue three-story cottage. He also has a home in Helena, Montana.

Author of nineteen books, Ambrose was born in Whitewater, Wisconsin, the son of a U.S. Navy doctor and a housewife. He received a B.A. and Ph.D. at the University of Wisconsin at Madison. While still in graduate school, he wrote a biography of General Henry Halleck that caught the attention of President Dwight D. Eisenhower. On reading it, Eisenhower called him up and asked him to edit the Eisenhower papers. Soon after, he commissioned young Ambrose to write his biography.

Among Ambrose's works are *D-Day* (1994), *Undaunted Courage* (1996), *Nixon: The Triumph of a Politician* (1997), *Citizen Soldiers* (1998), and *Lewis and Clark: Voyage of Discovery* (1998). Ambrose was a consultant for Steven Spielberg's film *Saving Private Ryan.* He is founder of the Eisenhower Center and President of the National D-Day Museum in New Orleans.

Return to Highway 90 to Pass Christian.

Pass Christian

This beautiful old town is called simply "the Pass" by locals. "Pass" refers to the deep-water marine pass, discovered in 1699, which runs between the barrier islands and the coastline; "Christian" commemorates a seventeenth-century French settler, Christian L'Adnier. Edwin Corley (1931–1981), author of *Long Shots*, *Shadows*, and other novels, lived here.

James Albert Harrison (1848–1911) was born here, although the family moved to New Orleans before he entered school. A remarkable teacher, scholar, lecturer, and writer, Harrison was educated at the University of Virginia. He taught modern languages at Randolph Macon and Washington and Lee. His Creole tales were collected in *Autrefois*, published in 1888.

He is best known as editor of the *Complete Works of Edgar Allan Poe* (1902, seventeen volumes) and as writer of the highly valued biography of Poe included in the collection. Called the Virginia Edition, it was for years considered to be the most authentic and correct collection of Poe's work, and it served to increase critics' regard for Poe. Harrison also published subsequent, independent biographies of Poe, *Life and Letters of Edgar Allan Poe* (1902, two volumes) and *Life of Edgar Allan Poe* (1902), as well as a biography of George Washington.

Site of Dorothy Dix House

730 West Beach Boulevard (Highway 90)

Here once stood the home of Elizabeth Meriwether Gilmer (1861–1951), better known as Dorothy Dix. She was the earliest syndicated newspaper feature writer in America and became America's most trusted adviser. The cottage she bought here in 1929 burned in 1955.

Born on a plantation in rural Tennessee, she attended female institutes in Clarksville, Tennessee, and Botencourt Springs, Virginia. At age twenty-one, she married George Gilmer, a mentally and financially unstable man. He had a mental breakdown. Soon after, when she too suffered a breakdown, she turned to fiction to sustain herself, psychologically and financially. She remained with her husband through all of his difficulties.

Her stories appeared in the New Orleans *Picayune* and the *Nashville American*. From the Nashville paper, she won a prize of a hundred dollars for her story "How Dan Won the Christmas

Stakes." A reviewer for the *Clarksville Chronicle* wrote, "Whatever other distinction may be accorded the writer, Mrs. Gilmer has established her fame for knowing just when and how to kill a boy." She wrote about racehorses, trapping rabbits, and old-time ceremonial tournaments, complete with men bearing their ladies' colors.

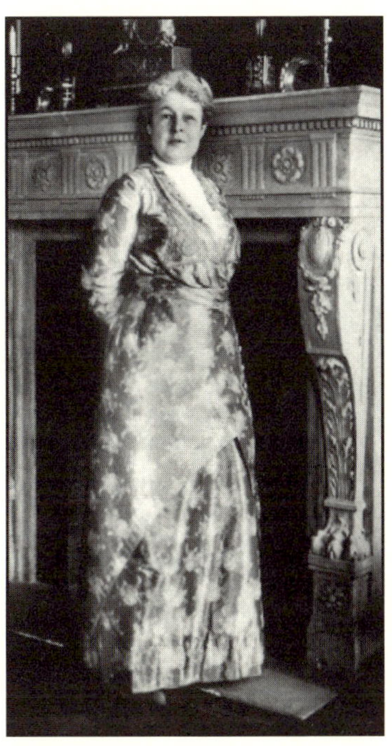

Dorothy Dix

Her career as a newspaperwoman began on a family trip to Bay St. Louis when her father fortuitously rented a cottage next door to Eliza Jane Poitevant, also known as the poet "Pearl Rivers" and owner of the New Orleans *Picayune* (see Picayune). Meriwether was given a position on the paper. As Dorothy Dix, she wrote a wildly popular advice column, the first one appearing in 1895. With over sixty million readers, her columns appeared all over the world. To one distraught wife of a philandering husband who showed up at her door with plans to kill her husband's mistress, Dix cooly suggested, "Why don't you kill *him*?"

In 1952, historian Harnett T. Kane published a biography about her, *Dear Dorothy Dix*. He called her an "oracle and an arbiter of morals and customs." In their famous sociological study of America, *Middletown*, Robert Staughton Lynd and Helen Merrell Lynd concluded that Dix's column was a better representation of Middletown's views and values than any other source.

She bought this cottage at Pass Christian as a respite from her busy schedule in New Orleans. Here she would work in her beloved garden filled with lemon and orange trees. At age eighty-eight, she was writing at her desk when she suffered a fatal stroke. Her estate was estimated to be worth nearly two and a half million dollars.

Long Beach

Friendship Oak

USM Gulf Coast–Gulf Park Campus
730 East Beach Boulevard

Gulf Park College is now part of the University of Southern Mississippi. The towering tree called Friendship Oak dominates the south campus. The tree is reputed to be more than five hundred years old, predating Columbus's voyage. It has a foliage spread of 150 feet. According to legend, friendships made under the spreading limbs are eternal.

The tree became a literary site in 1923 when Illinois poet Vachel Lindsay (1879–1931) taught here. In the branches of the tree, he and his students would gather while he read them poetry, often his own. Lindsay also spent time visiting in the home of Greenville writer William Alexander Percy. After a quarrel with his wife, Lindsay, known to be unstable, killed himself by drinking a bottle of Lysol.

Gulfport

The second-largest city in Mississippi, Gulfport owes its existence to Pennsylvania oil millionaire Captain Joseph T. Jones. In 1894 when the Gulf and Ship Island Railroad ran out of money, Captain Jones invested $1.5 million to save it because he liked the climate. After he assumed control of the railroad, he created a harbor that made the town a seaport. When he hired Thomas Sully, who had designed the St. Charles Hotel in New Orleans, to draw up plans for the Great Southern Hotel, Gulfport was on its way to becoming the resort it is today. Jones is rightly called the "father of Gulfport." Among Gulfport writers are memoirist Gary Harrington and novelists Anne Long and Patricia Boatner.

Poet Natasha Trethewey (1966) was born in Gulfport. She is the recipient of several fellowships, including a Bunting Fellowship from Radcliffe, and her poems have appeared in *Agni*, *The American Poetry Review*, *The Best American Poetry 2000*, and elsewhere. Her first poetry collection, *Domestic Work* (2000), won the 1999 Cave Canem Poetry Prize and the poetry award from the Mississippi Institute of Arts and Letters in 2001. Her second collection, *Bellocq's Ophelia*, is forthcoming in 2002 from Greywolf Press. She is assistant professor of creative writing at Emory University.

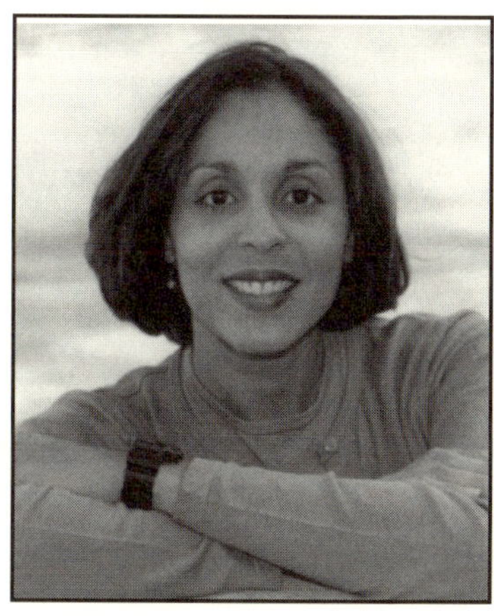

Natasha Trethewey

Ashton Hall

Once located between Gulfport and Biloxi, Ashton Hall is no longer standing. It was the fashionable summer home of Judge Allan Kimbrough and his family, including a daughter who would grow up to be the writer Mary Craig Kimbrough Sinclair (see Greenwood). The house was built by slaves out of hand-sawn lumber.

In her autobiography *Southern Belle*, Sinclair describes extensively the blissful vacations at Ashton Hall where their nearest neighbors were their friends the Jefferson Davises. About Ashton Hall, she wrote, "The old house was set well back from the beach road in the midst of wide-spreading liveoak trees. It was spacious, and hospitable-looking, with wide galleries, roofed, and with banisters on all sides."

Continue on Highway 90 to Highway 49 which is also 25th Avenue. Take a left. Take a right in the next block onto 13th Street. Take a left onto 24th Avenue.

Dixie Press

1417 24th Avenue

Clayton Rand (1891–1971) grew up in poverty and learned early how to be tough. He would become known as the "fighting editor of the Deep South." From Wisconsin, the Rands moved to Bond, Mississippi, in 1898 when Clayton's father took a job in a sawmill. But this common laborer who performed backbreaking work in the sawmills also loved Robert Burns and quoted the classics. Through him, young Clayton came to love literature.

Determined to get an education, Rand paid his way through Mississippi Agricultural and Mechanical College (now Mississippi State University) by setting up a peanut concession. Soon the money he made from his concession exceeded the salary of the college president. After earning a B.S. degree there and a second one from Harvard, he married May Ella Smylie, his childhood sweetheart. Having studied law only a short time while at Harvard, he passed the Mississippi bar exam and settled in Jackson. Always the entrepreneur, while dealing in land speculations in Neshoba County he impulsively bought the *Neshoba Democrat*, inadvertently launching his future career as a newspaperman.

He rose to prominence when he and his family moved to Gulfport after he purchased the *Dixie Press.* Here he conceived and started up the *Mississippi Guide*, the first newspaper in Mississippi to carry photographs. He was a crusader for community improvement and liberal causes, and he received national attention when he wrote about such subjects in a daily syndicated column called "Crossroads Scribe." In 1925, he was elected president of the Mississippi Press Association. He wrote five books about the newspaper business, the best of which is the autobiographical *Ink on My Hands* (1940).

Return to Highway 90.

Ship Island

Gulfport Yacht Harbor
Highway 90

Mississippi has four offshore islands, two with strong literary associations. (See Ocean Springs regarding Horn Island.)

Ship Island, twelve miles offshore, is rich in history and legend. The island, which is now a part of Gulf Islands National Seashore, was cut in two by Hurricane Camille in 1969. Access to West Ship Island is provided through regularly scheduled day trips from the Gulfport Yacht Harbor. The island offers tours of

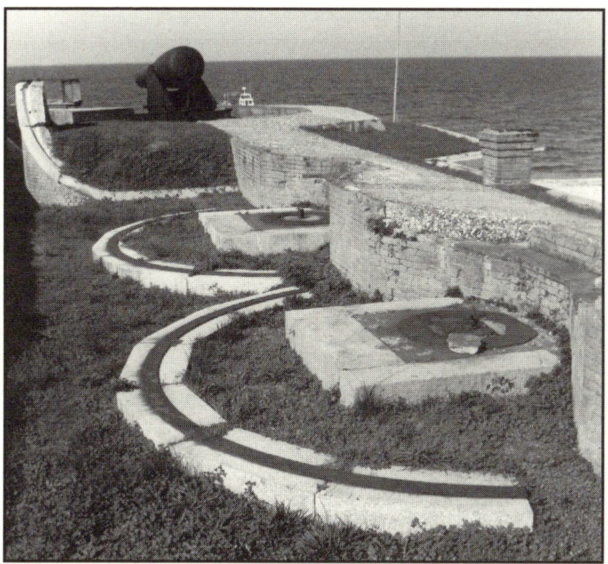

Ship Island

Fort Massachusetts, a long boardwalk, and the best beach on the Gulf Coast.

Fort Massachusetts served as a Union prison during the Civil War. It was a refuge for pirates who raided the Spanish galleons sailing the Gulf of Mexico, a port of entry for French colonists, and a base for the English navy during the War of 1812. Ship Island appears in Walker Percy's *The Moviegoer* and in Elizabeth Spencer's story "Ship Island." Spencer's book *The Salt Line* is also, in part, set here.

Biloxi

The Biloxi Bay area is the oldest permanent settlement in Mississippi. The French arrived here in 1699, naming the bay for a friendly, local Indian tribe. Originally settling at Ocean Springs, the French made New Biloxi the capital of Louisiana in 1720. By 1722 the capital was moved to New Orleans, but Biloxi struggled on.

In its early life Biloxi was sustained by its fishing industry and boat building, but in the nineteenth century, tourism was born.

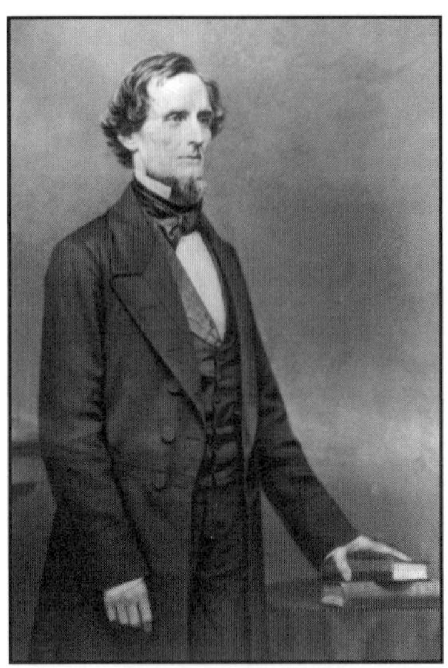
Jefferson Davis

Travelers, hearing of its mild climate, luxurious vegetation, and sparkling waters, flocked in. Today its numerous golf courses and casinos attract people from all over the nation. Contemporary writers associated with Biloxi include Jack Nelson, Murella Powell, Glenn Robert Swetman, and Charles Griffin.

Beauvoir

2244 Beach Boulevard

Sarah Ann Dorsey (1829–1879) of Natchez bought this house and fifty-one additional acres in 1873 for the health of her elderly husband, who died before they could move. Dorsey came to Beauvoir alone, and, when Jefferson Davis returned homeless from Europe in 1877, she invited him to live at Beauvoir and write his memoirs.

While living here Dorsey became the first female member of the New Orleans Academy of Sciences and wrote her novel, *Panola: A Tale of Louisiana* (1877). In 1879, when her illness was diagnosed as cancer, Dorsey sold Beauvoir to Jefferson Davis. (See Natchez regarding her early life.)

Jefferson Davis (1808–1889), president of the Confederate States of America, spent the last twelve years of his life at Beauvoir. He initially rented the East Cottage (now called the Library Pavilion) from Mrs. Dorsey when he arrived at Beauvoir in 1877. In 1879 Sarah Dorsey sold Beauvoir to Davis, but in her will that same year left the house to Davis and his daughter. Her family in Natchez hotly contested the will, but Davis prevailed and lived out his life at Beauvoir with his wife, Varina, and daughter, Winnie (Varina Ann).

In the Library Pavilion, he completed his memoirs, *The Rise and Fall of the Confederacy* (1881), a thick two-volume work not well received by a nation ready to move on. After his Confeder-

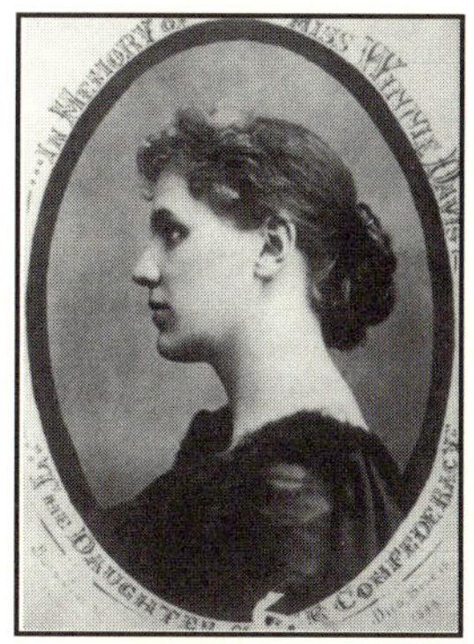
Winnie Davis

acy book was published, he continued to write articles on such diverse themes as Indian policies and states' rights; a school text, *A Short History of the Confederate States of America* (1889), was published after his death. He wrote sketches of Robert E. Lee and John Calhoun, as well as a short autobiographical piece. Davis was first buried in New Orleans, where he had died; then his body was moved to Richmond, Virginia. At the time of his death he was still stripped of his citizenship, which was not restored until 1978 by the U.S. Congress.

The handsome Jefferson Davis Presidential Library was built in 1998. Beauvoir was named a National Literary Site in 2001 by the Friends of Libraries U.S.A., and the grounds are designated as part of the Misssissippi Statewide Arboretum.

Varina Howell Davis (1826–1906) assisted her husband in the research for his work, and after his death wrote *Jefferson Davis, Ex-President of the Confederate States of America: A Memoir*, two volumes, over sixteen hundred pages; it was published in 1890. In her old age she sold Beauvoir to a veterans' association for a token sum. It was used as a home for indigent Confederate veterans. Where the museum now stands a hospital was built for the veterans and for their widows, orphans, and slaves. After her husband's death, Varina moved to New York to live with her daughter, Winnie. In New York, Varina continued to write magazine and newspaper articles until her death in 1906. She, too, was buried in Richmond, Virginia. (See Natchez regarding her early life.)

Varina Ann (Winnie) Davis (1864–1898) was born in Richmond in the White House of the Confederacy. After the surrender of the Confederate states and the imprisonment of her father, her mother took the children to live in Canada. When Jefferson Davis was released from prison in 1868, the family lived in Europe for several years. Winnie stayed on to be educated there, and Jef-

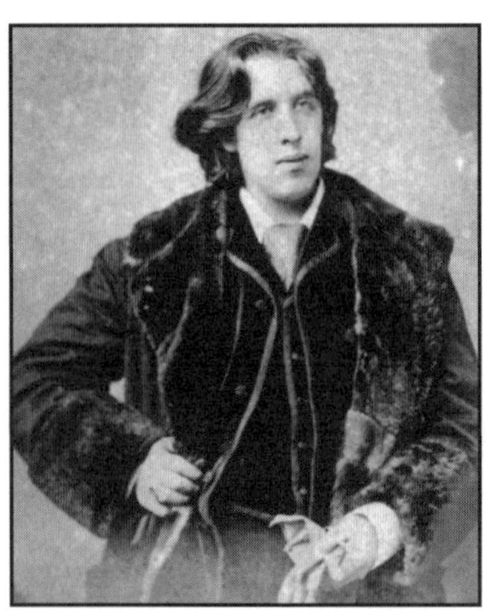
Oscar Wilde

ferson Davis celebrated the publication of his book by going to Paris to bring her home to Beauvoir. She was sixteen. At age twenty-three she fell in love with a Yankee, but the reluctance of her mother to accept him and Winnie's image as "the daughter of the Confederacy" prohibited the marriage. She turned her energies to writing, first producing a biography of Irishman Robert Emmet (1888), and then, in her few remaining years, publishing two novels. Her last book, *A Romance of Summer Seas* (1898), showed great promise for her literary future. She died at the age of thirty-four, preceding her mother in death by eight years.

Beauvoir has two other literary associations.

It is the site of a meeting between Jefferson Davis and Oscar Wilde, truly an odd couple. Twenty-six-year-old Wilde, famous playwright and lecturer on the new aesthetics of Great Britain, came on a lecture tour of America in 1881. He spoke in Vicksburg the night of June 14 and expressed a desire to meet the ex-president, Davis. Varina Davis, who admired Wilde's work, invited him to stop by Beauvoir the next day en route to Mobile. Wilde and Davis reportedly sat on a bench overlooking the gulf and chatted. No record exists of their conversation, but one can imagine the flamboyant Wilde bewildering the stiff-backed gentleman of the Old South. Davis made excuses to retire early, leaving Wilde to entertain the ladies of the house, which he did past midnight. When Varina chided Jefferson for absenting himself, he replied, "I did not like the man." Wilde, for his part, left Davis a photograph of himself inscribed "To Jefferson Davis in all loyal admiration from Oscar Wilde, June '82—Beauvoir." The photograph is on file in the Jefferson Davis Presidential Library at Beauvoir.

Beauvoir Cemetery contains the grave of Prentiss Ingraham (see Natchez for his biography), the most prolific writer Mississippi, and perhaps the nation, has ever had. His burial plot has a simple marker engraved only with his name, place of birth, and rank of colonel, which was bestowed on him in the Cuban war. He spent his last days at Beauvoir as a Confederate army veteran, apparently impoverished.

1428 West Beach Boulevard

This was once the home of Abram Joseph Ryan, "poet of the Confederacy," a sobriquet based on his subject matter: the experience of war and Reconstruction in the South. One of his most popular poems was "The Conquered Banner," written when he heard of General Lee's surrender.

Ryan, a native of Maryland, was a Confederate army chaplain who saw military action himself. After the war he was pastor of St. Mary's in Mobile. He lived and wrote in this house, perhaps used as a vacation retreat.

The Episcopal Church of the Redeemer

Beach Boulevard and Bellman Street

The church that Jefferson Davis and his family attended was the first Church of the Redeemer. A new church was built on this site in 1874, using components of the old church. A third church structure, built in 1891, was destroyed by Hurricane Camille in 1969. Parishioners searched through the debris and reclaimed some of the Davis memorial items, including the Davis family communion set, the Jefferson Davis pew, and fragments of the stained glass windows memorializing Davis. The glass fragments were used to construct "The Window of Hope," which was placed in the bell tower, a survivor from the 1891 church. The transept of the current church is from the original church built in 1874.

Old French House Restaurant

Highway 90, East of Beau Rivage

Built in 1737, this structure is on the National Register of Historic Places and is the oldest building in the city. The flamboyant Mary Mahoney opened the restaurant in 1964 and built it into a landmark on the Mississippi coast before her death in

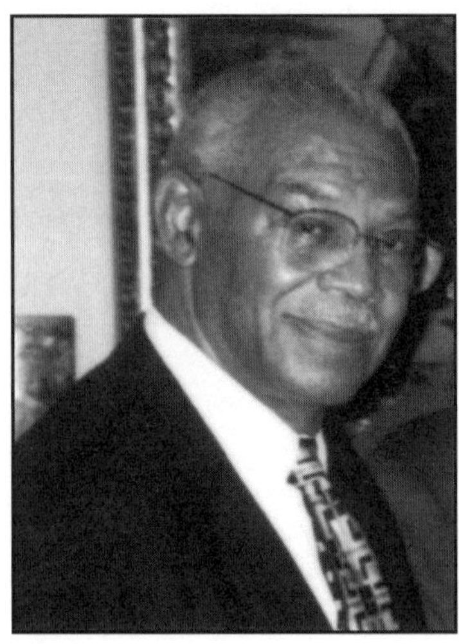
Gilbert Mason

1986. The restaurant is mentioned in John Grisham's *The Runaway Jury* and *The Partner*. Edward Lepoma, a native of Biloxi, has written a biography of Mahoney, who was the child of immigrant Yugoslavian parents and who rose to fame as a restaurateur; the book is entitled *A Passion for People: The Story of Mary Mahoney and Her Old French House Restaurant* (1999).

Biloxi Beach

Along Highway 90

The white sand beach that stretches along the Gulf of Mexico for twenty-six miles from Biloxi to Pass Christian was created in the late 1940s. West Beach at Biloxi became the site of intense civil rights battles in the 1960s. In chilly April waters Dr. Gilbert Mason defiantly swam alone through the choppy sound to protest the "whites only" policy which kept blacks off the Mississippi beaches. A series of rallies resulted in a riot in which two young black men were killed, but Mason's action ultimately led the way to desegregation of the beaches. Mason was the first African American to be admitted to the Mississippi Academy of Family Physicians. His memoir is entitled *Beaches, Blood, and Ballots: A Black Doctor's Civil Rights Struggle* (2000).

Ocean Springs

Ocean Springs, a town that embraces all of the arts, can perhaps claim the most varied writing community in the state—mystery writer Micah Hackler, romance writer Carolyn Haines, poet Al Young, history writers Ray Skates and Ray Bellande, and, on the Shearwater compound, the poets, mystics, and nature writers of the Anderson family.

The Walter Anderson Museum

510 Washington Avenue

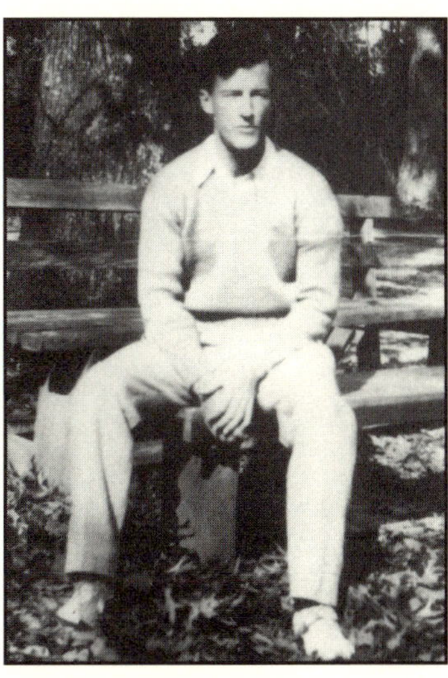
Walter Anderson

Walter Anderson (1903–1965) is Mississippi's greatest artist, as this museum, created in 1991, attests. He was also a poet and a writer who attempted to interpret the natural world of the Gulf Coast, once even attempting to write down the vocabulary of pelicans. At his death, eighty-two volumes of his journals were discovered. *The Horn Island Logs of Walter Inglis Anderson* (1973) contains portions of these journals, mostly written on Horn Island. A revised edition was published in 1985; both were edited by Redding Sugg, Jr.

The murals by Anderson are as intensely poetical as his writings. The most famous of these can be seen in the community center adjoining the museum and within the museum. A small room of his house, filled with wall murals he had painted, was moved to become part of the museum. Redding Sugg, Jr., tells the story of these breathtaking murals in *A Painter's Psalm* (1978); a revised edition was published in 1992.

Shearwater Pottery

102 Shearwater Drive

Walter Anderson's mother, Annette McConnell Anderson, bought this property in 1918 for a summer retreat and artists' colony. It has become a true art colony; four generations of Andersons have made it their home. Just inside the compound on the right are the workshops of Shearwater Pottery, where Peter Anderson began his business. Christopher Maurer has chronicled the history of the pottery and the Anderson family in *Dreaming in Clay on the Coast of Mississippi* (2000).

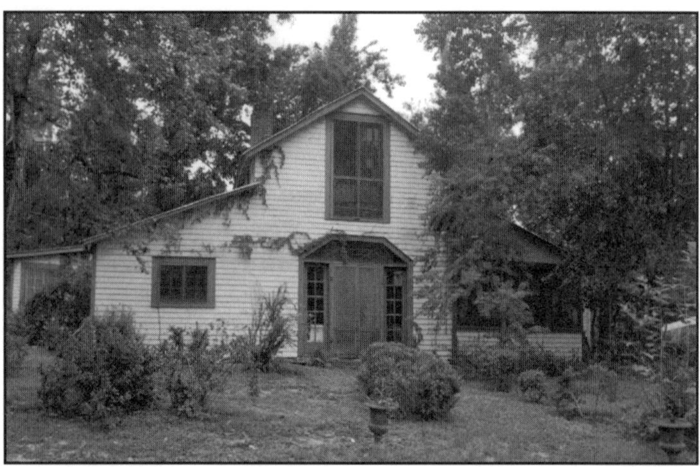

The Barn, Shearwater

The next building on the right is the cottage where Walter Anderson and his bride, Agnes Grinstead, began their marriage. It figures prominently in her memoir, *Approaching the Magic Hour* (1989). Agnes Anderson, called Sissy, was a prolific writer. In addition to her diaries, she wrote poetry, letters, and sparkling vignettes about the natural world. (See Gautier for more about her life.)

Across from the pottery showroom, next to the cottage, is the barn, which was the last home of Walter Anderson's mother, Annette McConnell Anderson (1867–1964), an artist and writer. She was a long-time journal keeper and essayist, but her major writing consisted of poetry, published by her family in *Possums and Other Verses* (1960).

Living on the compound are other accomplished writers. Mary Anderson Pickard has devoted much of the last thirty-five years to writing about her father, Walter Anderson, in countless articles and catalogs; she is a poet and essayist as well. Another daughter, Leif Anderson, a dancer and poet, published *Dancing Through Airth* (1986) and has completed a memoir. Patricia Anderson Findeisen is also a poet who lives on the compound; she is the daughter of Peter Anderson, founder of Shearwater Pottery. Her mother, Patricia Grinstead Anderson, was also an eloquent journal keeper.

Louis Sullivan Houses

509 East Beach Boulevard

6 Holcombe Boulevard

St. John's Episcopal Church

Porter Avenue

When Louis Sullivan, later to become one of America's foremost architects, visited New Orleans in 1890, he was persuaded to come to the Mississippi Gulf Coast to see the rapidly developing resort of Ocean Springs.

Enchanted with the climate, azaleas, magnolias, and sparkling Mississippi Sound, he bought property here and built an airy vacation cottage overlooking the sound and Deer Island. Sullivan returned to Ocean Springs to stay a part of each year for eighteen years. During his residence here, he designed the two houses listed above and St. John's Episcopal Church. Because the parishioners added a steeple to his original design for the church, he declined to take credit for it.

In 1924, Sullivan published *The Autobiography of an Idea* describing his first visit to Ocean Springs in 1890.

Music permeates the work of writer Al Young (1939). He was born in Ocean Springs and lived here for half of his childhood, attending Kingston Primary School. When his father returned from World War II, the family moved to Detroit, where Young graduated from high school. He attended the University of Michigan and moved to San Francisco to pursue a music career. In 1969, he graduated from the University of California at Berkeley the same year that his first volume of poetry, *Dancing*, was published.

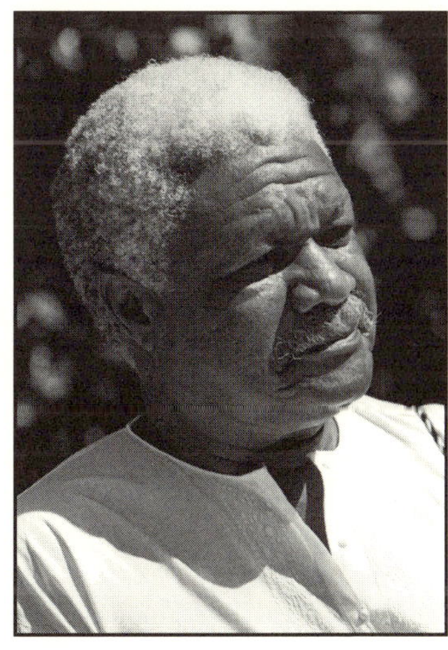

Al Young

His *Bodies & Soul* (1981), *Kinds of Blue: Musical Memoirs* (1984), and *Things Ain't What They Used to Be* (1987) are memoirs inspired by American music.

His work includes four books of poetry, five novels, and four books of nonfiction, as well as film scripts. He has taught at Stanford University, Colorado College, the University of Washington, and the University of California. His works have been anthologized and translated into eight foreign languages.

With Ishmael Reed, Young founded *Yardbird Reader*, the nation's leading multicultural literary review. Together they edit *Quilt*, an international journal also devoted to multicultural writing. He has received a National Arts Council Award for poetry, the Pushcart Prize, a National Endowment for the Arts Fellowship, a Fulbright Fellowship, a Wallace Stegner Fellowship, and a Guggenheim Fellowship. His book *Heaven: Collected Poems* was published in 1988.

John Ruskin Oak

Ruskin Avenue

At the height of his fame, John Ruskin (1819–1900), England's influential art critic and author of *Stones of Venice*, came to America in 1885 for the world's fair in New Orleans. While in New Orleans he came to Ocean Springs to visit a friend in a summer cottage built beside this tree. The story goes that parties were staged under and around the tree to honor him then and for years after his visit. One of the oldest live oaks in the country, it is a member of the national Live Oak Society and is among the most famous trees in Mississippi. It is also registered with the Societé des Arbres.

Horn Island

Horn Island, twelve miles out, was made famous by *The Horn Island Logs of Walter Inglis Anderson*, published in 1973 and reprinted in 1985, and by his hundreds of watercolors made on the island from 1940 until his death in 1965. The island was his laboratory of life, the site of a spiritual quest, and a means of "realizing reality." He left more than eighty-five journals of the time spent on Horn Island. The island also figures in the memoir of his wife, Agnes Anderson, who continued to visit there after his death. Now a part of Gulf Islands National Seashore, the island has no regular access by public boat. The Gulf Islands National Seashore office at 228-875-9057 can supply the names of companies that offer private transportation.

Gautier

Formerly known as West Pascagoula, Gautier, named for a pioneer family, came into its own after the railroad gave its creosote industry a boost. Like its neighbors on the coastal plain, the area has been in the timber and naval stores business since the eighteenth century. Its famous literary site, Oldfields Plantation, was once a large cattle farm. In addition to the Anderson family, Gautier can claim poet Sue Wright Entrekin.

Oldfields

Agnes Grinstead Anderson (1909–1991) published her poignant memoir, *Approaching the Magic Hour: Memories of Walter Anderson*, in 1989. This is the house where she was born and spent much of her childhood. Her father, an attorney in Louisville, Kentucky, and Chicago, bought this antebellum property in 1904. At that time the house was surrounded by four hundred acres of woods and marshes. Both Agnes and her sister Patricia were born here. The sisters married the Anderson brothers, Walter and Peter, from Ocean Springs, and moved there as young brides. Agnes and Walter Anderson returned to live at Oldfields from 1941 to 1946. Those years, difficult for Agnes but productive for the artist Walter Anderson, are described both in Agnes's memoir and in *Dreaming in Clay on the Coast of Mississippi* (2000) by Christopher Maurer.

Agnes Anderson's published memoirs represent only a small fraction of her writing. She was a poet, nature writer, and journal keeper, and she wrote a memoir of her childhood at Oldfields that is not yet published. Her correspondence with Walter Anderson

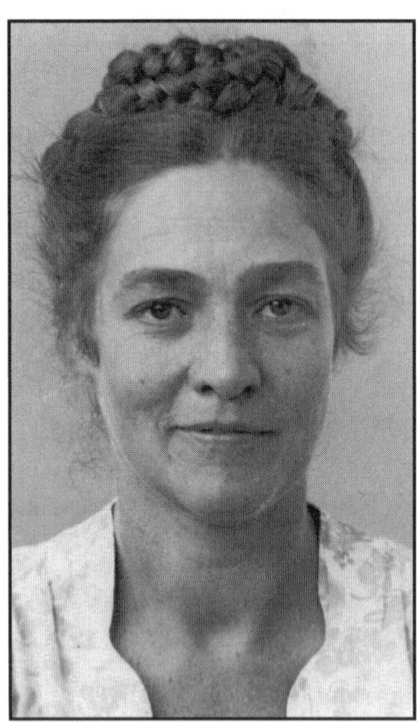
Agnes Grinstead Anderson

during their courtship is currently being edited for publication.

Another literary legacy that emanated from this house is a cache of some nine thousand sketches that Walter Anderson made while reading here at night. An avid reader, Anderson illustrated for his own pleasure dozens of literary classics including *Hamlet, Don Quixote, The Divine Comedy, Paradise Lost,* and *Alice in Wonderland.*

Pascagoula

The Mississippi Gulf Coast is anchored on the east by Pascagoula, which is less than ten miles from the Alabama state line. Named for the Indian tribe who lived near here, this town on the Gulf of Mexico boomed after 1870 when the railroad came, facilitating transportation for the timber industry, commercial fisheries, and pecan culture. During World War I, its ascendancy as a major shipbuilding center began and continues today.

An interesting variety of writing has emerged from Pascagoula. Ira Harkey earned his Pulitzer Prize here (see below). Martin Hegwood of Canton, who launched the Jack Delmas mystery series with *Big Easy Backroad* in 1999, was born and raised here. Prieur Jay Higginbotham traced local history. The poetry of Eunice D. Barnes, Mildred R. Henderson, and Brenda B. Finnegan appeared in *Lyric Mississippi.* After Charles Hickson and Calvin Parker were reportedly picked up by a spaceship from a Pascagoula pier, Hickson, with William Mendez, wrote a memoir of that encounter entitled *UFO Contact at Pascagoula* (1983). Down on the beach, distinguished visitors Henry W. Longfellow and Willliam Faulkner left their marks.

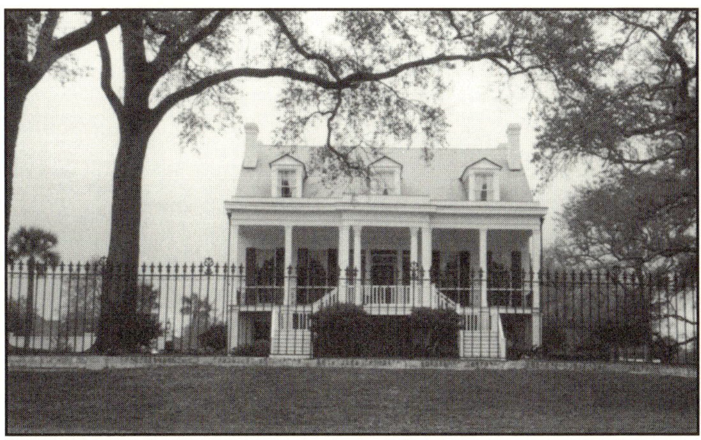

The Longfellow House

West Beach Boulevard

Between Pascagoula Street and Market Street

In the summer of 1925, Faulkner came here to a beach house owned by Myrtle Lewis and Jack Stone, Phil Stone's brother. Called "The Camp," it was a simple four-room house with a magnolia and a live oak growing through it. Faulkner found a favorite work place on a board seat that encircled the big oak. A wooden bench supported his small typewriter, and he worked there for hours on revisions of *Soldiers' Pay*, his first novel. He also swam, sailed with friends, courted Helen Baird, and spent time lounging on the pier and in bars where the Pascagoula fishermen congregated. He returned in the summer of 1926, still attempting, unsuccessfully, to court Helen Baird and working on *Mosquitoes*, which he dedicated to Helen.

Several years later, in 1929, William Faulkner and his bride, Estelle Oldham, honeymooned here, and in 1939 Faulkner used the Gulf Coast as a setting for *The Wild Palms*.

Longfellow House

3401 Beach Boulevard

Henry Wadsworth Longfellow wrote of Pascagoula's "sunny bay" in his poem "The Building of a Ship." He came to vacation at this

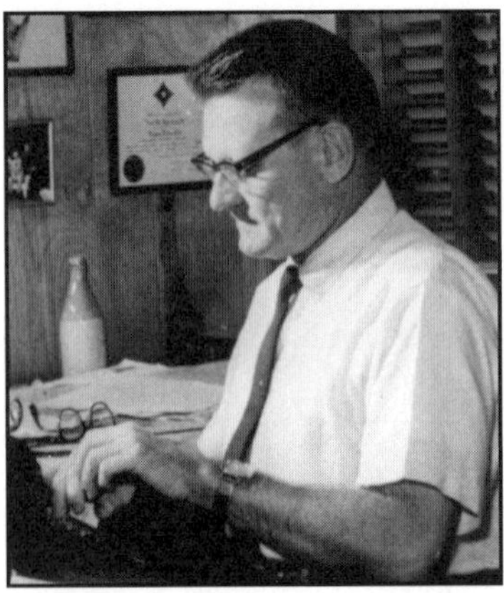
Ira Harkey

house in the 1850s when it was still owned by Mr. and Mrs. Daniel Smith Graham, whose wealth had been secured by slave trading in New Orleans. The house, built in 1854, and its surrounding acreage were called Bellvue Plantation. It has had a long succession of owners including Robert Ingalls of Ingalls Shipbuilding who used it to house visiting dignitaries. Ingalls acquired it in 1940 and named it The Longfellow House. For the last quarter of a century it has been operated as a resort hotel. Even so, Longfellow might recognize the house. He could still watch shipbuilding from the front porch and feel the breezes from "the sunny bay."

Ira B. Harkey (1918), editor of *The Chronicle*, was a 1963 Pulitzer Prize winner "for his courageous editorials devoted to the processes of law and reason during the integration crisis in Mississippi in 1962." Harkey piloted *The Chronicle* for fourteen years. He was born in New Orleans, and graduated from the Isidore Newman School and Tulane University. He later earned his M.A. and Ph.D. from Ohio State University.

After serving in the navy during World War II, he worked for the New Orleans *Times-Picayune* and began looking for a weekly newspaper to buy in Louisiana or Mississippi. With a partner he bought Pascagoula's *Chronicle-Star* in 1949. He sold the newspaper in 1963 after enduring harassment by some and ostracism by others in the community for his views on civil rights. He joined the academic world as a professor and visiting lecturer for several years before moving to the corporate arena. His autobiography, *The Smell of Burning Crosses*, was published in 1967. In recent years he has lived in Texas and published biographies of other distinguished men.

Moss Point

Moss Point's history has always been entwined with its pine trees, from the days of refitting the early vessels of the French, Spanish, and

British navies to its current-day paper mill. Named for the ubiquitous hanging moss, the town was settled in 1721 around a sawmill and eventually became the largest pine lumber export center in the United States, until 1910 when Gulfport took the lead. No literary activity was recorded in those heady days, but a poet, Jerry Ward, has emerged from the contemporary milieu.

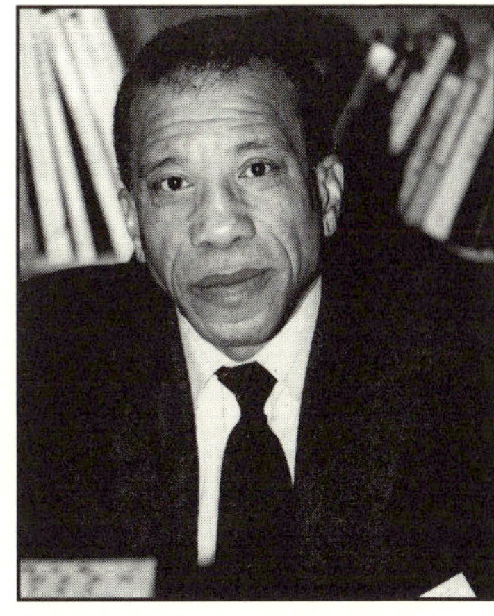
Jerry Ward

3501 Barnett Street

Jerry W. Ward, Jr. (1941), professor of English, literary critic and scholar, and poet, grew up in Moss Point. Born in Washington, D.C., he moved to Moss Point with his parents when he was a small child, and attended public schools here. He earned his B.S. in mathematics from Tougaloo College (1964), his M.S. at the Illinois Institute of Technology (1966), and a Ph.D. from the University of Virginia (1978). He served in Vietnam before taking a professorship at Tougaloo College, where he has been chair of the English department. He has also been a member of the Mississippi Humanities Council and the U.S. Civil Rights Commission. During his tenure at Tougaloo he has taken leaves of absence to accept the United Negro College Fund Distinguished Scholar award, to be scholar-in-residence at Talladega College, and to work for the National Endowment for the Humanities.

Ward's poetry offers a black perspective on art and society. He wrote, "The years I've called Mississippi home have been inspiration and substance for my poetry . . . Mississippi is a culture of profoundest joys and pains. Its writers have a moral obligation to face naked truths squarely and articulate them for the future." His poems and reviews have appeared in such magazines as *Iowa Review, New Orleans Review, Obsidian, Callaloo, Black American Literature Forum*, and *The Black Scholar*. He is currently working on a collection of poetry.

Moss Point is the end of the Gulf Coast tour.

Credit List

Page 7 William Alexander Percy home, Greenville. Courtesy of Mississippi Department of Archives and History.

Page 7 William Alexander Percy. Courtesy of Mississippi Department of Archives and History.

Page 9 Walker Percy. Courtesy of Rhoda K. Faust, photographer, Maple Street Book Shop, New Orleans.

Page 11 Hodding Carter. Courtesy of Mississippi Department of Archives and History.

Page 16 Bern Keating. Courtesy of Franke Keating.

Page 17 Beverly Lowry. Courtesy of Nancy Scanlan, photographer.

Page 19 Shelby Foote. Courtesy of Mississippi Department of Archives and History.

Page 22 Caroline Stern home, Greenville. Pen and ink, courtesy of Greenville Writers' Exhibit.

Page 23 Steve Yarbrough. Corrinne Hales, photographer; courtesy of Steve Yarbrough.

Page 24 Craig Claiborne. Courtesy of Ann Chwatsky, photographer.

Page 27 Lewis Nordan's childhood home, Itta Bena. Marion Barnwell, photographer.

Page 37 Morris home, Yazoo City. Marion Barnwell, photographer.

Page 37 Willie Morris. Courtesy of Hunter Cole, photographer.

Page 47 Thomas Harris studio, Lula-Rich. Marion Barnwell, photographer.

Page 51 Tennessee Williams. Humanities Research Center Library, The University of Texas at Austin.

Page 60 Clifton Taulbert. J. B. Petersen Photography, Inc.; courtesy of Clifton Taulbert.

Page 60 St. Mark MB Church, Glen Allan. Marion Barnwell, photographer.

Page 61 Ellen Gilchrist. Courtesy of Mississippi Department of Archives and History.

Page 65 Harris Dickson. Courtesy of Mississippi Department of Archives and History.

Page 66 Myrlie Evers-Williams. Courtesy of *Clarion-Ledger*, Jackson.

Page 69 Biedenharn Museum, Vicksburg. Marion Barnwell, photographer.

Page 71 Rosemont, Woodville. Courtesy of Mississippi Department of Archives and History.

Page 72 Site of McGehee House, Bowling Green. Marion Barnwell, photographer.

Page 77 Dumas Malone. Courtesy of University of Virginia.

Page 79 James Seay. Courtesy of Hunter Cole, photographer.

Page 81 Donna Tartt. Courtesy of Tay Tartt Weatherall.

Page 83 Elizabeth Spencer. Courtesy of Hunter Cole, photographer.

Page 85 Melany Neilson. Courtesy of Fred Slabach, photographer.

Page 87 Hosford Fontaine. Courtesy of John Fontaine.

Page 93 Alice Walker. Courtesy of Lynda Koolish, photographer.

Page 94 Walker/Leventhal home, Jackson. Marion Barnwell, photographer.

Page 95 Margaret Walker Alexander. Courtesy of *Clarion-Ledger*, Jackson.

Page 96 Beth Henley. Courtesy of Hunter Cole, photographer.

Page 98 Eudora Welty. Robert L. Williams, photographer; courtesy of Mississippi Department of Archives and History.

Page 99 Welty home, Pinehurst Street, Jackson. Marion Barnwell, photographer.

Page 101 Ellen Douglas. Courtesy of Kay Holloway, photographer.

Page 102 Charlotte Capers. Courtesy of Mississippi Department of Archives and History.

Page 103 Welty home, North Congress Street, Jackson. Courtesy of Mississippi Department of Archives and History.

Page 104 Richard Ford. Courtesy of Kay Holloway, photographer.

Page 106 Richard Wright. Courtesy of Beinecke Library, Yale University.

Page 114 Stevens shed, Liberty. Marion Barnwell, photographer.

Page 115 Will Campbell. Courtesy of Mississippi Department of Archives and History.

Page 116 Anne Moody. Courtesy of Christine Wilson, photographer.

Page 121 Sherwood Bonner. Marshall County Historical Society.

Page 125 Ida B. Wells Art Gallery. Courtesy of Mississippi Department of Archives and History.

Page 129 Colonel W. C. Falkner. Ripley Public Library.

Page 130 W. C. Falkner's house, Ripley. Ripley Public Library.

Page 133 Borden Deal. Sketch by Richard Brough.

Page 135 William Faulkner. Courtesy of Mississippi Department of Archives and History.

Page 138 Lafayette County courthouse, Oxford. Courtesy of Mississippi Department of Archives and History.

Page 142 Stark Young. Courtesy of John Pilkington.

Page 144 John Faulkner. Courtesy of Mrs. John Faulkner.

Page 150 Rowan Oak. Courtesy of Hunter Cole, photographer.

Page 153 Barry Hannah. Courtesy of Hunter Cole, photographer.

Page 155 Larry Brown. Courtesy of Tom Rankin, photographer.

Page 156 Taylor Grocery, Taylor. Courtesy of Jane Rule Burdine, photographer.

Page 157 John Grisham. Courtesy of Mitchell Memorial Library, Mississippi State University, John Grisham Papers.

Page 162 Dunleith, Natchez. Courtesy of Mississippi Department of Archives and History.

Page 163 Sarah Ellis Dorsey. Courtesy of Beauvoir Collection, Biloxi.

Page 167 John R. Lynch. Courtesy of Mississippi Department of Archives and History.

Page 169 Varina Howell Davis. Courtesy of Beauvoir Collection, Biloxi.

Page 170 Mount Repose, Natchez. Courtesy of Mississippi Department of Archives and History.

Page 173 Greg Iles. Courtesy of Geoff Iles.

Page 175 Chapel, Laurel Hill Plantation, Natchez. Courtesy of Mississippi Department of Archives and History.

Page 176 Joseph Holt Ingraham. Courtesy of Mississippi Department of Archives and History.

Page 177 Prentiss Ingraham. Courtesy of Mississippi Department of Archives and History.

Page 179 Irwin Russell. Courtesy of Mississippi Department of Archives and History.

Page 180 Temple Gemiluth Chassed, Port Gibson. Courtesy of Mississippi Department of Archives and History.

Page 181 Berry Morgan. Courtesy of Berry Morgan.

Page 182 Rosa Vertner Johnson. Courtesy of Eudora Welty Library, Jackson.

Page 184 Sterling Plumpp. Courtesy of Sterling Plumpp.

Page 185 Nevada Barr. Courtesy of Center for the Study of Southern Culture.

Page 187 James Meredith. Courtesy of Center for the Study of Southern Culture.

Page 190 James Robert Peery. Courtesy of Suzanne Peery Schutt.

Page 195 Frances Jones Gaither. Courtesy of Mrs. Hoyt Wilder.

Page 196 Thomas Hal Phillips. Courtesy of Sue Elam, photographer.

Page 198 George E. Allen. Courtesy of George E. Allen Library, Booneville.

Page 201 Reuben Davis. Courtesy of Mississippi Department of Archives and History.

Page 202 Frank Trippett. Judy Ross, photographer; courtesy of Robert Trippett.

Page 206 Tennessee Williams's birthplace, Columbus. Courtesy of Mississippi Department of Archives and History.

Page 209 Red Barber. Courtesy of Cincinnati Historical Society.

Page 211 Paul Ruffin. Courtesy of Paul Ruffin.

Page 213 T. R. Hummer. Courtesy of T. R. Hummer.

Page 216 Florence Mars and Turner Catledge. Courtesy of Mississippi Department of Archives and History.

Page 218 Ed Kimbrough. Courtesy of Julius Feazell.

Page 219 Howard Bahr. Courtesy of Steve Cook, photographer.

Page 222 James Street. Courtesy of Ruth Giles.

Page 226 Eliza Jane Poitevant Nicholson. Courtesy of the Historic New Orleans Collection.

Page 227 Noel Polk. Courtesy of Noel Polk.

Page 230 Laurel Wood, Pearlington. Courtesy of Mississippi Department of Archives and History.

Page 231 Stephen Ambrose. Courtesy of the University of New Orleans.

Page 233 Dorothy Dix. Courtesy of the Historic New Orleans Collection.

Page 235 Natasha Trethewey. Courtesy of Natasha Trethewey.

Page 237 Ship Island. Courtesy of Mississippi Department of Archives and History.

Page 238 Jefferson Davis. Matthew Brady, photographer; courtesy of Mississippi Department of Archives and History.

Page 239 Winnie Davis. Courtesy of Mississippi Department of Archives and History.

Page 240 Oscar Wilde. Courtesy of Beauvoir Collection.

Page 242 Gilbert Mason. Courtesy of Mississippi Department of Archives and History.

Page 243 Walter Anderson. Courtesy of Estate of Walter Anderson.

Page 244 The Barn, Shearwater. Courtesy of Mississippi Department of Archives and History.

Page 245 Al Young. Courtesy of Lynda Koolish, photographer.

Page 248 Agnes Grinstead Anderson. Courtesy of Estate of Walter Anderson.

Page 249 The Longfellow House. Patti Carr Black, photographer.

Page 250 Ira Harkey. Courtesy of Ira Harkey, Jr.

Page 251 Jerry Ward. Courtesy of Center for the Study of Southern Culture.

Index

Numbers in **boldface** indicate an illustration on that page.